The International Politics of Race

The International Politics of Race

Michael Banton

polity

First published in 2002 by Polity Press in association with Blackwell
Publishers Ltd, a Blackwell Publishing Company

Editorial office:
Polity Press
65 Bridge Street
Cambridge CB2 1UR, UK

Marketing and production:
Blackwell Publishers Ltd
108 Cowley Road
Oxford OX4 1JF, UK

Published in the USA by
Blackwell Publishers Inc.
350 Main Street
Malden, MA 02148, USA

ISBN 0-7456-3048-0
ISBN 0-7456-3049-9   (pbk)

A catalogue record for this book is available from the British Library and
has been applied for from the Library of Congress.

Typeset in 10½ on 12 pt Palatino
by SNP Best-set Typesetter Ltd., Hong Kong
Printed in Great Britain by TJ International, Padstow, Cornwall

This book is printed on acid-free paper.

Contents

Acronyms

CERD	Committee on the Elimination of Racial Discrimination
CHR	Commission on Human Rights
COE	Council of Europe
ECHR	European Convention on Human Rights
ECRI	European Commission Against Racism and Intolerance
ICCPR	International Covenant on Civil and Political Rights
ICERD	International Convention on the Elimination of All Forms of Racial Discrimination
ICESCR	International Covenant on Economic, Social and Cultural Rights
ILO	International Labour Organization
NGO	Non-governmental organization
OSCE	Organization for Security and Co-operation in Europe
UN	United Nations
UNESCO	United Nations Educational, Scientific and Cultural Organization
WHO	World Health Organization

Preface

UNESCO's constitution of 1945 declared that 'Wars begin in the minds of men.' It went on to aver that the recent war had been 'made possible by the denial of the democratic principles of the dignity, equality and mutual respect of men, and by the propagation, in their place, through ignorance and prejudice, of the doctrine of the inequality of men and races'. Though it was not called that at the time, this was the beginning of the anti-racist movement in international politics.

This book is an examination of the movement and of its inherent weakness, namely, the tendency to recycle some of the very ideas that it opposes. That anti-racism could itself be racist was recognized by Jean-Paul Sartre (1948:xiv, xli) at the movement's birth when he asserted that the elaboration of an 'anti-racist racism offered the only route which could lead to the abolition of racial differences'. In a preface to an anthology of poems by black writers celebrating the philosophy of *négritude*, Sartre wrote of the theoretical and practical affirmation of white superiority as a thesis that was opposed by *négritude* as the weak phase in a dialectical progression that would impel human history towards a non-racial synthesis. Sartre thought the impulse would come from political action rather than from the realm of ideas. In places this book echoes the conception of a dialectical progression by describing first the thesis of natural inequality, as this was developed in Europe in the nineteenth century, and then its antithesis, which was publicized under UNESCO's leadership in the 1950s. Any description of the new trends that started in the 1960s as a synthesis of the preceding phases quickly becomes artificial because they were so complex, but the beginning of a new century is a good time at which to ask whether a reformulation of currently prevailing ideas about relations between black, brown, white and yellow-skinned peoples could help promote a non-racial synthesis.

The international anti-racist movement was a coalition. Some persons and groups, like the drafters of UNESCO's constitution, wished to combat the *doctrine* of racial inequality. Others, like Sartre, were critics of European imperialism, which they represented as a source of a larger ideological complex that encouraged the spread of the belief that whites were naturally superior to blacks. They presented racial doctrine as a product of political relations. My contention is that the central international problems stemmed from unequal development, because as long as whites were relatively rich and blacks relatively poor economic differences were bound to be associated with the physical differences. Racial doctrine had devastating consequences in Nazi Germany but the leaders of the anti-racist movement tended to exaggerate its significance on the post-war international scene, presumably because they had to simplify if they were to mobilize support and persuade others that their objective was attainable. The reduction of the international economic differences posed, and continues to pose, much more complex problems.

The process that is now called globalization has been in operation for many centuries, as peoples have spread out from the lands of their birth to trade with others, and sometimes to settle overseas. The colonization of foreign parts by the British, Dutch, French, German, and other West European nations was but one prominent component of globalization. Encountering others, peoples fashioned new conceptions of themselves. When groups were of distinctive physical appearance, and when their relations were competitive, what later generations have come to call 'race' complicated the picture. The social structures within which peoples came into contact could be of vital significance in the formation of group conceptions, none greater than the institutions of chattel slavery as that developed in the United States of America. That country's first civil rights act, in 1866, referred to 'citizens of every race and color', thereby authorizing use of the word 'race' to designate groups. It was a fateful step.

The population of the USA comprised millions of individuals differing in their physical appearance. The most obvious kind of difference was that of skin colour, though there were lesser differences of hair form and facial structure associated with it. Because of the country's history, these differences were also associated with the socio-economic and cultural differences that developed during and because of the regime of slavery. These were all statistical associations, so there were persons of African or partly African appearance who did not fit easily into a two-category scheme. It was individuals who differed in physical appearance, just as they differed in socio-economic status; had anyone been able to plot the differences on a chart they would have formed a pattern of continuous variation. To ascribe individuals to 'races' was to:

- assign them to discontinuous categories, distracting attention from differences within categories and from characteristics shared across categories;
- identify biological differences with social and political differences, suggesting that the former caused the latter.

This may be deplored, but that does not remedy the consequences. For the United States, the dilemma was embodied in Justice Blackmun's dictum in the *Bakke* case, that: 'in order to get beyond racism, we must first take account of race. There is no other way. And in order to treat some persons equally, we must treat them differently. We cannot – we dare not – let the Equal Protection clause perpetuate racial supremacy.' Others will wish to add that the methods chosen for 'taking account of race' should not make racial divisions worse.

The US was not the only country to use the word *race* as a classifier, but in the late nineteenth century its practice was the most systematic. Since then, and because of the power of the US and its mass media, US assumptions about people belonging in racial categories have been spread to other world regions. The international anti-racist movement has never known quite what to do about the way in which the language of race can reinforce the identification of biological and social differences. National anti-racist movements, by contrast, have tended to start from the popular usage of their own countries and have tried to correct the misconceptions embedded in those usages. It was ironical that Jean-Paul Sartre should have written of '*racial* differences' because France has been the leading nation to oppose the US conception of racial belonging. The French have long insisted that it is citizenship that matters, and that any differences between citizens that are irrelevant to their rights and duties as citizens must be disregarded. That was their national solution to the problem of nomenclature.

The Swedish parliament has also expressed concern about these misconceptions. In appointing a committee to consider new legislation (Dir. 1999:49) the government stated: 'The Riksdag has declared that there is no scientific justification for dividing humanity into distinct races and from a biological standpoint consequently

no justification for using the word race with reference to humans
. . . the government in international connections should try to see
that usage of the word race with reference to humans is avoided in
official texts so far as is possible.' Since 1994 Sweden has had a law
against *ethnic* discrimination that covers racial discrimination,
rather than the other way round.

As the twentieth century drew towards a close it began to look
as if the appeals that had inspired the anti-racist movement, both
internationally and nationally, no longer evoked the same enthusiasm. Racial matters had never attracted more attention in the
mass media of the West, but it was only old ideas that were
rehearsed. In 1997 the president of the USA appointed an Advisory
Board on Race to advise on 'matters involving race and racial
reconciliation . . . promote a national dialogue . . . increase understanding . . . bridge racial divides . . . [and] identify solutions'. The
Board, under the chairmanship of Professor John Hope Franklin,
had seven members and a substantial staff. Its report, *One America
in the 21st Century* (Franklin, 1998), discussed ways to build a more
united and just America, summarizing the effect of 'race' upon
civil rights enforcement, education, poverty, employment, housing,
stereotyping, the administration of justice, health care and immigration. It ended with ten suggestions on what individuals could
contribute (like 'make a conscious effort to get to know people of
other races').

The assumption that individuals belong in, or to, races, is double-
sided. This can be appreciated by considering the situation of
someone of mixed ancestry who could be assigned to more than one
category. Others may decide in which category such an individual
belongs, or the individual can decide for himself or herself. The two
decisions may lead to the same result, but do not always. It is also
possible that someone can belong in a particular category for certain
purposes but not others. In the US, as in other countries, belonging
in a racial category is legally irrelevant to the enjoyment of constitutional rights, but consciousness of such differences is heightened
when there is a possibility of close social relations, such as marriage
across a line.

In everyday speech few people talk about 'racial categories'. In
the US they are more likely to ask 'is he black or white?' The whole
process of assignment has been bound up with the use of these two
names and with the assumption that anyone with a small quantity
of African ancestry belongs in the black category. It still operates
in a way that restricts the individual's freedom of choice to decide whether, in particular circumstances, he or she wishes to be
identified with a racial category, and, if so, with which one. The

composition of the population is changing with more immigration from Latin America and Asia and the new groups do not fit easily into a system of categories designed for different circumstances.

The Franklin board recognized 'the inadequacy of our existing language' for working through the issues that 'surround race', but it was caught in a trap embodied in the language of race that President Clinton had employed. Though it seeks to overcome differences, the metaphor of dialogue is divisive in assigning individuals to groups. Group representatives are trapped, too. Since they are in some measure accountable to those they represent, they have to prioritize the interests peculiar to their groups rather than the interests shared across group boundaries. A dialogue is based upon what differentiates the two parties, not upon what they have in common, and so instead of bringing them together the dynamics of the relationship can push the groups further apart.

Recognition of the danger that talking about race makes people more conscious of group differences, even when they should be irrelevant, informed the suggestion during the Nixon presidency that the best policy for the federal government was that of 'benign neglect', enforcing the law but not attempting to influence the ways in which people relate to one another for fear that if a government gets deeply involved it does more harm than good. That was not a popular suggestion. Activists, being conscious of the existing disparities, wish to intensify their struggle and are impatient with hesitations over what they see as points of detail. Until recently there has been no alternative set of concepts that could both appeal to the practically minded and pioneer a way out of the language trap. Now there is one. This book contends that the report *One America in the 21st Century* could have offered a vision of how to impel policies forward from the civil rights movement of the 1960s had it jettisoned the language of dialogue in order to concentrate upon discrimination as a violation of shared values. It could have looked beyond the USA's national conception of constitutional rights to the international conception of human rights. The language of human rights is practical in the highest degree because it is grounded in international law and in national laws; it encompasses everyone, not just victim groups. Yet it is not simple. It takes time to learn how to use this language.

After offering a concise analysis of what the new movement had to combat, this book turns to the history of international anti-racism. Ideas of racial distinctiveness had been opposed from the outset, particularly by Christians committed to the Biblical account of human origins. World War II heightened concern about the dangers of racial doctrine. The international movement drew upon the support of national movements but went beyond them to influence decisions on a higher level. The principal organs of the United Nations, like the General Assembly and the Economic and Social Council, are political bodies, lacking any competence to pronounce on matters of scientific knowledge, so, as chapter 2 notes, they gave the task of reviewing the scientific issues to the UN's educational, social and cultural agency, UNESCO. The mandate was limited by what were seen as the political imperatives of the 1950s and 1960s. Chapter 3 describes the actions of the General Assembly subsequent to what appeared a threatened revival of Nazi ideology in Germany in 1959. Four years later, in the Declaration on the Elimination of All Forms of Racial Discrimination, the Assembly 'affirmed the necessity of speedily eliminating racial discrimination throughout the world'. The Declaration assumed that racial discrimination sprang from doctrines that were generated by social structures like those of fascism and colonialism. This was a noble lie. It was empirically false, but its acceptance made possible in 1965 the adoption of the International Convention on the Elimination of All Forms of Racial Discrimination (ICERD), which has been of inestimable practical value.

The Convention incorporated two distinct conceptions of the nature and causes of racial discrimination, which I call Thesis One and Thesis Two. They have contrasting implications for the anti-racist movement. A strategy based upon Thesis One and upon concepts of human rights would enable the anti-racist movement to overcome its tendency to recycle the ideas it opposes. No 'dialogue on race' can do this because of the internal contradiction embodied in this use of the word. The manner in which implementation of the Convention has been monitored since 1970 is summarily described in Chapter 4; subsequent chapters review experience in selected countries. In some, like the USA and the United Kingdom, national action against racial discrimination preceded the adoption of the Convention. In others, the international movement influenced national action, though governments often had domestic reasons for what they did. In virtually all countries the international dimension is now important. As an illustration of the Convention's potential, Chapter 5 singles out the dispute over whether the Australian government's recent legislation on Aboriginal land rights is in conformity with the legal obligations it accepted in 1975. Chapter 6 discusses the reception, in August 2001, of the initial report of the USA. This was the first occasion on which a US government has submitted its policies in this very sensitive field to official oversight by an international body of experts. In view of the pride of contemporary US governments (and most governments are proud!), this was a major event. This chapter, and the next one about Britain in Europe, both argue that the vocabulary of human rights offers the best prospect for avoiding the language trap.

The international anti-racist movement started as an elite movement. In the 1960s the national anti-racist movement in the USA became a mass movement, one that succeeded in changing the definition of *racism* to encompass more than doctrine. As explained in chapter 3, this change had immediate effects upon the international stage. Then in 2001 the UN World Conference Against Racism, which is described in chapter 8, showed that the commitment to combat racism in its expanded sense offered an opportunity for many kinds of group to publicize their grievances. By making such extensive use of the idea of *racism* did the activists breathe new life into the idea of *race*? The inter-governmental discussions on the text of the conference declaration threw into relief different views about the adequacy of the language of race. The fifteen states of the European Union stated their shared objection to any wording that might appear to endorse belief in the existence of different human races, but there was little support for their point of view. While agreeing that 'races' were not biologically distinctive, some states insisted on their social distinctiveness. Because some other states suspected the EU of trying to weaken international action against racial discrimination, the arguments were often heated and acrimonious. In the end its representative read out a formal statement of the EU's position, which, together with other such statements, forms part of the official report of the conference.

The statement stressed the fundamental nature of the 1978 proclamation of the General Conference of UNESCO that 'All human beings belong to a single species.' It noted that for the purpose of applying the International Convention the concept of race might be helpful for identifying the basis of discrimination, and went on: 'The member States of the European Union consider that the acceptance of any formulation implying the existence of separate human "races" could be a retrograde step as it risks denying the unity of humanity.' They expressed concern lest any use of the terms 'race' and 'racial' by the Conference might imply acceptance of doctrines that they rejected.

In the long run the only way of displacing misleading conceptions (of race, as of other things) is to find and promote better conceptions. Chapters 9 and 10 therefore discuss the merits of human rights concepts in the sphere of public policy and as aids to progress in social science. Whereas fifty years ago it was essential to attack misconceptions about race, much current teaching about racism tends, in spite of itself, to recycle nineteenth-century scientific waste. The history of science shows that the best method for the disposal of such waste is the development of improved explanations, and the same principle can be applied to popular language.

Those who disagree with other arguments in the chapters that follow may nevertheless agree that the idiom of race in contemporary parlance can constitute a trap, and that the problem of how to avoid it is of surpassing importance. Social scientists should be able to offer a lead in the search for a solution.

1

Race as Species

When people identify themselves and others as Americans, British, Canadians, French and so on, they use proper names. When they describe a group as a nation or a race, they classify it with supposedly similar groups and distinguish it from dissimilar ones. This is the origin of the idea of race as a belief or assumption that human individuals belong in races. The assumption that physical differences determine the contours of what are really social groups has been reinforced by popular English-language usage.

Any attempt to correct the resulting misunderstandings is more likely to succeed if it benefits from knowledge of how a word with such powerful biological associations came in the first place to be used as a designation for certain kinds of social group. In summarizing this, as other histories, it is important not to force the evidence into the moral categories of a later age. If some of the statements made in the 1850s were repeated today they might appropriately be called 'racist' with all the moral condemnation that implies. Any such description would rest on some assumption about the intention behind the statement. To come to any conclusion about a person's intention it is necessary to know quite a lot about that person's world and the knowledge that was available to him or her. People today may say things they believe correct but that in a future era may look decidedly dubious.

Yet members of a later generation can use new knowledge to get a better understanding of what went on in earlier periods. They can spot the blind alleys and concentrate on the developments that proved significant. The very notion of summarizing a history implies as much, though different writers may summarize it in different ways according to the story they seek to tell. This chapter simplifies a complicated history by claiming that the notion that human races resemble animal species constitutes a thread that runs through two hundred years of writing about race and this helps the reader understand what the fuss was about.

A two-dimensional concept

According to the *Oxford English Dictionary* the origin of the word *race* is obscure. It seems to come from the Old Norse, in which it meant a running or a rush of water. Many of its early meanings relate to a sense of movement either in space (like a horse race) or over generations, as in its use from the middle of the sixteenth century to denote a line of descent. When used to identify such a line it is two-dimensional, the vertical dimension being the distinctiveness over time (as in 'the race of Abraham') and the horizontal one being the distinctiveness at a particular moment in time (as in 'the Eskimo race').

Between the sixteenth and eighteenth centuries the English people's ideas about themselves and other peoples were dominated by the anthropology of the Bible. All humans descended from Adam and differences between them were to be explained genealogically. Such explanations could be of political significance. Thus in the fifth edition of a book first published in 1605 called *Restitution of Decayed Intelligence*, Richard Verstegan asserted 'Englishmen are descended of German race and were heretofore generally called Saxons.' The author went on to explain that 'the Germans are a most noble nation' because, according to the Roman historian Tacitus, 'the authority of the kings is not unlimited'; 'on minor matters, the chiefs deliberate; on larger questions the whole tribe'; and 'the King or chief is attended to more because of his authoritative persuasion than of any power to command'. Verstegan, who was supporting the parliamentary cause against the claims of the Stuart monarchs to rule by divine right, had constructed a genealogy that undermined these claims. It is an example of the way that, in this period, the word *race* was used in the sense of its vertical dimension. This was no aberration, for at much the same time it was being used in a similar fashion in the writing of French history. There *race* was a way of identifying the Franks and the Gauls, also in the course of an appeal to Tacitus, but this time to try to resolve disputes about the privileges of the aristocracy. So in both Britain and France the word had become a counter in internal politics, well before it was used in explanations of the differences between Europeans and non-Europeans (Banton, 1977:13–26).

Some thought that differences between peoples might also be explained genealogically. The Bible seemed to say that all humans descended from Adam and Eve, but some doubters found passages in Genesis that could support a belief that Adam was the ancestor of the Jews alone, and that his group was not the only one in the region at the time. The first belief was known as monogenesis; to it was opposed the doctrine of polygenesis, or multiple origins.

Genealogies embody the vertical dimension, but a group constituted by common descent is necessarily distinct from other descent groups, so the horizontal component of race as a classification is as inherent to the idea of race as the vertical one. Nevertheless the word could be used in ways that gave differing emphases to the two dimensions. This created an ambiguity that became troublesome in the eighteenth century when scholars abandoned the use of Latin to write in the vernaculars. When classifying plants and animals Linnaeus and his followers had distinguished *genus, species* and *varietas* as categories. Then in English and in French some anthropologists started to use *race* as a category without explaining its relationship to the existing categories. This was an ominous mistake. There was no avoiding the two-dimensional significance of the word *race* in ordinary language but scientific taxonomy needs to be systematic. If the Linnaean scheme of *genus, species* and *varietas* was in some way unsatisfactory it could be modified. It was wrong to try to insert into it another category without agreement about how it was to relate to the existing categories.

Yet this is what happened. Some writers used *race* as a synonym for *species* as a class in the horizontal dimension consisting of anatomically similar humans who might be of distinctive origin. Others used it as a synonym for *varietas*, a class of persons who were the present representatives of a line of descent that must at some time have shared a common ancestor with persons belonging to other similar classes. In the mid-1780s the philosophers Immanuel Kant and Johan Gottfried von Herder both commented on the disturbing ambiguity. Kant distinguished between *Naturbeschreibung* (nature-description) and *Naturgeschichte* (natural history). The former was static, a classification at a moment in time that was based upon similarities between specimens ordered into genera, species and varieties. Where nature-description took up the horizontal dimension, natural history dealt with relations between genera, species and varieties over time and reflected the vertical dimension. Kant wrote: 'The wolf, the fox, the jackal, the hyena and the house dog are so many kinds of four-footed beasts. If one assumes that each of them has had to have a separate ancestry, then they are that many species, but if one concludes that they could all have descended from the one stem, then they are only races thereof' (Greene, 1961:363n15; for reviews of writing about racial classification, see Banton, 1986, 1998a).

Lévi-Strauss (1952:5) maintained that the original sin of anthropology was its confusion of the idea of race in the biological sense with groups produced by human action. If any one writer bore a special responsibility for this it was his compatriot, the great French anatomist, Georges Cuvier. He popularized the horizontal sense of the word *race*, using it as a synonym for *variety*. When his magisterial work *Le Règne animal* of 1817 was translated into English in London in 1827, Cuvier's references (in the French) to *races* were translated as *varieties*, but in the next English translation (published in New York in 1831) any attempt to correct possible misunderstandings was abandoned. The designation *race* was maintained. The leading English anthropologist of the period, James Cowles Prichard, protested in 1836 about the way a word that denoted a succession of individuals propagated from a given stock was being wrongly used to imply a distinction in the physical character of a series of individuals. His objection passed unheeded.

The long and unilluminating debate in nineteenth-century British and French anthropology about the status of the race concept came to no clear conclusion. To write about blacks, whites and yellows as if they were distinct species within the genus *Homo sapiens* was to represent the differences between them as similar to the differences between lions, tigers, leopards and jaguars as different species within the genus *Panthera*. Lions, tigers, leopards and jaguars were accounted distinct species because they did not interbreed. Much of the discussion at the time centred upon the mule, which is the sterile offspring of a horse and a donkey; the inability of mules to produce offspring was taken as proving that horses and donkeys were distinct species. Since it was evident that blacks, whites and yellows interbred and produced fertile offspring, the accepted criterion for the definition of species constituted an obstacle that was never overcome by those who maintained that they resembled separate species. They also found the public hostile to the suggestion that the human races were of separate origin. It might be thought that a theory of permanent differences would have been welcomed in the Southern states of the USA as offering an intellectual justification for the enslavement of blacks, but, up to the Civil War of 1861–5, that was not the case. Public opinion was committed to the belief that Adam was the ancestor of both blacks and whites. Justifications for slavery could be found in the Bible. In the early part of the century it was believed that blacks had been held back by the African environment and that they would eventually catch up with

other races. Only after the war did the theory of permanent difference get a hold.

Prichard and other advocates of the doctrine of monogenesis had
to confront a different challenge, also centring on the Bible. The
book of Genesis seemed to say that God had created the earth and
the human species about six thousand years ago. In that event,
and since everyone could see that children usually resembled their
parents, how could the physical differences between blacks, whites
and yellows have come about? Was it the influence of environment?
There was no good evidence in support of such a hypothesis, which
made the idea of separate creation seem more plausible. From a
twenty-first-century perspective it looks as if the mid-nineteenth
century was a period waiting for Darwin to disperse the clouds
of confusion by discovering the principle of natural selection and
explaining how evolution operated, though that was not how it
appeared at the time.

Racial typology

The first theory to attempt to account systematically for the physical and cultural differences between groups known as races was
one best called the theory of racial typology. Formulated in the late
1840s and early 1850s by writers in France, Britain and the USA, it
held that:

1   Variations in the constitution and behaviour of individuals are
    the expression of differences between underlying types of a
    relatively permanent kind, each one of which is suited to a
    particular continent or zoological province.
2   Social categories in the long run reflect and are aligned with the
    natural categories that produce them.
3   Individuals belonging to a particular racial type display an
    innate antagonism towards individuals belonging to other racial
    types, the degree of antagonism depending upon the relation-
    ship between the two types.

The typologists argued that just as kangaroos are found only in
Australia, so are humans of the Australian Aboriginal type found
only there, and for similar reasons. The natural world was divided
into provinces, each with its distinctive fauna, including its own
kind of humans.

Robert Knox, a strident typologist, opened his 1850 book *The
Races of Men* with the proclamation: 'That race is in human affairs

everything, is simply a fact, the most remarkable, the most comprehensive, which philosophy has ever announced. Race is everything: literature, science, art – in a word, civilization depends upon it.' Knox was a Scotsman, but his book was published in London. Readers there may have thought that they had heard something like this already, for in his novel *Tancred* (1847) the future British prime minister Benjamin Disraeli made one of his characters wind up a similar discussion of the historical success of the English with the conclusion: 'All is race; there is no other truth.' According to Knox's version of typology humans needed to understand the ways in which they were limited by natural laws; it was useless for a race to try to colonize a territory for which it was not adapted. In France Arthur de Gobineau sketched an even more pessimistic version, arguing that race-mixing had gone past the point of no return so that Europeans could look forward only to progressive degeneration and mediocrity, benumbed in nullity like a buffalo grazing in the stagnant waters of a marsh.

In subsequent decades a related idea that the British, the Germans and the Nordics were the contemporary representatives of a superior race, the Aryans, received a cordial welcome in West European societies being transformed by industrialism. New sections of the population were learning to read and to take an interest in developments overseas. They were receptive to a message that flattered them. Writers like Houston Stewart Chamberlain rewrote history as the story of racial superiority, while the forerunners of the Nazis selected the parts of Gobineau's writing that suited their purposes and ignored the rest.

How the idea of race was used to build a philosophy that could, in simpler form, be used to mobilize less educated sections of the population can be seen from the writing of the Nazi movement's chief ideologist, Alfred Rosenberg (1970:101–8). Holding forth on the subject of Nordic religion, he presented love and pity, honour and duty, as the driving values of almost all races and nations capable of culture. Nowhere was the struggle for primacy between love and honour more tragically evident than in the conflicts between the Nordic races and their surroundings. The Vikings were said to be without breeding, uninhibited by cultivated reflection upon purpose, but motivated by a sense of personal honour that drove them to new regions in which there was land to master. Christianity did not understand the idea of honour, even if the leaders of the church sought power in the same ways as other princes. It was racial-*Volkish* thinking that inspired the Vikings and protected them from the greatest of dangers, race-mixing, and therefore from descent into racial chaos.

This is not to say that Hitler himself accepted all of Rosenberg's ideas. In *Mein Kampf* he had set out a simpler scheme, dividing humankind into 'culture-founders', 'culture-bearers' and 'culture destroyers'. The bearers of cultural development were 'the Aryans', who needed to preserve 'racial purity' to fulfil their mission. In later years there were Nazi leaders who felt quite out of place in the audience for Wagnerian operas but were there because the Führer gave them to understand that these embodied values central to their movement. The Nazis were careful in the use they made of Darwinian ideas of race; they drew more upon racial typology because that gave them greater freedom to manipulate the idea.

Selectionism

Natural selection accounted for the characteristics of species and sub-species. Darwin wrote of certain kinds of butterfly as 'geographical races, or sub-species' being 'local forms completely fixed and isolated'. Because they were isolated they did not interbreed and so 'there is no possible test but individual opinion to determine which of them shall be considered as species and which as varieties'. Darwin used the word *race* in the same sense as Kant and Prichard, but he introduced a new understanding of the process of change.

There was a rush to apply Darwin's ideas to the study of society, giving rise to an intellectual movement that has been called social Darwinism. Some individuals within this movement (like Sir Arthur Keith) drove its ideas to an extreme in formulating what may be named the selectionist theory of racial relations. It held that:

1 Evolution may be assisted if interbreeding populations are kept separate so that they can develop their special capacities (as in animal breeding).
2 Racial prejudice serves this function and in so doing reinforces racial categories in social life.
3 Therefore racial groups are products of evolutionary processes of inheritance and selection.

It should be noted that whereas the typological theory implied that pure races had existed in the past, the selectionist theory implied that they were in the process of creation. Blacks, whites and yellows were not species, but over the course of centuries they could become them. The typological theory had stressed the horizontal dimension of the race concept, implying that the correct classification of individuals and groups would explain why it was that some races were technologically more advanced. The selectionist theory stressed the vertical dimension. Writers of a later generation have described both theories as examples of scientific racism, but the name fits the selectionist theory much better.

Another strand within the social Darwinist movement was that embodied in the doctrines of eugenics. Its founder, Sir Francis Galton, collected evidence to show that a streak of genius ran in certain families. There were other families that produced a more-than-average number of intellectually backward or physically handicapped children. Was it not desirable to encourage childbirth among those biologically best endowed (positive eugenics) while improving the environmental conditions surrounding reproduction in the poorer classes and preventing reproduction by those likely to give birth to handicapped children (negative eugenics)? The eugenics movement had a scientific aura that appealed to social reformers. In the United States eugenics provided a rationale for arguments that immigration policy should be based upon quotas favouring persons from countries where the population had the best biological inheritance. In Europe it was an important influence upon the political culture of the period in which racial theories were at their height (Mazower, 1998:77–101). In Britain before World War I there were fears that insanitary conditions in the cities were causing physical decline, and a movement for 'racial hygiene' advocated elementary measures for the promotion of good health. The need for national efficiency became a slogan crossing party lines. Sweden and Switzerland maintained policies for the compulsory sterilization of the unfit until the 1960s. While the birth of a deformed or handicapped child can be an individual tragedy for a family, it also poses questions about the causes of physical handicap. In some African cultures the birth of a deformed child can be taken as indicating that the mother has committed adultery. More generally, such misfortunes contribute to folk beliefs about inheritance and can be an indirect influence upon racial thought.

The establishment of population genetics in the 1930s completed Darwin's revolution of 1859 by showing that inheritance has to be analysed statistically. For the typological theory to be persuasive it would be necessary to find discontinuities between racial gene pools, but research reveals only differences of degree, sometimes measured as 'clines'. The new understanding was expressed in the statement 'there are no races, only clines'. There are important differences in the inheritance of certain medical conditions between the groups popularly called races. Further research in behaviour genetics, in socio-biology and in evolutionary psychology may well show that processes of selection are relevant to the explanation of some kinds of group difference. Any problems that such discoveries may appear to cause will not be resolved by condemning nineteenth-century scientific mistakes. The troubles may lie in the popular understanding of so-called racial differences.

Popular usage in English

Botanists and zoologists assign specimens to classes in the course of developing theories to account for their special characteristics. In human social life individuals may be assigned, or assign themselves, to classes that are popularly called races, and that may in some degree correspond to biological classes. There may be disputes about whether an individual has been assigned by others to the correct class or about whether the classes themselves are correctly defined. In so far as a recognition of so-called races helps explain their characteristics, much depends upon whether individuals identify themselves with such groupings.

The popular understanding of a word like *race* is influenced by an interaction. When the mass media write about an individual's social attributes they need to use expressions that will be understood by their readers. When the legislature drafts laws to regulate conduct they need to do likewise. The decisions they take then influence popular understanding. If the legislature prohibits discrimination 'on racial grounds' it will define those grounds and, inevitably, lend authority to a certain conception of race. In similar fashion, if the government holds a population census and requires members of the public to identify themselves in terms of racial or ethnic origins, this will have an important influence.

The language employed in the first US Civil Rights Act in 1866 may well have been fateful. It declared that all persons born in the United States were citizens thereof, and that 'such citizens of every race and color . . . shall have the same right to make and enforce contracts' and to do various other things. This may have been the first time that Congress used the word 'race' to designate groups in this way and to refer to the protection of constitutional rights 'without distinction of race or color'. The Act could have referred to citizens of every colour; it was not obliged to use the term 'race' as well and thereby to add legal authority to the idea that individuals belonged in racial categories. Though it recognized a plurality of races in the USA it was primarily concerned to establish the equal rights of blacks and whites. It reinforced the assumptions that all (or most) citizens were either black or white, that these classes or groups were properly called races, and that the individuals within them were further divided according to their ethnic origin.

Thereafter the use of 'race' as a designation for sub-groups within the population of the US became a feature of everyday speech that is rarely challenged. To an observer on the other side of the Atlantic who has not had the opportunity to make a systematic study of this usage, it looks as if the distinction between black and white became the paradigm case for the US understanding of the nature of race. In situations of tension between two groups identified by race there is likely to be a high level of agreement within each group, and disagreement between them, as to what the main issues are, and, because of the tension, they will be political issues. Tensions were strongest in the Deep South, so it was this region that most often called the tune. The white Southern definition of race, exemplified in the rule that one drop of African blood meant that a person was accounted black, was taken over by blacks as well and was spread to other regions of the country and of the world. By naming socio-political groups *races* the usage implied that some hereditary factor distinguished them in perpetuity from other similar groups and magnified the differences between groups.

In the age of Theodore Roosevelt and Taft, according to Lauren (1996:68) US political leaders were as much inclined to imperialist rhetoric and to prophecies of racial war as any politicians in Europe. The sociology of race relations which developed in the US between World Wars I and II offered a more sober assessment. Nevertheless, it tended to accept the folk, or popular, conception of race, high-lighting the consciousness of racial difference as a variable. It was not until after World War II, with the publication of a magisterial treatise by a Trinidadian-born born author (Cox, 1948), that the legitimacy of the folk concept as a term in a sociological analysis was seriously called into question. Cox's argument is described in chapter 10.

On the eastern side of the Atlantic there was no situation such as that of the Deep South to crystallize popular attention. Some have thought that a racial ideology was fashioned on the imperial frontier and brought back to the metropolitan country, but the historical evidence does not support this hypothesis. It was the intellectuals at home who formulated racial theories. As already mentioned, there was the seventeenth-century thesis based on Tacitus that the English were 'of German race', and the eighteenth-century environmentalist theory, based on the writings of travellers, that Africans were inferior because they had been held back by the unfavourable environment in which they had developed, whereas in a new environment they could catch up with Europeans (Barker, 1978). Popular use of the word *race* in nineteenth-century Britain was also influenced by events nearer home. Movements in many European countries that demanded greater political rights for the ordinary people took forms that were usually called nationalist. Race was commonly a synonym for nation. In explaining what stimulated him to write his *Essai sur l'inégalité des races humaines*, Gobineau referred explicitly to 'the great events, the bloody wars, the revolutions' of 1848. That year was described by T. H. Hodgkin, the English physician and philanthropist, as 'remarkable for the savage atrocities which have signalised those wars of races'. Whether a man like Hodgkin thought he explained the character of the conflicts better by calling them wars of races is difficult to determine, for in the middle years of the century the word was used in so many ways, as in a reference to 'the race of lawyers'. Charles Kingsley could assert that 'there is no more beautiful race in Europe than the wives and daughters of our London shopkeepers' and 'undergraduates are an affectionate race'.

In Britain, arguments about race sometimes overlapped with arguments about West Indian slavery and the motivation to work. The abolitionists had thought that once freed from coercion black labourers would work harder because they would be working for themselves. Yet it turned out that ex-slaves put a high value on their leisure and were not motivated by the prevailing wage levels. The report that cane crops in Demerera were rotting for want of harvesters drove Thomas Carlyle to despair. In 1847 he was but recently back from a visit to famine-struck Ireland. In his notorious 'Occasional Discourse on the Nigger Question' he maintained that all men must work, if not voluntarily, then by compulsion. The British had overestimated the power of a free market and by 'emancipating' the West Indies had turned them into a black Ireland, 'like our own white or sallow Ireland, sluttishly starving from age to age on its act of parliament "freedom"'. Arguments about British policy in Ireland often made use of racial doctrine. Frederick Engels, writing of the condition of the English working class in 1844, maintained that the Englishman, 'who is not yet wholly uncivilised', expected a higher standard of living than the Irishman, who, by competition, could drag the Englishman's wages and standards of living down to his own level.

Conflicts within Europe, of a kind that would now be called nationalist, may have done most to stimulate use of the idea of race to explain events. Discussing the rise of nationalist sentiment in the Balkans, E. A. Freeman (1877:211) remarked:

It is only in quite modern times, under the direct influence of the preaching of the doctrine of race, that a hard and fast line has been drawn between Greeks and Bulgarians. That doctrine has cut two ways. It has given both nations, Greek and Bulgarian alike, a renewed national life, national strength, national hopes . . . but . . . it has arrayed them against each other.

The doctrine of race to which Freeman referred was one that asserted that political life had to be based on the map of nationality. Everyone was to be grouped with others of the same descent and governed as part of a homogenous unit. It was, he wrote, 'a learned doctrine . . . an inference from facts which the mass of mankind could never have found out for themselves'. Unlike some others, Freeman did not see race as an unconscious determinant of group behaviour. A little later, in his 1906 book *Macedonia: Its Races and their Future*, H. N. Brailsford was still using a contemporary idiom when he wrote about 'the muddle of racial conflicts' in the Balkans. Ideas of race were not then identified with differences of colour.

At the end of the nineteenth century the idiom of race was sometimes used as a mode of collective self-congratulation. Joseph Chamberlain, on appointment as secretary of state for the colonies, could proclaim that one of his qualifications for office was that: 'I believe in the British race. I believe that the British race is the greatest of governing races that the world has ever seen. I say this not merely as an empty boast, but as proved and evidenced by the success we have had in administering the vast dominions which are connected with these small islands.' Three years later Lord Roseberry could ask: 'What is Empire but the predominance of Race? How marvellous it all is! . . . Do we not hail, in this, less the energy and fortune of a race than the supreme direction of the Almighty?' Chamberlain seems to have been appealing to a conception of race as comprising the people of the United Kingdom, English, Scottish, Welsh and Irish, and to their political qualities. Whether he thought these qualities to be biological in origin is uncertain. Roseberry seems to have thought that differences between peoples were part of God's design.

References to a 'race problem' or a 'colour problem' multiplied but remained inchoate, in part, perhaps, because there was no political pressure to crystallize thoughts about the subject. The conflict between the interests of Africans and settlers of European origin in South Africa might have had such an effect, but at the end of the century British opinion was more concerned by the political conflict between the Boers and the settlers of British origin. At that time it was more usual to refer to Boers and Britons as races than to write of black and white races. Some of the confusion stemmed from an inability to separate the idea of a problem into its component elements. For example, the British Institute of Philosophical Studies held a meeting in 1926 on 'The Problem of Colour in Relation to the Idea of Equality'. The first contribution was from Sir Fredrick Lugard, a distinguished former colonial administrator. He emphasized the importance of starting with a precise definition of the nature of the 'Colour problem', but regretted that it was difficult to find two people who could agree on such a definition. Without explaining what he understood by colour prejudice, he asked whether it was intuitive or acquired; was it a natural law restricting miscegenation; was it reciprocated by the Coloured races towards the Whites; did it operate between the Coloured races themselves? Nor was he confident about the definition of race, for he wrote of the Southern races of Europe, and of the Nordic races, as if in these circumstances it was not important to differentiate races from nations. Looking further afield, he also wrote of the Portuguese creating 'virile half-caste races' and of Negroes in the United States as a distinct race. He spoke of the desirability, in circumstances such as those of the USA, of each race 'pursuing its own inherited traditions, preserving its own race purity and race pride' (Lugard et al., 1926:8). Neither of the other contributors to the same symposium, Morris Ginsberg and a labour expert, H. A. Wyndham, gave any clear meaning to the concept of a colour problem. Ginsberg reviewed the evidence on the inheritance of intelligence; he discussed the idea of equality and questioned Lugard's advocacy of 'equality in things spiritual; agreed divergence in the physical and material'. Wyndham contended that if racial groups in South Africa and elsewhere could attain economic equality this would bring a solution to 'the problem of political control'.

That there should have been so little clarity about the nature of the 'colour problem' is interesting. Much of the history and sociology of imperialism was taken for granted, such as the proposition that the expansion of European power had been bound to lead to European control in regions of economic interest to the colonizers. There had been other empires in which people from one ethnic group ruled those of another. Were the results any different because the Europeans were of a skin colour different from that of those they came to rule? Were the results any different because the idea of race was so widespread? In the European empires of modern times, political superiority was associated with a difference of colour or race, but the association may have been fortuitous. In the terminal phase of European imperialism its critics exploited the association.

Mrs Eleanor Roosevelt, reflecting on her service in the early years of the UN, wrote of the intense feeling among persons from Africa and Asia 'that we, because our skins are white, necessarily look down upon all peoples whose skins are yellow or black or brown. This thought is never out of their minds' (quoted Lauren, 1996:241). In such a sentence it is the word *because* that should prompt reflection. Maybe most people of European origin did look down on most Africans and Asians, but was it simply because of their skin colour? Many Africans and Asians may have believed this, but the differences of colour may have mattered to whites because they signalled differences in living standards and culture. Much of the resentment over racial inequality, and much of the criticism of colonialism, sprang from resentment over unequal development. This led the UN in 1986 to proclaim a right to development and to insist that it was a human right, even if it was of a different character from the right to be protected from discrimination. Sometimes it is difficult to separate the idea that humans belong in races from concerns about unequal development.

In the British as in other empires, control was exercised by a very small officer class. In British India there was one Briton to 3,000 Indians, in Nigeria one to 2,000 Nigerians (Mason, 1970:64). Officer classes tend to keep themselves apart socially and to cultivate ideas that help them function as a team and justify their privileges. Depending heavily upon mutual trust and loyalty, they have to put pressure on any of their own number who might deviate from group norms. The admission to their circle of persons from the ranks of the ruled – whether in the colonial service or in the armed forces – is regarded as very tricky. The first British anti-discrimination law was one passed in 1833 when parliament included in the Government of India Act a clause that stated that no native of India 'shall by reason only of his religion, place of birth, descent, colour, or any of them, be disabled from holding any place, office or employment' in the East India Company, but those who were supposed to give effect to this law found excuses for ignoring it (Lester and Bindman, 1972:383–418).

In 1885 a Polish sociologist, Ludwig Gumplowicz, had written of the process 'by which tribes became peoples, peoples nations, nations grew into races' that underlay 'the perpetual struggle between races for dominance, the soul and spirit of all history'. That white solidarity would evoke the solidarity of the far more numerous non-white population was a prospect of which the next generation was acutely conscious. F. Ashton-Gwatkin, the author of a 1921 British Foreign Office memorandum entitled *Racial Discrimination and Immigration*, put it bluntly: 'Great Britain, the

Dominions and the United States are all equally interested in avoiding a discussion of the subject' because the 'white and the coloured races cannot and will not amalgamate . . . one or the other must be the ruling caste' (Lauren, 1996:109; Füredi, 1998:4). Discussion would only increase racial consciousness and accelerate the progression towards the ultimate confrontation. Frank Füredi assembles much evidence in support of his argument that while a sense of race gave Western elites a confidence in themselves and a coherent view of the world, it made them worry about whether their race was maintaining its quality, and generated great apprehension about the long-term future. The reaction to Nazi race science was in his view less important than fears about the development of race consciousness among the non-white peoples of the empire. Füredi believes that this was a major problem for British and US foreign policy, and that it was the more troublesome because it could not be discussed in public.

Chinese and Japanese feelings that whites looked down upon them had been exacerbated by the immigration policies of the US and Australian governments. They underlay the Japanese proposal, advanced at the Paris peace conference in 1919, that the Covenant of the League of Nations should include an affirmation of racial equality (Lauren, 1996:58–63). The Japanese delegation presented a resolution: 'The equality of nations being a basic principle of the League of Nations, the High Contracting Parties agree to accord as soon as possible to all alien nationals of States members of the League equal and just treatment in every respect making no distinction either in law or fact on account of their race or nationality.' Many delegations were sympathetic; when others demurred, drafting amendments were proposed, but every solution was resisted by the Australian prime minister; the British delegate, although generally unopposed, was unwilling to overrule him (Lauren, 1996:82–107; McKean, 1983:16). Twenty-five years later there was a repeat performance at the Dumbarton Oaks conference (which considered plans for the creation of the United Nations and established the IMF and the World Bank). China proposed that in the Charter of the UN 'The principle of equality of all states and all races shall be upheld.' Initially the proposal was resisted, but later a similar objective was achieved by the wording of the second and third paragraphs of the Charter's first Article (Lauren, 1996:158–60).

That the Foreign Office should have used the word *discrimination* in 1921 is itself remarkable, because that word was rarely used in the discussion of racial relations until after World War II and the word *racism* entered the English and French languages only in the 1930s. One reason why the report of the Institute of Philosophical

Studies discussion in London in 1926 reads so strangely to a modern reader is that what he or she will perceive as the issues had not been identified in the 1920s. Just as political pressure crystallizes issues, so philosophical analysis is needed to refine them. Political pressure may encourage the study of issues regarded as problems but it rarely offers any incentive to the examination of the concepts used in popular debate. The search for an escape from the language trap within the idea of race requires scholarly imagination and inspiration.

Nazi racial policies had a crystallizing effect in some quarters. Huxley and Haddon's 1935 *We Europeans*, published in the same year as the Nuremberg laws, was only partially successful in separating what was at one time called biological race from social race. In retrospect, the book seems a weak response to a major threat, but for its time it was a path-breaking advance. Perhaps the most shocking feature of the Nazi era was the ease with which Germans were persuaded to retract their moral boundaries. Jews, Gypsies, mentally handicapped people and homosexuals were made to appear 'other', outside the boundary of humans who had a moral claim upon other humans. The doctrine of racial superiority played a major part in a process of social and moral exclusion, and the suspicion must linger that, in similar circumstances, other nations would have been as ready to revise their moral ideas as the Germans were. If doctrines can exert such influence within nations, the international community must be able to react.

The British Colonial Office was preoccupied with the practical problems of particular colonies and reluctant to consider abstract principles about racial equality. After the fall of Singapore in 1942 its officials had to work desperately to influence policy-makers in the USA who wanted a promise that after the war India and the colonies would become independent. They devised a new political language for a post-war world; imperialism was to be transformed into a partnership for promoting development and welfare, while the metropolitan power was to protect the minorities that might suffer were sovereignty too quickly transferred to representatives of the largest ethnic group (Wolton, 2000). The transformation was driven by international politics and these changed the significance given to the word *race*.

Young Europeans in the latter part of the twentieth century were inclined to disparage any suggestion that the maintenance of social distinctions associated with rank could help maintain discipline, but many human rights reports to the UN in recent times have drawn attention to the problem of impunity, referring to localities in which troops and armed police can abuse members of the public without any expectation that they will be disciplined for so doing. The parties may now be of the same colour, but the corruptions of power remain. Though democracy requires the elimination of any exclusiveness based on ascribed characteristics, like those of race, few political tasks are more difficult than engineering a gradual sharing or transfer of power from one group to another. The British tried again at the time of decolonization in the late 1950s to Africanize their colonial service, but an analysis of the options open in practice to the European district officer in East Africa (summarized in Banton, 1983:174–5) demonstrated that goodwill was not enough. There are limits to the social engineering of human relations.

The tangled web

What Sartre called the practical affirmation of white superiority seems unproblematic, but this chapter must surely conclude with doubts about the relation between the practical and the theoretical affirmations.

There could be no doubting white supremacy as a matter of fact. European expansion into other regions of the world was an expression of unequal development, a phase in the process of globalization. Technologically and economically the European region was far ahead. The long-term effect of its expansion may be eventually to reduce regional inequalities, but its medium-term effect has been to increase consciousness of them, for the regional inequalities have been recreated in the parts of the Third World that white influence has reached. In some parts the Europeans wanted the land for their own settlement and they adopted genocidal measures when dispossessing the indigenous peoples. Some colonialists sought ideological justifications for their actions; others were not bothered. In other parts the Europeans were more interested in trade and they imposed their own rule on top of the political system they found in place. They had a much greater capacity for collective action; when required, they could summon troops from elsewhere or signal for a gunboat. The indigenous peoples could not co-operate to the same extent and imperial policy was to keep it that way. It was expressed in the Roman maxim: *divide et impera*, divide and rule.

As the designation *white* indicates, the rulers and the ruled were distinguished by their appearance. They differed in many respects, in language, religion, skills and so on, but it was complexion that came above all to serve as the sign of where a person belonged in the new social order. Those who tried to describe that order

frequently called upon a word that had acquired biological connotations, *race*, to identify a whole cluster of non-biological differences. This gave extra plausibility to the claim that there was a
theoretical affirmation of white superiority. That claim had two
components. First it pointed to the propagation of doctrines, particularly those here called selectionist, that interpreted the superior
development of the countries inhabited by whites as the product of
biological evolution. Second, and more contentiously, it maintained
that these doctrines served a political function in that they raised
white morale, rationalized the means used by the whites to secure
their rule, and lowered the morale of those they dominated.

The doctrines in question conceived of human races as species or
groups in the process of becoming species and supported the belief
that white superiority could be traced to biological causes. But the
word *race* was used in other senses also. When used as a name for
a sub-species it supported the belief that the group differences were
of environmental and cultural origin. Often the word was used
in a way that had no biological content. As theories, the racial
theories of the nineteenth century were attempts to account for
the unequal development of nations and peoples. They probably
contributed to white arrogance, even among those who recognized
that unequal development was too complex an observation to be
explained by any single theory. The notion that, for whatever
reason, they were superior to Third World peoples doubtless gave
the whites extra confidence and made them more effective rulers.
For the subjugated peoples, especially those who did not profess a
major religion like Hinduism, Islam or Buddhism, and were mili-
tarily weak, the magnitude of the inequality in development could
have a shattering effect and stimulate bizarre attempts to account
for it, like the 'cargo cults' of the Pacific and the Ras Tafari movement in Jamaica. Many of the effects of contact between unequally
developed peoples seem to have been independent of the colonial
context in which many of them occurred, and independent of the
propagation of racial doctrines.

The theoretical affirmation of white superiority was often an
affirmation of a temporary superiority, for there was an acceptance
that the new empires might last no longer than earlier ones. This
acceptance was recalled every time congregations sang a popular
hymn with its lines: 'Crowns and thrones may perish, kingdoms
rise and wane.' It is probably right to conclude, with Füredi, that
many whites expected and feared a developing solidarity among
the non-white peoples. They may have seen this as the Number
One problem for the future, but they did not describe it as a
race problem. The claims, advanced by a minority, that whites were

naturally superior were undermined by the serious fears of racial decline that were given elaboration by the eugenics movement, and by a general scepticism about attempts to explain the unequal development of different world regions as the product of inheritance.

2

UNESCO

In 1948 the UN's Economic and Social Council advised UNESCO of the interest of the United Nations in effective educational programmes in the fields of prevention of discrimination and protection of minorities. It asked UNESCO to initiate and recommend 'the general adoption of a programme of disseminating scientific facts designed to remove what is commonly known as racial prejudice'. UNESCO's General Conference, a political body composed of representatives of member states, two years later instructed its director-general 'to study and collect scientific materials concerning questions of race; to give wide diffusion to the scientific information collected; to prepare an educational programme based on this information'.

Scientific facts

UNESCO began by assembling an international committee of experts, representing both the biological and the social sciences, who prepared a fifteen-paragraph 'Statement on Race'. This was published in 1950. Among other things, it stated 'A race, from the biological standpoint, may therefore be defined as one of the group of populations constituting the species *Homo sapiens*.' It went on to explain that 'when most people use the term "race" they do not do so in the sense above defined', so that 'the biological fact of race and the myth of "race" should be distinguished' and that 'it would be better when speaking of human races to drop the term "race" altogether and speak of ethnic groups'. 'According to present knowledge there is no proof that the groups of mankind differ in their innate mental characteristics . . . biological studies lend support to the ethic of universal brotherhood; for man is born with drives towards co-operation, and unless those drives are satisfied, men and nations alike fall ill.' The statement was primarily concerned with the horizontal dimension, with race as classification, but in referring to 'the biological fact of race' it touched upon the other dimension, of race as heredity.

Last-minute withdrawals from the meeting had meant that biological science was not as well represented as had been intended. This helps explain why the statement was criticized by biologists who, while not rejecting its general spirit or its main conclusions, believed that it went beyond the scientific facts (e.g. in the reference to 'drives towards co-operation') and confused the biological and social uses of the word 'race'. To clear up any possible misunderstanding, UNESCO assembled another group, this time including physical anthropologists and geneticists who had expressed disagreement with the first Statement. They drew up the 1951 Statement on the Nature of Race and Race Differences. UNESCO considered it important to avoid any suggestion that it was issuing an authoritative manifesto as the last word on the race question, so it sent out the draft to a further ninety-six scientists. Sixty-nine submitted observations; further comments were received from others as the draft was passed round. Nearly half approved the draft unreservedly. Others had suggestions as to presentation and relevant evidence. In a booklet entitled *The Race Concept*, UNESCO then published the Statement, a selection of observations and comments, three alternative suggested statements, and a reformulation of the 1951 Statement prepared by L. C. Dunn of Colombia University, the rapporteur of the 1951 meeting.

The 1951 Statement declared: 'The concept of race is unanimously regarded by anthropologists as a classificatory device providing a zoological frame within which the various groups of mankind may be arranged and by means of which studies of evolutionary processes can be facilitated.' This sentence combines the horizontal and vertical dimensions of the concept. The new statement summarized the factors influencing hereditary differences among populations, stating that 'existing races are merely the result, considered at a particular moment in time, of the total effect of such processes on the human species'; there were 'processes of race formation and race extinction'. It outlined the problem of deciding on which characteristics a classification should be based, while emphasizing that 'equality of opportunity and equality in law in no way depend, as ethical principles, upon the assertion that human beings are in fact equal in endowment'.

Dunn's reformulation began by acknowledging that in common usage the word *race* had so many meanings that confusion resulted. He addressed one prime confusion by writing: 'Race is determined by biological heredity, by descent from particular parents and thus cannot properly be used to describe groups whose association is political (national), religious, or due to a community of language, or to other cultural or social factors, since these are not biologically inherited.' That sentence appealed to the vertical dimension of race. The author went on to imply that some of the difficulty in agreeing a statement arose because geneticists thought of race as heredity, whereas anthropologists were concerned with the horizontal dimension, if not of race as species then as something resembling it. Dunn wrote:

> For those most closely concerned with the races of man, the physical anthropologists, races are categories required for the classification of the varieties of mankind, and for arranging them in an order which may reveal their relationship and descent . . . For students of hered-ity, geneticists, race has a double significance: first for classifying groups of men according to their hereditary characters and, second, as a stage in the process by which populations become different from each other and adapted or fitted to the different environments in which they live.

Some of the geneticists who were most critical of the 1951 Statement thought that they too had to wrestle with an ideological manipulation of the evidence on the part of their colleagues. They suspected that, in the service of egalitarianism, others were engaged in a well-intentioned effort to minimize the real differences that existed.

In 1964 another international expert group was convened to bring up to date the Statement published thirteen years earlier. Most of its members came from university departments of anthropology, which by this time were making more use of the advances that had been pioneered by the geneticists. The 1964 statement, entitled 'Proposals on the Biological Aspects of Race', insisted that 'the concept of race is purely biological' and referred to both its horizontal and vertical dimensions. More clearly than its predecessor, it broke with the race-as-species conception by stating that smaller units, groups of populations or single populations within major stocks, could be called races. One of the experts who participated in the meeting (Hiernaux, 1969:15) believed that the major original contribution of the 1964 text lay in what it said about the interaction between genetic and cultural factors. It declared that the human capacity for intellectual development depended upon genes that had a universal biological value for the survival of the whole species, irrespective of environment; and that human evolution, over many thousands of years, appeared to have been based on the transmission of cultural achievements rather than genetic endowment. The Proposals concluded: 'The biological data given above stand in open contradiction to the tenets of racism. Racist theories can in no way pretend to have any scientific foundation', but it offered no criteria for deciding whether a theory was racist.

In the mid-1990s a group within the American Association of Physical Anthropologists prepared a revision of the 1964 Proposals. The text was approved by the International Union of Anthropological and Ethnological Societies and submitted to UNESCO. The revision took account of the way that new data from prehistory and palaeontology, combined with new techniques for measuring and conceptualizing the sources of human variation, have modified earlier notions of human variation. Given the complexity of the issues, the 1964 text had been relatively brief and the updating was achieved without lengthening it.

To give wide diffusion to scientific opinion UNESCO published a series of little books, 'The Race Question in Modern Science'. They were: *Race and Culture* (Leiris), *Race and Psychology* (Klineberg), *Race and Biology* (Dunn), *Racial Myths* (Comas), *Race Mixture* (Schapiro), *The Roots of Prejudice* (Rose), *Race and History* (Lévi-Strauss), *Race and Society* (Little), *The Significance of Racial Differences* (Morant), *The Jewish People: A Biological History* (Schapiro), and *Race Relations and Mental Health* (Jahoda). These were later supplemented by essays on 'Race and Contemporary Genetics' (Dubinen); 'Race, Caste and Ethnic Identity' (Béteille); 'Tribalism and Racism' (Essien-Udom); 'Racialism and the Urban Crisis' (Rex); 'The Changing Position of the Chinese in South-East Asia' (Tjwan); and 'New Dimensions of Change, Conflict and Settlement' (Gluckman), published in a volume edited by Leo Kuper (1975).

The booklet that gives the best indication of the ideas UNESCO wished to combat was the one entitled *Racial Myths*, written by a member of the 1950 group, Juan Comas. The group had described the use of 'race' as a name for national, religious, geographic, linguistic and cultural groups as constituting a myth, so this is perhaps the first of the ideas to be combated. Whether this is the correct use of the word 'myth' is another matter. Longman's *Dictionary of the English Language* cites 'a myth of racial superiority' as an example of the use of this word, defined as 'a belief given uncritical acceptance by a group, especially in support of existing institutions or practices'. A myth is not simply an error; it can be a story, like the myth of Oedipus, that gives expression to fundamental values.

In the booklet, Comas described the general tendency, which today would be called ethnocentrism, of peoples to believe that their own group is better than other groups. He identified four errors, which he described as: the myth of blood and of the inferiority of cross-breeds; the myth of Negro inferiority (and the associated 'one drop' rule in the USA); the myth of a Jewish race; and the myth of 'Aryan' or 'Nordic' superiority (with a variant called Celticism). He stated that: 'Racism involves the assertion that inequality is absolute and unconditional, i.e., that a race is inherently and by its very nature superior or inferior to others quite independently of the physical conditions of its habitat and of social factors.'

UNESCO did not believe that racial conflicts could be resolved simply by bringing the findings of scientists to the knowledge of the public. Other dimensions, moral and intellectual, had to be considered. So the moral teaching of world religions was summarized in the series 'The Race Question and Modern Thought'. This included, from 1954, essays on *The Catholic Church and the Race Question* (Congar); *Jewish Thought as a Factor in Civilisation* (Roth); *The Ecumenical Movement* (Hooft); *Buddhism and the Race Question* (Malasekera and Jayatilleke); and *Islam and the Race Question* (Kāmil).

In another series, 'Race and Society', UNESCO from 1952 published *Race and Class in Rural Brazil* (Wagley); *Racial Equality and the Law* (Berger); *Equality of Rights between Races and Nationalities in the USSR* (Tsamerian and Ronin); and *The Defence of Human Rights in Latin America (Sixteenth to Eighteenth Centuries)* (Zavala). The first of these titles is a reminder of UNESCO's part in encouraging research in Brazil in the belief that experience in that country offered lessons for North America, given that many people of European origin then thought that the subordination of blacks by whites in South Africa and the Deep South of the USA was an inevitable expression of natural differences. The UNESCO-sponsored research in Brazil described a very different pattern of black–white relations. This helped the anti-racist movement in the West argue that the so-called 'race problem' could be solved when there was sufficient political will.

UNESCO's contribution to educational research included an interesting study of the benefits of having a teacher from Ghana take charge of a class in an English school (James and Tenen, 1953) and the preparation of a handbook for teachers, *Race, Prejudice and Education* (Bibby, 1959). After the reports of what appeared a revival of anti-Semitism and Nazism in Germany UNESCO mounted comparative research in Britain, France and Germany into the social acceptability of various minorities. Melvin Tumin, who directed this

research, was unable to raise sufficient funds to complete his analysis of its findings, though a table based upon them has been
published (Banton, 1967:389) showing the relative social acceptability in Britain at this time of Americans, Germans, Jews and West
Indians. Comparative tables for the other countries are lacking.

In 1960 the General Conference of UNESCO adopted a Convention on Discrimination in Education. In implementation of it, the
director-general has since conducted periodic consultations on
progress towards equality of opportunity in education, including
opportunities for persons belonging to minorities, refugees and
indigenous people.

Science and politics

Looking back after a half-century, the contrast between the observations on the biological and the sociological aspects is still striking. The biologists had found a way of superseding pre-Darwinian
ideas of race. They could offer an introduction to the new explanatory framework developed in population genetics. The social scientists had no comparable intellectual orientation. The objectives
for their research had not been properly identified. Such knowledge
as they had assembled had not been systematized.

A 'programme of disseminating scientific facts designed to
remove what is commonly known as racial prejudice' needed to
consider the nature of such prejudice and whether the material that
was being publicized had the desired effect. The director-general of
UNESCO at this time was Sir Julian Huxley, who, in *We Europeans*
written with A. C. Haddon and published in 1935, had opened the
final paragraph with the words:

> The violent racialism to be found in Europe today is a symptom of
> Europe's exaggerated nationalism: it is an attempt to justify nation-
> alism on a non-nationalist basis, to find a basis in science for
> ideas and policies which are generated internally by a particular
> economic and political system, and have real relevance only to that
> system.

If 'the doctrine of the inequality of men and races' had been generated by an economic and social system, it was the system that had
to be addressed, not the doctrine. A study of the evidence might
indicate that the prevention of discrimination and protection of
minorities required something more. Reviewing the publications in
the 'Race and Society' programme, Leo Kuper (1975:24) discerned
a trend in this direction. Whereas the original authors had been on
the defensive, their successors had moved into attack. They showed

a greater theoretical emphasis on the structures of power within which racist ideas were expressed, in place of the former preoccupation with prejudice and discrimination; and they were more concerned with the international context and implications of race relations.

As an illustration of the difficulties confronting UNESCO, the Statement on Race and Racial Prejudice of 1967 is of particular interest because, in retrospect, it looks as if there had been two weaknesses in the 1950 Statement. First, that statement appears to assume that once the erroneous nature of racist doctrines had been exposed, the structure of racial prejudice and discrimination would collapse. The eminent scholars who composed the document did not themselves believe this, but the committee did not consider explicitly the other sources of racial hostility. Second, because of the circumstances of the time, the group was primarily concerned with the equal potential of different racial groups and did not refer to the social consequences of contact between groups.

In 1967 another panel of experts, including sociologists, lawyers, a social psychologist, an ethnographer, a historian and two geneticists, were asked to prepare a statement covering the social, ethical and philosophical aspects of the problem. They had one week for what some would consider an impossible task. Is there one single, distinctive problem, or are there many problems? Since any person's view of the social, ethical and philosophical aspects must be saturated with political preconceptions that cannot always be reconciled, was this not a task for a political body rather than a panel of experts? Social scientists, and sociologists especially, were then, as now, deeply divided on the question of whether they should cultivate a detachment from political issues. Some believe that, if they are to make a distinctive contribution, they must limit themselves to what can be established as factually undeniable. Others believe that they have special insights into the overcoming of conflicts and that they should seek, through political involvement, to apply them. Sometimes they claim that it is better to follow the model of the medical scientist and to regard certain features (like racism) as diseases that have to be fought.

To have followed the course of detachment would have entailed grappling with issues which a heterogeneous panel could not resolve in the course of a week. As Ruth Benedict (1942:151) had written, 'to understand race conflict we need fundamentally to understand *conflict* and not *race*'. The study of race conflict spreads into almost all areas of society, for there is no separate kind of 'racial behaviour' that can be separated from other kinds of social behaviour. In the event, the committee of 1967 accepted the suggestion

that there was a single problem and preferred the course of engage-
ment to that of detachment. Their statement comprises a diagnosis,
a warning and a series of recommendations. It differs from its three
predecessors in starting from a description of a political threat:
'Racism continues to haunt the world'; it 'stultifies the development
of those who suffer from it'; 'it seeks to make existing differences
appear inviolable'; it 'finds ever new stratagems for justifying the
inequality of groups'; etc. The authors depict racism as a social force
possessing the autonomy of a social and political actor.

The experts in 1967 agreed that there are various causes of racial
hostility and that they vary in importance from one situation to
another. One cause was 'racism, namely, antisocial beliefs and acts
which are based upon the fallacy that discriminatory intergroup
relations are justifiable on biological grounds' (a definition that
according to Miles (1989:50) inflates the concept so much that it
reduces its utility). Surprisingly, they ignored the 1950 proposal
that groups distinguished by physical characteristics would be
better referred to as 'ethnic groups'. Their text reflects the international concerns of its time. In a later age, mindful of the atrocities
that marked the conflicts associated with the break-up of Yugoslavia
and the Soviet Union, the slaughter in Rwanda, Burundi and the
Congo, the attacks on ethnic Chinese in Indonesia, and many
similar horrors, informed opinion is reluctant to accept the assumption that racial hostility is a distinctive kind of hostility distinguished by beliefs about biological differences. To put so much
emphasis upon the power of such beliefs tends to recycle them. It
contributes to an image of racism as a mighty spectre overhanging
the world when in fact a very great deal has been learned about the
various causes of racial hostility and about the methods by which
it can be reduced. The challenge remains, but there has been
progress in responding to it.

UNESCO's campaign had been launched on the assumption that
doctrines of racial superiority generated discriminatory behaviour.
It did not deny that there could be causal influences in the opposite
direction: that discriminatory behaviour could encourage ideas of
superiority; but it prioritized the examination of one causal relation
among many interrelated ones. In the 1950s through to the late
1960s there was a significant degree of agreement among the
specialists concerned that the complex was three-dimensional.
What were then called 'race relations' could be approached from
three main standpoints. There was the dimension of ideology, with
racism as its basic concept; the psychological dimension, with the
concept of prejudicial attitudes; and the behavioural dimension
concerned with social relationships, which started from the concept

of discrimination (Banton, 1967:8). Under the impact of the black leadership of the civil rights movement in the USA this changed, so that the word *racism* came to be used as a name for the whole complex (Carmichael and Hamilton, 1967). This shift was reflected in the 1967 statement's description of racism. Increasingly the word came to be used as an epithet and to be applied to individuals and their attitudes. By the late 1960s also (as noted on p. 129), a further shift could be discerned in the arguments of those considered sympathetic towards racism, away from biological justifications for racial segregation and towards cultural ones.

When reviewing the contributions to the 'Race Question in Modern Science' series, Leo Kuper (1975:25) wrote approvingly of the passionate involvement displayed in the 1967 statement. He maintained that the basic conflict of values could be addressed only on the level of values, demanding personal and social commitment. This did not, he wrote, dispense with the growing need for the most careful scholarship in the field. Kuper did not elaborate upon the relationship between scholarship and personal involvement. A sociologist who participated in the drafting of the 1950 Statement, Morris Ginsberg (1947:256–7), touched upon this in a 1939 address about the function of reason in morals. He took as an example a question that may seem strange to a later generation, that of 'race mixture', and listed the many matters of fact that would have to be established before anyone could decide whether or not such mixture was desirable. The social scientist can learn from John Locke, who described the philosopher's task as that of an 'under-labourer', clearing the ground and removing some of the confusions that lie in the way to knowledge. Similarly, the student of racial discrimination can ascertain the relevant matters of fact, analyse the categories of thought in which they are presented and clarify the issues for political decision. What he or she does will at some points be influenced by personal values, but there is a world of difference between trying to minimize these and the use of the occasion as an opportunity to make propaganda for them. If those who take political decisions read the social scientist's work they will notice the stance the author has adopted and will be more easily persuaded if they conclude that he or she has disciplined any personal commitment.

In 1978 the General Conference of UNESCO, consisting of representatives of all member states, adopted by acclamation a Declaration on Race and Racial Prejudice. In its eleventh preambular paragraph it stated that it bore in mind 'the four statements on the race question adopted by experts convened by UNESCO', and went on to note that 'racism, racial discrimination, colonialism and *apartheid* continue to afflict the world in ever-changing forms'. In Article 1 it proclaimed that 'All human beings belong to a single species'; 'All individuals and groups have the right to be different, to be considered as different, and to be regarded as such'; 'The differences between the achievements of the different peoples are entirely attributable to geographical, historical, political, economic, social and cultural factors.' Article 2 stated that there was no scientific foundation for theories of racial or ethnic superiority; it listed components of racism and declared that racial prejudice was without justification. Further articles covered the incompatibility of discrimination with an international order guaranteeing respect for human rights; apartheid as a crime against humanity; the responsibility of educational and mass media institutions to combat racism; legislation; the encouragement of natural and social scientists to undertake objective research; the restructuring of the international economy; and the contribution of international organizations.

The Second World Conference to Combat Racism and Racial Discrimination in 1983 recommended that UNESCO should 'continue its studies and research on the factors of influence in the maintenance, transmission and alteration of prejudices and on the causes and effects of the various forms of racism and racial and ethnic discrimination'. This recommendation recognized that the causes of ethnic prejudice are manifold; it called for a more imaginative response than simply combating the dissemination of dubious doctrines. Yet, sadly, when the Third World Conference was convened eighteen years later UNESCO had nothing to report on this element in its mandate. Resolutions passed in international meetings regularly stress the importance of educational measures as means for reducing racial discrimination, but despite the rhetoric there is still little systematic knowledge of what can be accomplished by what methods. There is evidence, much of it anecdotal, that whatever is taught in the classroom, children and adolescents adopt the values of their social environment. Among the less successful adolescents a counter-culture can develop that disparages what the teacher stands for. By the values they encourage and the images they transmit, the mass media can be more influential than the school. Sometimes the most important measures are those that take the form of occupational training for adults who are already in post; a vital element in such training can be the explanation of the law's requirements and the punishments that can be imposed for failure to meet them. Law is one of the most important educational measures, but no country has found an effective way of relating proceedings in court to learning in the classroom.

Present problems

UNESCO's campaign started from an oversimplification. There were good political reasons for it to begin by concentrating upon scientifically unjustifiable beliefs about racial differences as one among many factors that had led to World War II, and to racial hostility in other times and places, provided it was clear that it was this that was being attempted. Moving on, it would have been desirable to try to specify the relation between this factor and other related factors in the generation and transmission of discriminatory patterns of behaviour. Having addressed the sorts of misunderstanding about racial differences that were current in the first decade following the war, the programme very properly went on to address the other factors that led to racial discrimination, but, motivated by a continuing sense of urgency, the programme tended to retain the original assumption about the centrality of belief in racial superiority.

In 1994 a new UNESCO social science programme on the Management of Social Transformations (MOST) became operational. One of its three themes, that relating to multiethnic and multicultural societies, is the intellectual heir to the earlier concern with prejudice, yet UNESCO did not choose to draw attention to its relevance to the Third World Conference Against Racism.

3

The UN General Assembly

From its earliest days, some delegations to the United Nations General Assembly expressed concern about racial discrimination, but, since the Assembly had other priorities, there was then no readiness to take any collective action. To appreciate the change of attitude in the 1960s it is necessary first to understand how the UN scheme for the protection of human rights was developed.

The Assembly's priorities had been established in the opening words of the Charter of the United Nations, signed in 1945 by the representatives of forty-six governments. It began: 'We the peoples of the United Nations determined to save succeeding generations from the threat of war', and continued in Article 1(3) to declare that one of the organization's purposes was to 'achieve international co-operation in . . . promoting and encouraging respect for human rights and for fundamental freedoms for all without distinction as to race, sex, language or religion'. So it was that on 10 December 1948, in the aftermath of what it called 'barbarous acts which have outraged the conscience of mankind', the General Assembly adopted the Universal Declaration of Human Rights. The governments of the day had seized an opportunity to secure a momentous agreement. Forty-eight state delegations voted in favour, none against, though eight abstained. Were a comparable proposal to have been advanced at any time in the last fifty years it would surely have been have been lost in the conflicts of the era. The achievement of 1948 therefore deserves to be celebrated. The General Assembly proclaimed the Declaration 'as a common standard of achievement for all peoples and all nations', listing the 'equal and inalienable rights of all members of the human family'. *Inalienable* is an important adjective, for it implies that even a democratically elected parliament, acting freely and unanimously, could not lawfully abridge one of these rights. At the head of them was the principle of non-discrimination embodied in the second article: 'Everyone is entitled to all the rights and freedoms set forth in this Declaration, without distinction of any kind, such as race, colour, sex, property, language, religion, political or other opinion, national or social origin, birth or other status'.

Treaties

The Universal Declaration is of great legal importance, for many courts can properly look to it when determining the application of other laws, both international and national. Since the UN can neither enact laws in the way that legislatures can, nor enforce agreements reached at its assemblies, the best way forward was for it to sponsor the preparation of a treaty to which states could become parties. They would thereby bind themselves to enact and enforce laws that would protect the rights and freedoms listed in it. The separate sovereign states always call the tune, and they, inevitably, are suspicious of one another's intentions. Treaties preserve the independence of states, though, as their scope extends, they constrain the exercise of that independence.

The General Assembly, acting on the recommendation of the Security Council, could expel a member state that persistently violated the principles of the Charter (which include a duty to encourage respect for human rights without distinction as to race), but a defaulting state could reply, as South Africa did, that the practices that were the object of criticism were within their domestic jurisdiction and therefore protected by Article 1.7. South African participation in the UN was eventually halted, not by suspension or expulsion, but by the General Assembly's refusal to accept the credentials of a delegation sent by the Pretoria government. The Charter binds all UN member states, so its authority is wide, but a treaty has the advantage that it can detail much more specific obligations, monitor their fulfilment, and create measures for enforcement.

A state may hesitate to ratify a treaty. It may want to prevent what it sees as abuses by other states but be apprehensive that, if it becomes a party to it, its enemies could use the treaty to make trouble. Many states therefore prefer the political route to the legal route as a way to combat racial discrimination. The political route runs from the Charter via the Assembly to bodies such as the Commission for Human Rights and programmes like the decades for action against racism described later (see pp. 53–8). The legal route runs from the treaties, but human rights treaties are not like other treaties. If two states make a treaty defining the limits of their territorial waters, the fishermen on either side will monitor one another's observation of the dividing line and there will be pressure to penalize any breaches. If one hundred and fifty states accept treaty obligations to protect human rights they cannot monitor everyone else's fulfilment of their obligations; so they elect a treaty body to do this for them. If one state fails to fulfil its obligations, it is for the other states to take what action they consider appropriate, but by ratifying a treaty a state is surrendering some of its sovereignty to legal determination by government-appointed lawyers whom it may not trust.

The logical course would have been to draw up a single treaty that translated the Universal Declaration into legal form with a full-time monitoring body or court to examine the parties' compliance with their obligations. No such proposal would have been acceptable. The delegations from the Eastern bloc had abstained from voting on the Universal Declaration, saying that it did not go far enough in the protection of economic and social rights; they wanted to follow the principle that 'human rights begin after breakfast'. States of the Western bloc prioritized civil and political rights, as if 'human rights begin in the police station'. (Unlike some other constitutions, that of the USA guarantees only civil and political rights.) Each group was apparently ready to accept obligations to protect what it regarded as core rights and hesitant about the others, while the Eastern states were so suspicious of possible Western manoeuvring that they were unwilling to allow even the International Court of Justice to pronounce upon disputes between states concerning human rights. For such reasons it became politically expedient to draft two treaties, called covenants to emphasize their special status: the International Covenant on Economic, Social and Cultural Rights (ICESCR) and the International Covenant on Civil and Political Rights (ICCPR). To counter any suggestion that some rights are more important than others, UN texts regularly emphasize the indivisibility of human rights. A single covenant could have been supplemented by five protocols covering the rights that have since been set out in the conventions prohibiting racial discrimination, discrimination against women, torture, violations of the rights of the child and violations of the rights of migrant workers and members of their families. Yet that, again, was not the way the politics worked.

The Declaration, the two Covenants and the Optional Protocols to the second of them together constitute the International Bill of

Human Rights. This replaces older ideas of divine law or natural law as governing the relations between all humans. The representatives of states have simply agreed on an international legal code that, among themselves, constitutes positive law. The Charter's search for peace is now a search for peace amongst those states whose laws and practices are based on respect for human rights.

The text of Article 26 of the ICCPR, which is of particular relevance to this chapter, was agreed in the General Assembly in 1961, five years ahead of the adoption of the Covenant as a whole. Article 26 requires states parties to 'guarantee to all persons equal and effective protection against discrimination on any ground such as race, colour, sex, language, religion, political or other opinion, national or social origin, property, birth or other status'. The wording represents racial discrimination as one among many forms of discrimination inherent in the formation of social groups. Society is possible only because humans form families, communities, associations, nations and so on, conferring rights and duties upon members. Only when the less favourable treatment of non-members is extended to spheres in which it cannot be justified does it become unlawful. Judgements of what is unjustifiable change from one generation to another and the law should not impede this. Over many centuries social distinctions between males and females were built into institutions and came to be taken for granted as the outcome of natural differences. Many of them are no longer seen as biologically determined and are classed as discriminatory. In the early 1960s governments were more ready to support UN action against racial discrimination than against other forms because this suited their foreign policies. There was no external political advantage in pressing for legislation against discrimination on grounds of sex. When, in 1967, the General Assembly adopted a Declaration on the Elimination of Discrimination Against Women, and, in 1979, a similarly titled Convention, it did not blame doctrines of gender inequality for causing discrimination against women.

The noble lie

While the covenants were being drafted the political tide started to run against the colonial powers. In 1960 the General Assembly by resolution 1514(XV) adopted the Declaration on the Granting of Independence to Colonial Countries and Peoples, eighty-nine states voting in favour, none opposing, and nine abstaining. It declared that the subjection of peoples to alien domination was contrary to the Charter and, in paragraph 3, that: 'Inadequacy of political, social, economic or educational preparedness should never serve as a pretext for delaying independence.' The declaration was directed at 'salt water colonialism', the rule of dependencies on the other side of 'blue water'; no one at the UN then referred to Soviet influence over regions contiguous with Russia as exemplifying colonialism.

There was, of course, an excellent case for trying to ensure that all dependent territories became independent at the earliest opportunity, and the UN had taken over the responsibilities of the League of Nations for supervising the administration of the mandates allocated after World War I. As was mentioned in chapter 1, whenever a small class of persons is responsible for administering the affairs of another larger class the former maintain a degree of social separation. In Asia and in Africa such separation was identified with differences of skin colour considered to be 'racial'. This was incidental to relations of political subordination but it could be made to appear as if ideas about racial difference caused the subordination instead of reinforcing it. In the Soviet Asian republics the physical differences between the Russian and native populations were not thought of as racial even if the actual relations between the groups were not so very different. Now, after the dissolution of the USSR, it is more common to hear the Russian presence in these republics described as colonialist. In the 1960s the Soviets won the propaganda war at the UN, routing attempts by the West European delegations to overturn a biased conception of colonialism and the polemical claim that it was a major cause of racial discrimination.

At the end of the 1950s there were eleven states in the UN's African Group out of a total of eighty-five UN member states. Ten years later they had increased to forty-one out of 128. The African states shared a determination to use their newly found power to act against racial discrimination in southern Africa and to speed the process of decolonization. In this they were assisted by the Arab states, which were offended by the creation of the state of Israel and its government's policies, and by the states of the East European Group, which wanted to attack the Western states at what were seen as their most vulnerable points. In 1960 an opportunity to pursue such political objectives was presented by reports of attacks on synagogues and Jewish burial grounds in what was then West Germany, for they inspired fears of a revival of Nazi ideology. The UN Sub-Commission on Prevention of Discrimination and Protection of Minorities reacted to these reports in a resolution stating that it was 'deeply concerned by the manifestations of anti-Semitism and other forms of racial and national hatred and religious and racial prejudices which have occurred in various countries, reminiscent of the crimes and outrages committed by the Nazis prior to and during the Second World War'. To describe the attacks as manifestations of prejudice was to use an approach different from that of Article 26 of the ICCPR just quoted. It would not have been reasonable to describe the other forms of discrimination listed in that article as manifestations of some internal condition that had found a way to the surface. Article 26 defines the unequal treatment of other persons on certain grounds as something to be prohibited and prevented by governments just as they prohibit and prevent other kinds of behaviour that their societies define as criminal or socially deviant. The definition is consistent with the view that discriminatory behaviour is socially normal, just as crime or – more generally – deviance is found in all societies. The contrary view, implicit in the Sub-Commission's choice of words, was that racial and religious discrimination was a kind of social pathology to be found in certain societies only.

This latter conception carried the day in the UN and led to the General Assembly's adoption, in 1963, of the International Declaration on the Elimination of All Forms of Racial Discrimination. Two years later it made possible the adoption, on a unanimous vote, of the International Convention on the Elimination of All Forms of Racial Discrimination that translated the Declaration into a legally binding treaty.

Few delegations would have accepted that sexism or religious discrimination were pathological features characterizing certain forms of society or would have voted for a convention on the elimination of all forms of crime, but by presenting racial discrimination as a pathology of certain societies some delegations were able to persuade others not only that racial discrimination could be eliminated by international action, but that it could be eliminated *speedily*. There was a paradox in that a dubious assumption served a noble purpose. This led me, when reviewing the drafting history of the International Convention on the Elimination of All Forms of Racial Discrimination, to conclude that the Convention, like Plato's *Republic*, is founded on a noble lie (Banton, 1996:50). When setting out his design for an ideal republic, Plato recalled a myth that, when God made men, into some he put gold to make them capable of ruling; into the auxiliaries he put silver; into the farmers and craftsmen, iron and copper. If the citizens believed their abilities to be predetermined they would more readily accept their places in the prevailing social order. In some translations this myth is called a noble lie. Since human classes had not been created naturally unequal it was a lie, but, believing that it would contribute to the smooth running of society, Plato claimed that propagation of the myth was justified. In similar fashion, the axiom that racial discrimination *as defined in the Convention* can be eliminated is a lie, but because it made possible agreement on a treaty that now restrains racial discrimination in most of the world's states, it was a noble lie more honourable than Plato's.

The conception of racial discrimination as the manifestation of an internal essence or condition is an example of a mode of reasoning that Sir Karl Popper in *The Open Society and its Enemies* attacked as exemplifying 'the spell of Plato'. Popper (1945:vol. 1, 31–4, and 216; vol. 2, 9–21, and 287–301) taught that that in philosophy there have been two main traditions concerning definition. One, which derives from Plato and Aristotle and can be called *essentialist*, holds that a definition should grasp the essence of the thing to be defined. The other, which can be called *nominalist*, maintains that a definition should distinguish the thing being defined from other things with which it might be confused. A favourite illustration is to say that while an essentialist might define *Homo sapiens* as a rational animal, a nominalist would define *Homo* as a featherless biped! An essentialist might treat Nazism or apartheid as the paradigm case of racism, displaying the most extreme form of a kind of social, political and economic movement. A nominalist might treat racism as belonging in a family of related concepts such as anti-Semitism, fascism, nationalism and sexism, and would distinguish between doctrine, social practice and individual disposition.

One error of anti-racism has been the assumption that racism was an ontological unity, a distinctive and pathological form of behaviour. The contrast with conceptions of crime is helpful because most commentators would maintain that there are many forms of crime, committed for varied reasons, and that what causes them to be associated is the action of legislatures in criminalizing certain actions and providing for the punishment of the perpetrators. Just as crime is diverse and normal, so is discrimination. Humans can act in a discriminatory way on grounds of sex, religion, age, disability and other recognized social attributes just as they can on grounds of race. Like crime, discrimination is defined not by its presumed nature but by the manner of its prohibition.

Patterns of discrimination are the stronger when they are shared and embodied in institutional practice. They then look like the symptoms of a social disease. This might be a valid way of representing racial discrimination were it possible to identify a society in which there is no disposition to discriminate racially. Experience at the UN suggests that there is no such society. Certainly there are countries, often small ones, in which the entire population shares the same ethnic origin and is of similar outward appearance, but when strangers of different appearance enter they are in some contexts treated less favourably, showing that the disposition is there. Many contemporary Europeans who distance themselves from the real problems by representing discrimination on grounds of race as a sickness do not see discrimination on grounds of sex or disability in the same way. That is one of the reasons for believing that it is better if race, sex and disability are associated in legislation and in the procedures whereby members of the public may seek remedies.

Some discrimination can be traced to customary patterns of behaviour. Individuals grow up aware that people of a certain kind live in a particular part of the town or that certain positions are held by men rather than women, or by persons of particular ethnic origin, and they assume that this is right and proper. Only if they receive a jolt do they start to question the moral basis for their assumption.

That the disposition to discriminate on the basis of supposed group fellowship serves powerful psychological functions has been shown by a series of experimental studies from the early 1950s, notably those conducted by Muzafer Sherif, Stanley Millgram, Henri Tajfel and Philip Zimbardo. Their research demonstrated how easily mere differentiation could be transformed into group-based persecution; Sherif's research also showed that inter-group tensions could be dissolved when members of both groups were brought together in pursuit of shared superordinate goals. Other experimental research, notably that by Solomon Asch in the 1950s, showed that up to three-quarters of subjects will deny the evidence of their own eyes if they find that the other members of their group all report having seen something different. Even without any kind of threat, the innate pressures to conform can be powerful. The genocidal actions in Nazi Germany, Rwanda and Bosnia were the outcome of political manipulation, but they could not have been carried through without the active participation of normal people. If in 1965 the Convention was to be adopted, delegates had to close their eyes to this uncomfortable dimension to the problem.

The legal instrument: discrimination

The ICERD starts with twelve preambular paragraphs setting out the rationale for its adoption. The fourth begins: 'Considering that the United Nations has condemned colonialism and all practices of segregation and discrimination associated therewith'. This, together with the reference in the tenth preambular paragraph to the need 'to prevent and combat racist doctrines', is the only statement about the causes of racial discrimination. The claim that colonialism was a cause of racial discrimination was another lie. The falsehood lay in lumping together as colonialism so many historically different situations, for European settlement in South Africa, Kenya and Algeria had very different consequences from British rule in Nigeria, French rule in Ivory Coast or Belgian rule in the Congo. No way was found – probably none could be – of differentiating the racial element in the subordinate position of Africans from the political element, or from those elements associated with modern skills and technological sophistication. The misrepresentation of colonialism was a less noble lie than the claim that racial discrimination can be eliminated by political action, but it, too, served a worthy purpose in facilitating agreement on a convention to reinforce and expand upon Article 26 of the ICCPR. It should also be noted that the Convention's fifth preambular paragraph rehearses the wording of the Declaration adopted two years earlier that 'solemnly affirms the necessity of *speedily* eliminating racial discrimination throughout the world in all its forms and manifestations' (italics added).

Part One of the Convention consists of seven articles. Article 1.1 states:

> In this Convention, the term 'racial discrimination' shall mean any distinction, exclusion, restriction or preference based on race, colour, descent, or national or ethnic origin which has the purpose or effect of nullifying or impairing the recognition, enjoyment or exercise, on an equal footing, of human rights and fundamental freedoms in the political, economic, social, cultural or any other field of public life.

In so doing, it specifies five prohibited grounds of conduct, adding 'descent' and 'national origin' to the three grounds listed in the 1963 Declaration. This was an early example of the trend to expand the concept of racial discrimination to cover more inequalities of treatment. Article 1.2 follows with a most important exception: 'This Convention shall not apply to distinctions, exclusions, restrictions or preferences made by a State Party to this Convention between citizens and non-citizens.' This means that a government's decisions about who may or may not be admitted to citizenship are excluded from the definition of racial discrimination. Citizens of a country returning from a visit abroad have to be admitted. Non-citizens do not have to be. The Convention does not cover possible racial discrimination in the exclusion of aliens provided a government does not discriminate racially as between different classes of aliens (Article 1.3).

The conceptual difficulties may be clarified by first advancing three propositions:

1   The members of a national society are entitled to decide who else may be admitted to their society.
2   They are entitled (a) to restrict admission to persons willing to accept the principles on which their society is founded, and (b) to deny admission to those who, if admitted, would work to change those principles.
3   They are not entitled to deny admission on grounds of race.

A problem then arises if a class of persons distinguished by race is denied admission on the grounds stated in proposition 2. It may be alleged that the real motivation is racial. The problem is further complicated when religious differences overlap with racial or ethnic differences. The constitution of a national society may accord a special status to a given religion or may expressly separate the state from expressions of religious faith. Some adherents of some religions believe that their faith obliges them to see that state institutions serve the ends of their faith. Presumably it is both lawful and morally defensible for the citizens of a society to refuse citizenship to those who are unable to accept the principles on which their society is founded. Such rejection would not be religious or racial discrimination but an objectively justifiable expression of their political identity.

When the UN started work on these questions there was no accepted legal definition of discrimination. In fulfilment of a request from the Economic and Social Council, the secretary-general in 1949 submitted a memorandum on *The Main Types and Causes of Discrimination* (UN, 1949). In chapter III, on 'Sociological and Juridical Fundamentals for Defining Discrimination', he explained that some contemporary sociologists thought it was necessary to distinguish between inter-individual and social relations and that practices characterized as discriminatory were connected with social relations; they arose because of the functions persons were seen as performing:

> The fact that discrimination arises from the existence of social categories does not mean that all social categories are unjustified or bad. On the contrary, it is obvious that such collective patterns are inherent in any society and that among them there are many which are fully justified. Other social categories may become harmful when they give rise to prejudice or acts of discrimination.

The memorandum went on to state that the requirement of moral and juridical equality excluded any differentiation based on grounds that were not imputable to the individual and that should not be considered as having any social or legal meaning, such as colour, race, sex. The emphasis was on the elimination of inequality of treatment and on unfavourable treatment.

To decide whether treatment is unequal or less favourable, a comparison is necessary. It has proven easiest to develop anti-discrimination law in those settings in which agreement can be reached on what constitutes a fair comparison. It has proven difficult to develop that law in settings in which comparison is problematic. A notable example is the use of sex discrimination law to protect the interests of a woman who has been dismissed from employment when she became pregnant. There may be excellent reasons for protecting women in such circumstances, but can it be concluded that they have suffered less favourable treatment on grounds of their sex when men do not experience pregnancy? Is it proper to compare a pregnant woman's need for maternity leave with a hypothetical man's need for a similar period of leave to undergo hospital treatment? Another example of problematic comparisons arises when a racially distinctive group is treated less favourably, ostensibly on political grounds, and its treatment cannot be compared with that of a group similar in all respects except that of race or ethnic origin. Again, were not decisions about citizenship excluded from the Convention's definition of discrimination, there would be circumstances in which it could be very hard to agree upon an appropriate comparator when considering claims that immigration restrictions are racially discriminatory.

It is therefore unsurprising that the first definition of unlawful discrimination in a UN instrument should have been one for prohibiting discrimination in employment, a field in which it is relatively easy to identify a comparator. The International Labour Organization's (ILO's) Convention 111 defines it as including 'any distinction, exclusion or preference made on the basis of race, colour, sex, religion, political opinion, national extraction or social origin, which has the effect of nullifying or impairing equality of opportunity or treatment in employment or occupation'.

The ILO definition of discrimination is well suited to interpersonal relations in the workplace. Yet it is surprising that the definition in the ICERD should have followed it without considering how it might be adapted to circumstances in which there was no obvious comparator. International definitions of discrimination do not specify less favourable or differential treatment as a criterion, but it is difficult to apply their notions of distinction and impairment without attempting some comparison.

It is even more noteworthy that the General Assembly never connected its definition of racial discrimination for the Convention with its consideration of the forms of discrimination prohibited by Article 26 of the ICCPR. Much of the work drafting this article was done in 1947–52, while the text was finally agreed in 1961, so it should have been in the minds of delegates in 1963–5. Article 26 represented discrimination as a general and normal feature of society. The ICERD represented racial discrimination as a pathological social form characteristic of certain societies only. To relate the ICERD to Article 26 would have been to weaken the anti-colonial campaign, but the Western delegations missed their opportunity to argue for the alternative approach.

The legal instrument: protected fields

Article 2 lists the kinds of action states parties bind themselves to undertake. Articles 3–7 specify particular obligations: Article 3 to prohibit racial segregation; Article 4 to punish the dissemination of ideas based on racial superiority or hatred; Article 5 to ensure equality before the law in respect of civil, political, economic, social and cultural rights; Article 6 to assure to everyone within their jurisdiction effective protection and remedies; Article 7 to adopt measures, particularly in the fields of teaching, education, culture and information, to combat racial prejudices.

Part Two of the Convention (Articles 8–16) prescribes the manner of its implementation: Article 8 provides for the election of a treaty monitoring committee; Article 9 specifies the obligation of states parties to submit reports; Article 10 lays down procedure; Articles 11–13 offer a procedure for the resolution of inter-state disputes; Article 14 provides that a state party may allow individuals and groups to petition the monitoring body in connection with possible violations of the treaty; Article 15 concerns petitions and the monitoring of racial discrimination in Trust and Non-Self-Governing Territories. This article permits persons in these territories to petition the UN directly, unlike the provision in the previous article by which it is the government of the state or territory that grants this right. The justification for this exception to an important principle is the reference in preambular paragraph 4 to the 1960 Declaration on the Granting of Independence to Colonial Countries and Peoples. Article 16 ensures that recourse to remedies under the Convention does not rule out recourse to other remedies.

Part Three of the Convention (Articles 17–25) describes the means by which states may ratify or accede to it, may enter reservations to particular provisions, the duties of the UN secretary-general, its five languages, etc.

Political action

Implementation of the Declaration on the Granting of Independence to Colonial Countries and Peoples was entrusted to what later became known as 'the committee of twenty-four'. The representative of the USA on this committee during 1968–71 (Finger, 1972) has described its resolutions (which were purely rhetorical) as having been drafted by a group of communist members and representatives of anti-Western African and Arab states. They included an endorsement of armed struggle and suggested that member states were obliged to provide assistance for violent action. Thus General Assembly resolution 2621 of 1970, setting out a programme of action to implement resolution 1514, 'declares the further continuation of colonialism . . . a crime . . . reaffirms the inherent right of colonial peoples to struggle by all necessary means . . . Member States shall render all necessary moral and material assistance to the peoples of colonial Territories in their struggle to attain freedom and independence.' The compatibility of the committee's activities with the principles of the Charter was dubious. The opportunity to revise colonial boundaries as part of the decolonization process was overlooked. Western representatives advanced proposals for assisting exercise of the right to self-determination but were voted down. The United Kingdom and the United States then, in 1971, discontinued their participation in the work of the committee.

Mrs Roosevelt's comment on the intensity of feeling among delegates from Africa and Asia has already been quoted (p. 22). In her view, 'an age-old score' had come to light in the new discussions at the UN. She 'felt the weight of history for which the nations of the Western world are now to be called to account'. The accusation of racial motivation may have been unjustified, but the passions could carry the day. Looking back on the era of decolonization at the UN, the folly of the 1960 declaration that 'Inadequacy of political, social, economic or educational preparedness should never serve as a pretext for delaying independence' is evident. This rhetoric made it impossible to establish independent criteria for determining whether the political institutions of a candidate state were secure enough for it to be able to discharge the duties of a state towards its nationals and towards other states. The UN then admitted to membership states that soon proved unable to control their territory, so that they could not protect the human rights of their nationals. It is not necessarily preferable to be abused by someone of your own colour. Control of the government in many of the new states was used by the elites for their self-enrichment and for the establishment of kleptocracies, both civil and military. The anti-colonialist movement never envisaged the problems of corruption, despotism, military take-overs, the damage that could result from the unregulated extraction of valuable minerals, or the effect upon the economy of a country dependent upon a single export commodity when its market value collapsed.

A poignant example of the UN's failure to act as a proper trustee in protecting the interests of the ordinary people is that of Ruanda-Urundi. Before 1962 this was a UN trust territory administered by Belgium. In 1960 political parties representing the ethnic majority, the Hutu, won communal elections in both territories and provisional governments were established. In January 1961, following a coup, the northern section, Ruanda, declared itself a republic. In the southern section, Urundi, the provisional government agreed to exercise power jointly with the Tutsi king. In April 1961 the UN General Assembly's Fourth Committee (which deals with decolonization matters) reiterated (in resolution 1605) 'its conviction that the best future for Ruanda-Urundi lies in the accession of that Territory to independence as a single, united and composite State'. Elections held the following September under UN supervision were won by the Hutu party in Ruanda but by a predominantly Tutsi party in Urundi. The two states rejected a UN proposal to federate. Subsequent resolution of the Hutu–Tutsi conflict, which has cost so many lives, might have been easier had the UN insisted on the conviction it expressed in resolution 1605, bringing the separate kingdoms within a single political structure, as had been done in Uganda. The progress to independence did not have to be precipitate; it could have been planned, allowing for the Organization of African Unity to exercise an oversight. Instead, in a great rush, Rwanda and Burundi were admitted as UN Member States on 18 September 1962. Ethnic elites in both countries then used state power to further their sectional interests, with tragic results. (With the benefit of hindsight, it is apparent that if any of the colonial territories was to be split into two states because of ethnic differences, Sudan would have been a better selection.)

Nor were the states that set the pace for decolonization able to devise any formula for taking account of the difficulties facing the territories with small populations. As a result, the UN now has forty-four member states with populations of fewer than one million persons. Fifteen of them have populations of fewer than 100,000. The implications for the doctrine of the sovereign equality of states are ignored.

The decades

On the proposal of the Soviet Union, the General Assembly designated 1971 as International Year for Action to Combat Racism and Racial Discrimination. Then the ten-year period beginning on 10 December 1973 was declared a Decade for Action to Combat Racism and Racial Discrimination, being followed in due course by Second and Third Decades (though it was never explained why the UN should refer to racism as well as to racial discrimination, since it did not then specify and has never subsequently specified any difference in the meanings to be given to the two expressions). Any attempt to adhere to a dictionary definition would probably have been frustrated by the determination of the parties to advance or defend their political positions concerning colonial rule, apartheid, Zionism and the like.

It would in any case have been the more difficult for the UN to define racism because (as was explained in pp. 35–6) at this time the popular meaning given to the word in English was changing. The new trend subordinated the psychological and sociological dimensions of what had been called race relations to the ideological, which was congenial to the Soviet view of the issues. Doubtless it was this new conception of racism that carried the day in 1971. The question of definition also arises in connection with references to the forms of racial discrimination. No UN body has ever attempted to determine or enumerate these forms, though the secretary-general in 1972 (E/CN.4/1105; UN, 1972) prepared a report on studies of race relations, which in paragraphs 91–3 listed twenty-four such forms based on the denial of the rights listed in the Covenants. This report was submitted to the Commission on Human Rights (CHR) in fulfilment of the decision at the International Conference on Human Rights held in Tehran in 1968 to establish a new UN programme on racial discrimination.

Another implication of the addition of the word 'racism' may be mentioned. The word can be extended to cover possible racial discrimination in rules concerning eligibility for citizenship, although, as noted, this is excluded from the Convention's definition of racial discrimination. If the argument is expressed as one about racism rather than as about the Convention's definition of racial discrimination, there is more scope for one government to assert that another government is operating a racist immigration policy.

In present-day English-language usage a prime purpose in classifying something as *racist* or *sexist* is to disparage it. These two expressions became popular in the 1970s because of their utility as epithets. To call someone a racist was a stronger moral condemnation than to say that the person had engaged in racial discrimination. Consequently the word *racism* acquired high rhetorical value in mobilizing opinion against a great evil. Words that can be used in such a way are frequently overemployed.

Whether anything has been achieved by the institution of the three decades can never be determined because it is impossible to separate what has been done under them from other actions, many of which would presumably have taken place in any event. The programmes of the decades have been very general; that adopted in 1973 began by recalling that: 'The United Nations has opposed all manifestations of racial discrimination and has in particular condemned the policy of *apartheid* and similar policies based on racial theories'; it underlined 'the fallacy and injustice of racist dogmas and practices', accepting that there were 'kinds of situations that lead to racism'. It explained that:

> The ultimate goals of the decade are to promote human rights and fundamental freedoms for all, without distinction of any kind on grounds of race, colour, descent or national or ethnic origin, especially for eradicating racial prejudice, racism and racial discrimination; to arrest any expansion of racist policies, to eliminate the persistence of racist policies and to counteract the emergence of alliances based upon mutual espousal of racism and racial discrimination; to resist any policy and practices which lead to the strengthening of the racist regimes and contribute to the sustainment of racism and racial discrimination; to identify, isolate and dispel the fallacious and mythical beliefs, policies and practices that contribute to racism and racial discrimination; and to put an end to racist regimes.

The reference to 'the emergence of alliances' was inspired by reports of co-operation between the governments of South Africa and Israel.

According to the programme of action of the first decade, measures needed to be taken at national, regional, international and UN levels. The national level was the most important because it is at that level that laws are enacted and enforced, but the monitoring of national action, at least for states parties to the Convention, was a task allocated to the Committee on the Elimination of Racial Discrimination (CERD). It was therefore inappropriate for the UN's political bodies to involve themselves with matters that were being tackled by legal measures.

The national measures featured in the Programme of Action included 'assistance on a bilateral basis to peoples which are victims of racial discrimination'; no support for governments that practise racial discrimination; better legislation; adequate recourse procedures for victims; scholarships for youth from territories where racial discrimination prevails; research; publicity; universal ratification of the ICERD; improved educational programmes.

The regional and international measures were not separated, which meant that there was no recognition of the differences in the kinds of problem presented by racial discrimination in Africa, Asia, the Americas and Europe. Items (a)–(k) in this section included the following:

(a) a proposal for a world conference;
(b) the convening of seminars;
(c) the recognition of women's contribution to the struggle against racism and racial discrimination;
(d) the establishment of regional funds to support oppressed peoples suffering from racism and racial discrimination;
(e) denial of support to racist regimes, including policies aimed at depriving the indigenous people of their inalienable rights;
(f) the statement that 'states should adopt measures to prevent the activities of persons and groups which incite sectarian and racial passions that would provoke people to leave their land and settle in lands belonging to others in accordance with policies designed to consolidate settler-colonialism, or to settle natives in reservations, thus condemning them to a miserable existence';
(g) the isolating of racist regimes;
(h) support for liberation movements;
(i) the implementation of the ICERD;
(j) new instruments regarding racial discrimination and the suppression of the crime of apartheid;
(k) co-ordination of information.

Within the UN system there were to be programmes of research and study, of education, training and information, and the preparation of annual reports on the decade for presentation to the UN Economic and Social Council. Item (f) in the regional list has been quoted in full because it is not easily summarized and it shows the desire to include in the anti-racist programme action to minimize migration to Israel. The reference of settler-colonialism was not further developed in order to bring criticism of Israeli policies more clearly within the scope of UN action against colonialism.

In 1975 a set of proposals for implementing the programme came through the General Assembly's Third Committee to a plenary session. To it, in resolution 3379, was added the declaration that 'determines that Zionism is a form of racism and racial discrimination'. The US representative, Daniel Patrick Moynihan, insisted on keeping to the earlier definition of racism as an ideology, but to no avail, so after a bitter debate the resolution was carried by seventy-two votes to thirty-five. This led the USA to withdraw from participation in the first decade and damaged its programme. The vote aroused so much passion that for a long time delegations refrained from referring to it lest the bitter conflict be reopened. Then in 1991 the resolution was revoked by 111 votes to twenty-five.

Whether Zionism is or is not a form of racism and racial discrimination depends upon the meanings given to words, but seen from the standpoint of international politics the resolution casts light upon the utility of differentiating action at the regional and international levels. The policies of the government of Israel were a cause of great tension in the Middle East. A solution of the conflict could not be attained without the commitment of the powers within the region, including outside governments that had interests within it. In 1975 no solution was in sight. As the event showed, it was possible to recruit a majority by appealing to states outside the region who could not themselves contribute to a solution, but their involvement did not help and the passing of the resolution created strains that were too great for the normal processes of negotiation between delegations.

The first World Conference to Combat Racism and Racial Discrimination, in 1978, was convened to adopt effective measures for implementing UN resolutions on racism, racial discrimination, apartheid, decolonization and self-determination; it was also to promote implementation of human rights treaties. In the view of one senior UN official it was a disaster. When they learned that a majority of delegations were determined to vote for the inclusion in the conference's concluding declaration of certain draft paragraphs about racial discrimination against the Palestinians, the Western delegations withdrew from the conference. The USA had sent no delegation. Neither, of course, was there any delegation from the Republic of South Africa. In 1974 the General Assembly had refused to accept the credentials of a delegation from that state; it was not representative of the population. A member of CERD who attended the 1978 conference reported at the Committee's next session that there had been many ideological speeches that bore little or no relation to racial discrimination. He thought that one region had been trying to put another region in the dock (for a much less critical view, see Lauren, 1996:269–73).

When the second World Conference was being planned, the General Assembly removed topics relating to the Middle East from its agenda, but they still reappeared. The conference was held in 1983; Israel, South Africa and the United States did not participate (Lauren, 1996:286–7). The concluding declaration concentrated upon action against apartheid. That was understandable, but it is doubtful if it, or the programme of action for the second decade, added anything significant to the struggle against apartheid that was being waged on so many fronts. By condemning apartheid as 'the most extreme form of racism', anti-apartheid rhetoric encouraged a concentration upon certain specific characteristics of racial discrimination in one region at the expense of the more general human rights dimension embodied in Article 26 of the ICCPR. The draft declaration was adopted by 101 votes to twelve, with three abstentions. As is usual on these occasions, a variety of states (twenty-five on this occasion) issued statements clarifying their positions on certain matters and formulating reservations on others. The United Kingdom, for example, reiterated its refusal to endorse the use of 'all available means, including armed struggle' for the elimination of apartheid.

The decades for action against racism might (according to Lauren, 1996:298) just as well have been called decades for action against white racism. The programme for the first decade attracted little support from the states that contribute most to the UN budget. Activities had therefore to be funded from voluntary contributions to a trust fund. The situation in the subsequent decades was little better. The programme for the second decade began with a plan for action to combat apartheid and continued with sections on education, the mass media, minorities, recourse procedures, seminars and studies. Implementation of the plan was monitored by a report from the secretary-general to the General Assembly. After the change of government in South Africa in 1994 the programme for the third decade had to be revised; the same sorts of activity were featured, but the political impetus of 1973 had long since dissipated. The General Assembly regretted the lack of interest, support and financial resources that had limited implementation of the programme for the third decade but did not find it worthwhile to review the original conception in the light of subsequent experience.

Among the UN's specialized agencies, UNESCO was seen as playing a specific role in combating racial discrimination. The ILO received only subsidiary mention. That organization saw the elimination of discrimination as integral to all of its activities, in particular by monitoring implementation of the Discrimination

(Employment and Occupation) Convention 111 of 1958 and the Indigenous and Tribal Peoples Convention 169 of 1989. A further initiative, entitled 'Combating Discrimination against (Im)migrant Workers and Ethnic Minorities', was originated within the Migration Branch of the secretariat in 1989 (Zegers de Beijl et al., 2001). Since this was seen as a sensitive issue that would have difficulty attracting funds from the general budget, it was financed from outside donations. A report on 'Testing Discrimination in Natural Experiments' proposed research of the kind that had been so successful in Britain in 1967–8 to be conducted in eleven countries.

Studies in the Netherlands found that in one out of every three responses to advertisements of vacancies for semi-skilled employment, a Moroccan applicant received less favourable treatment than a Dutch applicant. When jobseekers had to apply by post even immigrants who had received a Dutch college education and spoke Dutch fluently were seriously disadvantaged. Only in Belgium, Germany, the Netherlands, Spain and the USA could the ILO plans be implemented as originally intended. The findings from all these countries reported an incidence of discrimination not greatly different from that found in the Netherlands and the United Kingdom. Studies were conducted into the efficacy of anti-discrimination legislation in ten countries. They showed that the criminal law is relatively ineffective in preventing discrimination at the workplace and in enabling its victims to obtain compensation. Other studies evaluated anti-discrimination training in six countries.

In its recommendations about educational measures for combating discrimination the UN has consistently focused on educational establishments like schools and colleges. It has neglected the influences to which young people are subjected when they leave such establishments and the importance of on-the-job training. One example of the latter that was not mentioned in the ILO studies was the British government's programme of judicial training in ethnic minority issues. In the years 1994–6 over £800,000 was spent on the training of some two thousand judges (Banton, 1998b).

In view of what is said about unequal development in other chapters of this book, it should also be mentioned that in 1986 the General Assembly adopted a Declaration on the Right to Development and that the UN Development Programme is allocated a significant share of the budget. The recent rapid technological advances in the West, such as those associated with the use of computers, mean that the gap between average incomes in developed and undeveloped societies has increased and will increase further. Inequality of development associated with ethnic difference will become ever more salient as an issue in international politics.

Universality

The different priorities that the states of the East and the West gave to economic and civil rights reflected long-standing philosophical differences about the nature of rights. In 1789 the French National Assembly had adopted a Declaration on the Rights of Man and the Citizen proclaiming that: 'The final end of every political institution is the preservation of the natural and imprescriptible rights of man. These rights are those of liberty, property, security and resistance to oppression.' Edmund Burke, in England, deplored this abstract claim, maintaining that there were only rights of men in civil society, enjoying rights that had been won for them by their ancestors. A person could enjoy a right only if he or she could exercise it against someone or something who acknowledged a corresponding duty, as citizens have rights against the state. A similar objection was famously expressed a few years later by Jeremy Bentham when he complained that: 'Right is the child of law; from real laws come real rights, but from imaginary law, from "laws of nature", come imaginary rights . . . Natural rights is simple nonsense: natural and imprescriptible rights, rhetorical nonsense, – nonsense upon stilts.' The difference of orientation could still be observed in the General Assembly in 1948, for when the Soviets (who thought of rights as conferred on citizens by the state) stressed the importance of the economic and social they were consistently supported by the delegate of France.

A parallel debate was instigated by the UN's convening, in Vienna in 1993, of the World Conference on Human Rights. The Asian states met beforehand and drew up the Bangkok declaration, which states that human rights instruments should be applied in ways that take account of 'national and regional peculiarities'. Since there is no distinctively 'Asian' perspective on human rights, entirely different from Western or other perspectives and unanimously shared by all Asian societies, the declaration was widely interpreted as an attempt by the political elites in a number of Asian countries to protect their authoritarian styles of government.

Diplomacy

Multilateral diplomacy, such as that of the decades, is not necessarily more effective than bilateral diplomacy. Sometimes a state is anxious to secure the support of some big and powerful state to assist in its own economic development or in some political dispute. In such circumstances it will pay careful attention to any representations made to it by the ambassador of the state whose favour it seeks. Nor is it necessary to document the extent to which some states have been dependent upon financial and military assistance from one of the major powers and the ability of the donor state to influence policies in the client state.

There have recently been multilateral pressures on the regional level. Many states in Eastern Europe have been anxious to secure admission to the Organization for Security and Co-operation in Europe (OSCE) and to the Council of Europe (COE) as stages on a path towards membership in the European Union, with the economic benefits expected to flow from that. When considering admission to membership in the OSCE and the COE the existing member states have looked to see whether the candidate states meet international standards in the treatment of minorities. It is worth noting, by way of example, that 'because of the unsatisfactory state of democracy in Croatia' (in which the treatment of minorities may well have formed a part) the International Monetary Fund at one time held up the availability to that country of a very substantial credit.

During the era of the Cold War (i.e., up to the end of the 1980s) many potential conflicts were suppressed by being forced into the bi-polar framework of international relations. The discussion of violations of civil and political rights was very selective. With the breaking of that framework more attention was paid to such violations and authoritarian states were subject to new criticism. This affected the proceedings of the CHR (a subsidiary of the Economic and Social Council, which itself is a subsidiary of the General Assembly) in ways that have been tactfully recorded in successive numbers of the *Human Rights Monitor*, a journal of the International Service for Human Rights in Geneva.

Each year a third of the members of the Commission are re-elected or replaced by the Council, which attempts to secure equitable representation of the different regions. The *Monitor* reported that the re-election of Pakistan, the Philippines and Iraq to membership of the Commission in 1989 had made it impossible for that body to agree on a condemnation of Iraq for its violations of human rights. It expressed distress that the Arab and Asian states should not have been able to nominate better candidates for election, and noted that authoritarian states were beginning to seek election in order to defend themselves from criticism. The following year the United Kingdom lost its seat, returning one year later at the expense of Denmark. Membership was expanded so that the CHR now consists of fifty-three states, but the USA has not always been able to secure election.

By the time of the fifty-second session of the Commission in 1996, a group of states, which came to be known as the Like-Minded Group, were demanding that decisions should be taken by consensus so that the minority could not be out-voted. In the following year the 'like-minded states', mostly Asian, combined, and debates became more politicized. The states that supported a resolution in 1999 demanding a change in the Commission's procedures are asterisked in the following list of the then member states: Argentina, Austria, Bangladesh, Bhutan*, Botswana, Canada, Cape Verde, Chile, China*, Colombia, Congo, Cuba*, the Czech Republic, the Democratic Republic of the Congo, Ecuador, El Salvador, France, Germany, Guatemala, India*, Indonesia*, Ireland, Italy, Japan, Latvia, Liberia, Luxembourg, Madagascar, Mauritius, Mexico, Morocco, Mozambique, Nepal*, Niger, Norway, Pakistan*, Peru, the Philippines*, Poland, Qatar*, the Republic of Korea*, Romania, the Russian Federation, Rwanda, Senegal, South Africa, Sri Lanka*, Sudan*, Tunisia, the United Kingdom, the United States of America, Uruguay and Venezuela. States that are not members of the CHR may participate as observers, and it may be noted that delegates from Afghanistan, Algeria, the Democratic People's Republic of Korea, Egypt, Iran, Jordan, Libya, Malaysia, Mauritania, Myanmar, Syria, Tanzania, Thailand, Vietnam and Yemen supported the proposals from the Like-Minded Group. One of the most active delegations in the minority was that of Cuba. According to the *Monitor* Cuba expressed preoccupations shared by many hard-line governments and the view that, were it to step aside, Pakistan and Algeria would be ready to take its place. At the Commission's fifty-sixth session in 2000 members of the Like-Minded Group, often speaking through the representatives of Cuba and Pakistan, succeeded in disrupting meetings through excessive numbers of interventions and a superior knowledge of the rules of procedure, which enabled them to run rings round other delegations, particularly those of the Western Group.

In considering the attitudes of some of these delegations it should be remembered that the first law of international politics is that governments seek to remain in power. Some nineteenth-century sociologists envisaged social evolution as an organic process by which small groups grew into larger ones, became nations, and would become a global community. Globalization was a more brutal process of unequal development by which colonial powers created some states by drawing lines on a map. Some of the resultant states were very difficult to govern and their systems did not have the checks and balances characteristic of the Western democracies. The new rulers were, of course, often self-interested. When in international forums they have been criticized by non-governmental organizations (NGOs), representatives of the rulers have described the NGOs as unduly influenced by Western attitudes. The UN grants consultative status to approved NGOs. This can occasion contention. In 1999, when the Commission considered the human rights situation in Sudan, the government condemned the murder by rebels of four men. An NGO called Christian Solidarity International nominated as its representative to address the Commission Mr John Garang, leader of the main rebel group. Later that year the UN Economic and Social Council voted by twenty-six votes to fourteen, with twelve abstentions, to withdraw consultative status from Christian Solidarity International. According to the *Monitor* some of the governments most exposed to criticism have created Gongos (Government-organized NGOs), which come to Geneva under orders to defend their governments and upset any concerted action by NGOs. 'As recent unproductive exchanges on Kashmir between pro-Pakistan and pro-India NGOs have shown, this slows down the Commission's activities.'

A UN body like the Human Rights Commission cannot discuss an issue on the basis of press reports. It requires an objective text setting out what appear to its own officials to be the facts of the matter. So in preparation for much of its business the Commission appoints a special rapporteur. Some are appointed to report on the situation in a particular country, others, called thematic rapporteurs, report on something that the Commission has identified as an issue. Proposals of this kind often originate within the Sub-Commission but the changing political balance in the Commission has led to a diminution in the scope of the Sub-Commission's activities, while many of its members are not truly independent experts.

The international politics of race were illustrated by the Commission's appointment in 1993 of a special rapporteur: 'to examine according to his mandate incidents of contemporary forms of racism, racial discrimination, any form of discrimination against Blacks, Arabs and Muslims, xenophobia, negrophobia, anti-Semitism and related intolerance as well as governmental measures to overcome them, and to report on these matters to the Commission'. In the eighth preambular paragraph to resolution 1993/20 the Commission expressed concern that: 'in many parts of the world, despite all efforts, racism, racial discrimination, xenophobia and related intolerance and acts of violence resulting therefrom persist, among them manifestations occurring particularly in developed countries', indicating that it wished the special rapporteur to give prior attention to developed countries and the situations of migrant workers and indigenous peoples. (The language is representative of current UN rhetoric about racism as resembling a sickness.) The special rapporteur would work under the authority of the UN Charter; there was no recognition that almost all the developed countries had accepted obligations under the ICERD, and that their fulfilment of them was being monitored by another body. Other statements in the course of the decades have demonstrated the desire to see action taken against discrimination directed against asylum-seekers, Roma, and minorities in general. When a resolution singles out certain examples of racism this is not to be seen as a philosophical definition but as a political statement indicating priorities to be observed. The addition of the expressions 'xenophobia' and 'related intolerance' exemplify further expansion of the concept of racial discrimination.

The special rapporteur, M. Maurice Glélé-Ahanhanzo of Benin, has reported on developments in many countries, based upon information received, and has undertaken missions to the USA, Germany, Brazil, France, the United Kingdom, Colombia, Kuwait and South Africa. The procedure is that on the conclusion of a visit by the special rapporteur a draft report is sent to the state for comment, and state comments are published together with the final report.

Commenting on the 1997 debate on the special rapporteur's report, the *Monitor* wrote: 'The noisy declarations of the delegates of Egypt and Indonesia . . . surprised observers . . . as the issue was a weak point for European countries, congratulations for the Special Rapporteur dominated the debate . . . which would seem to show that several government delegations had not read the report.' Then came a flood of protests when some delegations found that one paragraph quoted a document received from the government of Israel about trends in anti-Semitism, according to which anti-Semitic writers in the Middle East tended increasingly to rely on traditional sources, including the Qur'an. There was no suggestion that the special rapporteur shared this opinion, but as certain Islamic states considered it blasphemous the Commission deleted this sentence from his report. The *Monitor* regarded this as a dangerous challenge to the claim that special rapporteurs are independent experts.

In 2000, M. Glélé-Ahanhanzo wrote outlining 'three contemporary forms of racism', namely, discrimination against blacks, anti-Semitism and discrimination against Roma. Concerning the first he cited evidence from Amnesty International about the way in which the application of the death penalty in the USA bears disproportionately upon the African-American and Hispanic groups. He reported on the replies to his representations received from the governments of Australia, Canada, Germany, the Russian Federation, Spain and the United States, and on his missions to central European countries with large Roma populations. Once again, the debate on his report focused largely on Europe and the USA. NGOs drew attention to situations of racial discrimination in Austria, Burma (Myanmar), India (with particular reference to abuses under the caste system), Israel, Japan, Mauritania, the USA and Latin America, but not to great effect. The delegation of the USA joined the consensus by which the resolution on the special rapporteur's report was adopted. In an explanation of the vote it stressed the importance of unfettered freedom of expression for a fully functioning human rights system and as a step in combating racism. The message will have been lost on the delegates representing autocratic states.

A recent trend in the Commission has been to weaken the applicability of international human rights norms and to link international obligations to national legislation. Debates are increasingly politicized, while the European states have difficulty reaching a common position on human rights issues. The states appeal to international human rights standards but only occasionally are the appeals altruistic.

In 1965 the focus was on colonialism and fascism, with little recognition of the atrocities that could be perpetrated when humans were regarded as 'others' to whom ordinary moral norms were not applicable. The rape of Nanking by Japanese troops in 1938 can be cited alongside the Nazis' atrocities. Since then there have been the atrocities of a US military unit in the Vietnamese village of My Lai, the slaughter of Palestinian refugees in the Sabra and Chatilla camps in Beirut, the amputations of limbs by child soldiers in Sierra Leone, the genocide of the Aché in Paraguay and the Nuba in Sudan, the killings in Bosnia, Kosovo, Chechnya, Rwanda and Borneo, and the ethnic pogroms directed against Chinese in several parts of Indonesia at the time of the Asian currency crisis.

Little may be achieved by providing for the discussion of atrocities on the agenda of the CHR if it is to no concrete effect. Public discussions of disputes like that between India and Pakistan over Kashmir are a poor use of scarce time. Grave and persisting abuses of human rights may sometimes constitute a justification for interference in the internal affairs of states, but there is usually an opening for the state in question to argue that its critics are motivated not by altruism but by the pursuit of their selfish interests. In 2000, at the request of Arab states, the CHR convened a special session to examine the deterioration of the situation in Palestine.

The session was overshadowed by the almost contemporaneous meeting at which the parties, under the auspices of the USA, attempted to negotiate a resolution. The session concluded with a resolution condemning the Israeli use of force by nineteen votes to sixteen and with seventeen abstentions. Such votes achieve little.

Earlier in this chapter it was mentioned that the initiative that led to the preparation of the ICERD came from the Sub-Commission on the Prevention of Discrimination and Protection of Minorities. This body was created in 1947 as a subsidiary of the CHR and renamed in 1999 as the Sub-Commission on the Promotion and Protection of Human Rights. It consists of twenty-six experts acting in their personal capacity, elected by the CHR with due regard for equitable geographical representation. The politicization of human rights issues in the CHR has affected the Sub-Commission. About half these experts are diplomats who (according to the *Monitor*) 'often come from those States with a less than acute sense of human rights protection. Other experts are so closely aligned with their governments that they effectively represent them.' For more than thirty years a central task of the Sub-Commission has been the examination of situations where there are systematic violations of human rights, but since 1990 this work has been cut back, until in 2000 the CHR forbade the Sub-Commission to adopt resolutions relating to particular countries and reduced its meeting time. Many observers now doubt whether it has a future and some have expressed exasperation at the repetitive and unprofitable nature of its members' speeches about racism and other matters.

Two theses

This chapter has maintained that two mutually inconsistent conceptions of racial discrimination underlay the anti-racist strategies formulated at the UN in the 1950s and early 1960s. The differences are important to any consideration of how racial discrimination is best combated. The first conception (that racial discrimination is crime-like) was embodied in Article 26 of the ICCPR in 1961; the second conception (that racism is like a social sickness) informed the Declaration on the Elimination of All Forms of Racial Discrimination and the preamble to the ICERD agreed in 1963–5, although the operative articles of the Convention were in accord with the 1961 conception. The opposed views can be expressed as two theses:

- Thesis One: the less favourable treatment of a person because of his or her race, colour, sex or religion, or on any similar ground, constitutes discrimination. So defined, discrimination is characteristic of all forms of society. It is the duty of the state to prohibit discriminatory behaviour and to reduce it by means appropriate to the settings in which it occurs.
- Thesis Two: racial discrimination is the manifestation of a social pathology characteristic of certain forms of society. Ideas of group superiority and inferiority can become a partly autonomous social force acting upon individuals. Racism can be eliminated by changing the social relations that give rise to prejudice, preventing the prejudiced from acting in accordance with their beliefs and suppressing any manifestation of racial superiority.

In the last four decades of the twentieth century debate at international gatherings was usually based upon the second conception because this suited the political purposes of many states. Yet some who accepted Thesis Two might have been persuaded to change their minds had other delegations been better propagandists for the alternative conception. The delegates of the Eastern bloc and of some other states, like Cuba, were very well schooled in the importance of ideology and adept at recruiting support from among the non-aligned. They saw how the idea of race, supplemented by that of racism, could be an intellectual resource that could be used against the West. Some of their allies may not have been very open to argument, but Western diplomats, although brought up in an intellectual tradition that disparaged ideology, might have been better advocates for Thesis One.

4

A Living Instrument

It was a stroke of genius to give the name 'committee' to the body charged with overseeing the ICERD. The Convention included novel measures of implementation that must have made some states hesitate over ratification. A comparison with the Convention on the Prevention and Punishment of the Crime of Genocide, adopted in 1948, is instructive. That instrument defined the crime, included an undertaking of the parties to enact legislation to give effect to its provisions, and stated that any dispute between them relating to its interpretation or application should be submitted to the International Court of Justice. The ICERD went much further by requiring states parties to submit periodic reports to be examined by a body that would report on them annually to the General Assembly. Some states must have wondered what might happen if their enemies obtained control of this new organ. Choosing the familiar name 'committee' made it sound less novel and less threatening.

Ratification

The ICERD entered into force in January 1969 after the UN's receipt of the twenty-seventh instrument of ratification or accession. The first twenty-seven states parties were: Argentina, Brazil, Bulgaria, Costa Rica, Cyprus, Czechoslovakia, Ecuador, Ghana, Hungary, Iceland, India, Iran, Kuwait, Libya, Niger, Nigeria, Pakistan, Panama, the Philippines, Poland, Sierra Leone, Spain, Tunisia, the United Arab Republic, Uruguay, Venezuela and Yugoslavia. There were seven from the African group of states, six from the Asian group, seven from the Latin American group, five from the East European group, and two from the West European and Other group. States in which the treaty-making power is vested in the executive can ratify a treaty more rapidly than those in which a proposal has to be put before the legislature, or, as in the case of Switzerland, in which a referendum had to be conducted before the Swiss Confederation could become a party to the ICERD. Six months after the entry into force an election had to be held for the states parties to elect the members of the Committee. Each state party could nominate one candidate from among its own nationals. The Federal Republic of Germany, Ukraine, the USSR and the United Kingdom ratified in time to make nominations.

It is in the interest of every state to develop the scope of international law to restrain other states as much as possible, but at the same time every state wants to protect its own independence of action as far as it can. One such protection is provided by the power to enter reservations as to the obligations accepted. The costs of ratifying the ICERD, particularly in exposing their domestic affairs to external criticism, were high for some states relative to their benefits, but it was to their advantage to take part in order to reduce the risks that other states would use the Convention to create difficulties for them.

When the results of the first elections to the Committee were announced in 1969 it looked to Western diplomats as if indeed it would be controlled by the states that had been causing so much trouble in the decolonization committee. Of the eighteen members, four were from the group of African states (Ghana, Nigeria, Swaziland, the United Arab Republic); five from the Asian group (Cyprus, Kuwait, India, Pakistan, the Philippines); two from the Latin American group (Costa Rica, Ecuador), five from Eastern Europe (Czechoslovakia, Poland, Ukraine, the USSR, Yugoslavia) and two from the West European and Other group (the Federal Republic of Germany, the United Kingdom). There was no member from French-speaking countries. Nearly all members were diplomats or lawyers closely associated with their governments. The first chairman was from India (a country that was closely associated with the USSR in diplomatic matters) and the committee's rapporteur from Kuwait (for further details of elections and the history of the Committee, see Banton, 1996). It was recognized that the outcome had not corresponded to the Convention's stipulation that consideration be given to 'equitable geographical representation'; so agreement was reached that it would be desirable to have four seats for persons from each of the African, Asian and West European groups, and three from each of the East European and Latin American groups.

Given the novelty of the requirement of state reporting and examination of reports, and given the tensions in the arena of international politics, the heavy representation of diplomats on the Committee and its adoption of some of the conventions of diplomatic relations doubtless helped it secure acceptance among the delegations in New York. The influence of the diplomatic environment was illustrated by the incidence of casual vacancies in membership. The first such vacancy arose in 1972 when the Committee received messages from the government of the USSR stating that the Soviet member, a diplomat, would no longer be able to fulfil his duties as a member because he had been transferred to other duties, and submitting a biographical note about another Soviet diplomat whom it was presenting as a prospective member of the Committee. CERD insisted that notification of resignation had to come from the member. Between 1976 and 1986 there were fourteen casual vacancies, two as a result of deaths. In the other cases members from Argentina (twice), Austria, Bulgaria, Cyprus, Nigeria (thrice), Senegal and the USSR (thrice) were replaced. Not until 1999 was there another casual vacancy. There were so many between 1976 and 1986 because they were mostly diplomats nominated by governments who regarded Committee membership as simply one diplomatic duty among others. This also meant that CERD on occasion lacked the quorum necessary to start a session and the Committee had considered recommending states parties, when nominating and electing candidates, to take into account the availability of the candidate to attend meetings regularly. Since 1986 many states parties have been more inclined to see membership of a human rights treaty as calling for persons independent from governments.

Treaty monitoring

To start with, most states parties had a very limited understanding of the obligations they had accepted and tended to regard the Convention as directed against apartheid. Analysing the picture of racial discrimination portrayed in the initial reports from the first forty-five states, CERD's rapporteur found that only five admitted that there was any discrimination in their territory, and two of these explained that it was being practised by another state. Apparently, states that had ratified the Convention did not need it, whereas those that did need it had not chosen to ratify. Later it became more common for some states to refer to racial discrimination as part of their inheritance from the colonial era.

In the 1970s CERD acted as a tutor to state delegations, taking them through the various articles of the Convention and explaining to them any respects in which the actions of their governments fell short of what the Convention required. The Committee placed a particular emphasis upon Article 4, for two reasons. First, it was of a mandatory character, creating clear obligations upon governments to legislate. Some states, for example, simply pointed to provisions in their constitutions that prohibited racial discrimination. Committee members observed that this was insufficient: there had to be legislation ensuring that those responsible for certain actions were punished. Second, Article 4, regarded by many as the 'key' article of the Convention, was in line with the prevailing philosophy, which favoured the repression of expressions likely to incite discrimination and hostile to the belief that by permitting the maximum freedom of speech a government could in the long run do more to combat the evil in question.

The temper of the times was also illustrated by CERD's reading of Article 3 of the Convention. This obliges states to condemn racial segregation and apartheid and to 'prevent, prohibit and eradicate all practices of this nature in territories under their jurisdiction'. In 1972 CERD issued a General Recommendation calling attention to the passage in the preamble to the Convention in which states resolved 'to build an international community free from all forms of racial segregation and racial discrimination'; it went on to express the view that 'measures adopted on the national level to give effect to the provisions of the Convention are interrelated with the measures taken on the international level' and that therefore it welcomed the inclusion in states' reports of information regarding the status of their 'diplomatic, economic and other relations with the racist régimes in southern Africa'.

Many of the delegations that participated in the drafting of the Convention must have asked themselves whether there was any possibility of the Convention's being used against their national interests by other, possibly unfriendly, states. They may have concluded in 1971 that any such suspicions had been justified when they learned of claims made by Syria and Panama. Syria reported that its nationals resident in the Golan Heights had been deprived of their rights under the Convention and that it was the responsibility of the states parties to bring to an end the racist and discriminatory policies of Israel in the occupied territories. Panama claimed that while it was in all respects complying with the Convention, in that part of Panamanian territory known as the Panama Canal Zone the USA was violating the Convention by operating racially discriminatory salary scales. Cyprus adopted a similar approach after the invasion by Turkey, while Egypt and Jordan complained about discrimination in occupied areas of the Sinai Peninsula and the West Bank of the River Jordan. At the times in question, Israel, the USA and Turkey were not parties to the Convention. CERD was agreed that while it could not be indifferent to reports of racially discriminatory practices on the territory of states parties, such disguised inter-state disputes lay outside its competence.

The Cold War cast a shadow over the Committee's work during the 1980s, being particularly apparent in the examination of some reports, such as that from Bulgaria in 1986 at the time when the government was using illegal force in order to make the ethnically Turkish section of the population adopt Bulgarian names and Bulgarian culture. After the Committee elections of 1988 the atmosphere in the Committee started to change. Members could trust one another more. Though some of the diplomat members resisted proposals intended to make the examination of state reports more searching, the Committee succeeded in improving many of its procedures. A major advance was the securing of agreement on what became known as Concluding Observations, by which the Committee expressed a collective view on a report instead of offering readers a summary of what different members had said. Another important development was the appointment of Country rapporteurs to open the discussion. This improved the division of labour within the committee by designating one member to undertake a more detailed examination of the report.

Article 9 of the Convention states that the Committee shall report annually and 'may make suggestions and general recommendations based on the examination of the reports and information received from the States Parties'. It does not provide that states parties may send delegations to present their reports or that Committee members may draw upon their personal knowledge of situations or upon information derived from sources other than state reports. On occasion, members have argued that the Committee should limit itself to the state reports and have expressed concern when colleagues rely on press reports and similar information without making clear the ultimate sources of the information or giving the state party adequate opportunity to comment on its reliability. On the other hand, Article 9 uses the word *examination*, which implies more than mere acceptance, and Article 8 states that the Committee shall consist of experts. They are not there simply to endorse state reports. It has also to be recalled that on occasion there has been a change of government in a state and the new government has told the Committee that information supplied by its predecessor was not a truthful account of the situation. So the

Committee must be an independent body. This independence was asserted when in 1991 it formally decided that it would:

> continue to make its suggestions and general recommendations on the basis of the examination of the reports and information received from States parties . . . At the same time, in examining the reports of States parties, members of the Committee must have access, as independent experts, to all other available sources of information, governmental and non-governmental. . . .

The requirement that the Committee act on the basis of reports from states posed a difficulty when states failed to submit reports. Did they then escape all examination of whether or not they were fulfilling their obligations? Most of the legally qualified members maintained that the Convention provided no basis for Committee action in these circumstances (and some other treaty bodies have taken a similar position), but CERD decided that when a report was overdue by five years or more it would review implementation of the Convention in that state, based on the last report received, the consideration given to it by the Committee at that time, and other information available through UN sources. This enabled the Committee to take charge of the reporting process instead of simply reacting to incoming reports. It later extended this practice to situations in which a state had failed for more than five years to submit its initial report.

After the publication in 1992 of the UN secretary-general's *An Agenda for Peace*, with its emphasis on the need for preventive diplomacy, CERD agreed that it would include 'Prevention of Racial Discrimination' as a priority item in the agenda for all sessions. The Committee adopted a memorandum describing new early-warning measures and urgent procedures. Some states expressed apprehension about this initiative, but it was approved by the General Assembly. Theo van Boven (1998) has reviewed the use that has been made of these procedures. One clear-cut issue was presented by the shooting of Palestinians in the Hebron mosque in 1994. It was more difficult to determine whether reports of rebellion in Chiapas and of atrocities in Chechnya fell within the scope of the Convention.

The Convention's prohibition of segregation was given new life in 1995 by CERD's General Recommendation XIX. In effect, the Committee found within the Convention authority for action of a kind that had not previously been contemplated. The recommendation observes that while in some countries segregation may have been the result of governmental policies, a condition of partial segregation may arise as an unintended by-product of the actions of private persons. 'In many cities residential patterns are influenced by group differences in income, which are sometimes combined with differences of race, colour, descent and national or ethnic origin, so that the inhabitants can be stigmatised and individuals suffer a form of discrimination in which racial grounds are mixed with other grounds.'

In 1987 the Indian delegation was asked whom the Indian legislature had intended to protect in 1949 when it adopted a constitution that prohibited discrimination on grounds of race. The answer came in the report submitted in 1996, when it was said that those who drafted the section of the constitution on fundamental rights had wished to reflect provisions in the UN Charter and the United States constitution. That report acknowledged that castes and tribes were based on descent but maintained that the use of this word in the Convention 'clearly refers to "race" '. The government denied that its policies relating to caste came within the Convention. In its report to the General Assembly the Committee stated that 'the term "descent" mentioned in article 1 of the Convention does not solely refer to race'. It affirmed that 'the situation of the scheduled castes and scheduled tribes falls within the scope of the Convention', but included as an annex a set of comments from the government reiterating its dissent. In 2001, in its concluding observations on the reports of Bangladesh and Japan, CERD reaffirmed that in the Convention 'the term "descent" has its own meaning and is not to be confused with race or ethnic or national origin'; therefore the rights of castes in Bangladesh and of groups like the Burakumin in Japan were to be protected in fulfilment of obligations accepted by parties to the Convention.

In the 1990s CERD members asked many more questions about states' fulfilment of their obligations under Article 5 of the Convention. Since this covers so wide a range of rights, there are grounds for regarding this as the key article in the Convention.

Broadening the scope

During the 1990s there were signs that CERD had gradually been gaining authority, especially with the newer and smaller states. Governments almost invariably accept the invitation to send a delegation to present their reports to the Committee, but their obligation is to implement the provisions of the Convention, not to answer the questions asked by Committee members. The Committee is not a court; it issues opinions, not judgements. If one state does not fulfil its obligations, it is other states parties that have cause for complaint and it is they who can act against the defaulter. In practice they never do so. On the international level the main pressure for implementation of the Convention derives from states' desire for a good reputation. In the post-Cold War era this has become more important.

Prior to 1988 many of the reports from the Soviet Union, Ukraine, Belarus and East European states were categorical in tone. In the 1990s they changed dramatically, becoming much franker and ready to acknowledge deficiencies. Many of the new states created as a result of the dissolution of the USSR and Yugoslavia (notably Armenia, Azerbaijan, Croatia, Estonia, the Former Yugoslav Republic of Macedonia, Kyrgyzstan, Latvia, Slovenia and Uzbekistan) set about the task of protecting human rights with great enthusiasm and regarded the process of reporting under the Convention as very important.

Many of the states of Central and Eastern Europe have made it a priority to seek closer economic relations with the states of the West. The route to closer association is through membership of the OSCE, the COE and then the EU. Each of these bodies expects candidate states to meet its standards for the observance of human rights. The OSCE's high commissioner for national minorities took a very close interest in the language tests that the new Baltic states set for persons seeking citizenship; the levels of linguistic competence initially proposed were so high that it would have been extremely difficult for members of the Russian-speaking minority to meet them, so this became a matter of negotiation. The high commissioner's office has also taken a very close interest in discrimination against the Roma minority. To become a member of the COE, a state has to be a party to the European Convention on Human Rights (ECHR) and the Framework Convention on National Minorities. The Court of Justice of the European Union can now adjudicate upon allegations of racial discrimination in employment just as it does on cases of sex discrimination.

In general, states prefer to tackle their problems by bilateral action and have only limited confidence in international institutions. Some refuse to recognize established international law, as, for example, the US Supreme Court in the 1998 *Breard* case denied the self-executing character of the Vienna Convention on Consular Relations (Grant, 2000:318). US opposition to the establishment of the International Criminal Court has been well publicized. States have been reluctant to rationalize the treaty body system; they want to control others while preserving their own independence.

States have not hitherto disciplined those of their own number who fail to fulfil their obligations, though there was a major step forward when a former head of state of Chile, General Pinochet, was arrested in Britain in 1998 on a warrant issued by a Spanish judge. The judge was investigating allegations of the general's responsibility for the death of Spanish nationals. The central issue was the obligation assumed by Chile when its government ratified the Convention Against Torture. What if the warrant had alleged violations not of this convention but of the ICERD? A delegation of the Chilean government acknowledged to CERD in 1999 that the colonial society had marginalized the country's indigenous peoples and that there had been widespread discrimination against them. Yet there was no one corresponding to the Spanish judge to invoke international law on their behalf. The implementation of the legal content of the ICERD depends upon the action of states. Were an expert (such as a procurator or prosecutor) to be charged with assessing the current situation in international law with respect to some issue, he or she would set about the task by reviewing relevant treaties and tribunal decisions, noting the positions adopted by various states and the votes recorded when decisions have been taken. A unanimous judgement is more authoritative than a divided one. Such a person would study what has been the practice of states in order to draw inferences about the current legal position. In general, states yield to an international process some of their power to act independently only if by so doing they can advance their policy objectives by constraining the freedom of other states to act independently.

In recent years new states have become parties to the Convention, including Saudi Arabia (a state that did not vote for adoption of the Universal Declaration of Human Rights, on the grounds that the Qur'an was a sufficient guide), Indonesia, Japan, Switzerland (which was not then a UN member state), and the United States of America. Progress towards universal ratification of the Convention is steady.

In recent years also, the Committee has turned its attention to issues that previously received a low priority, notably to the rights of indigenous peoples. In 2000 it held a thematic discussion on discrimination against Roma and adopted a general recommendation on this. There has been some discussion of whether the forms of discrimination inherent in the Hindu caste system fall within the concept of descent listed among the Convention's prohibited grounds. As already mentioned, the Indian government disputes this, but there will probably be attempts in the future to consider the unequal treatment of untouchables, or Dalits as they are now often called, within the framework of the ICERD.

CERD is not entitled to expect a higher standard of fulfilment from the more developed states, though in practice this sometimes appears to be the case. In some Western states NGOs are active and submit to Committee members reports alternative to those of governments. In these circumstances state delegations may be questioned much more closely than when there are no such reports.

As has been explained, states and their delegations vary in their reactions to questions and comments from CERD members. To quote a somewhat extreme example, in August 1995, at the conclusion of the Committee's consideration of the thirteenth periodic report of Nigeria, the leader of the state delegation responded to questions from Committee members. He referred to the ongoing trial of Mr Ken Saro-Wiwa and other leaders of the Movement for the Survival of Ogoni People who, he said, had taken the law into their own hands, using the movement as a vehicle for murder, arson and vandalism. The Committee's country rapporteur (who was the present author), when making his final statement, objected, in tones of indignation, that the defendants were on trial charged with these offences and that if a government representative referred to them as responsible for murders this suggested that they would not receive a fair trial. The whole delegation, together with the Nigerian member of the Committee, burst into laughter at this observation.

In the 1990s NGOs and quasi-non-governmental organizations (Quangos) began to take notice of CERD's work. Thus in 1991 CERD received commentaries upon the ninth periodic report of the Netherlands from the Dutch section of the International Commission of Jurists, the state's Equal Treatment Commission, and the National Bureau against Racial Discrimination. In 1996 the thirteenth report of the United Kingdom was accompanied by a joint submission supported by twenty-two organizations within the country, together with seven further separate NGO submissions and documents from the Hong Kong Legislative Council and NGOs in that territory. Since then more such commentaries, sometimes called alternative reports or shadow reports, have been received.

In 1992 a private initiative in Switzerland led to the establishment of the Anti-Racism Information Service, an international NGO that services CERD. It notifies national NGOs of when state reports are likely to be considered by the Committee and helps them submit shadow reports. It takes up no positions itself, but simply assembles information and provides copies for any Committee members who ask for it. This service has greatly improved the Committee's examination of state reports.

Annual reports

CERD's annual report is considered by the General Assembly every October or November. For many years it was taken together with an agenda item on decolonization and some delegations used the occasion for speeches that had little to do with the substance of the report. Only rarely could it be inferred that any speaker had read any part of the report other than that relating to his or her own state or some state that the speaker's government wished to criticize. Since 1989 the report has been considered as part of a debate on the effective implementation of all human rights instruments, though separate resolutions are agreed on the status of the Convention and the work of the Committee.

General Assembly resolutions are almost invariably divided into two sections. The preambular section consists of paragraphs that rehearse precedents and set out the rationale on which the operative paragraphs in the second section are based. The wording of every draft paragraph is scrutinized by delegates. Once a set of words has been accepted it can be repeated in subsequent resolutions even if it has become obsolete; by contrast, it can be difficult to introduce new wording. I have called this the principle of the ratchet. Seeking to further their policies, states look for opportunities to move the ratchet up a notch and are alert to any attempts to undo previous agreements. From 1963 onwards, resolutions about racial discrimination made reference to only two causes: colonialism and the dissemination of doctrines of racial superiority. It took thirty-five years for small but significant changes to appear. In 1998 the General Assembly for the first time referred to 'intolerance in an increasingly globalised world', adding that it might be aggravated 'by inequitable distribution of wealth, marginalisation and social exclusion' and thus making a connection with unequal development. The same resolution (53/133), also for the first time, referred to 'the rise of racist and xenophobic ideas in political circles' without indicating whether it had any particular region in mind. With a Third World conference in prospect, the Assembly's reliance upon an oversimplified conception of racial discrimination was starting to weaken.

Communications

CERD became competent to consider communications received under Article 14 in 1984. From then until the middle of 2000, seventeen communications were received. It was ironic that the first should have been a case against the Netherlands, since twenty years earlier that country had taken the leading part in arguing for the inclusion in the Convention of an authority for CERD to act in this capacity. The communication turned on the dismissal from employment of a Turkish woman (*1/1984, Yilmaz-Dogon v. The Netherlands*). The employer had written:

> When a Netherlands girl marries and has a baby, she stops working. Our foreign women workers, on the other hand, take the child to neighbours or family and at the slightest set-back disappear on sick leave under the terms of the Sickness Act. They repeat that endlessly. Since we all must do our utmost to avoid going under, we cannot afford such goings-on.

Treaty body proceedings when considering such communications are confidential so I cannot refer to discussions within the Committee, but to any outside reader it will be apparent that the Committee had to decide whether the facts in the *Yilmaz-Dogon* case revealed an act of racial discrimination apart from any possible sex discrimination, and whether, since the Netherlands courts had found no breach of national law, the government had violated its obligations under the Convention. To do that they needed an agreed understanding of the definition of racial discrimination in Article 1(1) of the Convention. It was not necessary to consider whether the action in question had any relation to colonialism, racist doctrines, or the nature of Netherlands society.

The opinions reached concerning some other communications may give an indication of the scope of possible action under this provision. In the case of *Narrainen v. Norway* (*3/1991*) CERD found no violation of the Convention by the state, but was sufficiently concerned by the evidence relating to possible racial bias within a jury for it to recommend that the state give due attention to the impartiality of juries and, in connection with a periodic report from Norway, to urge a review of the procedures for composing panels from which juries are selected.

In the case of *L. K. v. The Netherlands* (*4/1991*), relating to threats made by neighbours to a man who had been allocated housing, the Committee stated: 'When threats of violence are made, and especially when they are made in public and by a group, it is incumbent upon the State to investigate with due diligence and expedition. In the instant case, the State failed to do this.' It went on: 'The Committee finds that in view of the inadequate response to the incidents, the police and judicial proceedings in this case did not afford the applicant effective protection and remedies within the meaning of

Article 6 of the Convention.' The government then revised its procedures to guard against the possibility of deficiencies in this
connection.

Opinions have been issued in three communications alleging that
Denmark has not provided the promised protections. In the case of
Habassi (10/97), the author of the communication had been refused
a bank loan on the sole ground of his non-Danish nationality. He
reported this to the authorities, but, in CERD's opinion, 'the steps
taken by the police and the State Prosecutor were insufficient to
determine whether or not an act of racial discrimination had taken
place'. In the case of *Ahmad (16/1999)*, in which the author of the
communication had been the subject of racial insults, the Committee found that the author was denied any opportunity to establish
whether his rights had been violated because the police and the
prosecutor had failed to continue their investigations of the allegations. Therefore there had been a violation of Article 6. In the
case of *B. J. v. Denmark (17/1999)*, an allegation of discrimination
had resulted in prosecution but there had been no award of non-
pecuniary damages to the victim. CERD found no violation of the
Convention but recommended further action by the state because:
'Being refused access to a place of service intended for the use of
the general public solely on the ground of a person's national or
ethnic background is a humiliating experience which, in the opinion
of the Committee, may merit economic compensation and cannot
always be adequately repaired or satisfied by merely imposing a
criminal sanction on the perpetrator.'

As more states make declarations under Article 14 and the availability of this remedy becomes better known, the number of communications will surely increase. The issuing of opinions on them
will become a more important part of the Committee's work and of
the international anti-racist movement.

Prospects

Especially since 1988, CERD has done a great deal to secure more
effective implementation of the Convention, but further advance
will be difficult without more support from the states parties on
behalf of whom the members work. The sporadic nature of the
states parties' collective activity illustrates the operation of the principle of the ratchet. A group of states takes an initiative, secures
agreement on a particular action, and then tries to use this as a foundation for a further step forward whenever an opportunity presents
itself. Once a form of words has been accepted it can be used again

or moved up a notch; this is the function of rhetoric in official conferences. It is difficult to disengage a ratchet and undo a previous agreement. Opportunities for tightening a ratchet and taking that further step may arise after a disaster when there is a feeling that 'something must be done', or when a special meeting – like a world conference – is convened to consider a particular problem.

When the ICERD was drawn up, no provision was made for action in the event of a state's failing to fulfil its obligations. Such a provision might have discouraged some states from ratifying. During the years 1986–90 and 1992 CERD was able to hold only half the number of its scheduled meetings, because states were not paying their assessments (which were graduated so that poor states had to pay relatively little). Appeals from the General Assembly had no effect, yet the states parties never considered suspending the rights of non-payers to vote in the elections for Committee members. (Since then the sums that were supposed to be met by such payments have been transferred to the general budget; even though the change is to their benefit, most states have failed to give formal approval to the change in order to give it legal effect.) Very few states submit reports every two years, as they have promised to do. Some reports are more than twenty years overdue. General Assembly resolution 49/178 in paragraphs 3 and 6 urges states parties to use their biennial meetings held to elect committee members in order to improve the reporting process. At each such meeting the states elect a bureau that could be authorized to communicate with states that have failed to submit the promised reports; in appropriate circumstances the electoral rights of such states could be suspended. There are other, smaller, changes that could be considered. For example, those persons who are elected to serve on certain of the human rights treaty bodies receive stipends as well as a payment for their expenses. CERD members receive no stipend. If states really want the Committee to consist of experts they might be expected to ensure that the members receive stipends. The record suggests that the states parties are not at present interested in taking any collective action to improve implementation of the Convention. Each individual state sees it primarily as an opportunity to report upon its national action.

Any proposal to reform implementation of the ICERD would have to take account of the other treaty-monitoring bodies, for the treaty body system is the product of separate initiatives. There are many inconsistencies that call for rationalization. In 1990 the CHR recognized this when it commissioned a report on the situation from Professor Philip Alston. He concluded that with rapidly increasing numbers of states parties, the treaty bodies were unable to keep up with the work required. The system functioned only because so many states failed to report, or to report on the due date. The growth in the workload was such that before long the system would be unable to cope in any meaningful way with the various functions entrusted to it. In an interim report he canvassed two possible reforms: (1) the consolidation of the existing committees into one or two new treaty bodies; and (2) that states would consolidate into a single document their reports under all the treaties they had ratified (Crawford, 2000). The states showed no enthusiasm for the first proposal, since it would increase the power of the supervisory system to a degree unacceptable to them. The second proposal would not help the larger states to meet their reporting obligations and took no account of the variations in reporting cycles of the different treaties. States have been slow to address the shortcomings because they want no closer supervision of their affairs and have insufficient confidence in the jurisprudence of the bodies they themselves have established.

In 2001 a Canadian professor, Anne F. Bayefsky, presented a report on a study of *The UN Human Rights Treaty System* prepared in collaboration with the Office of the High Commissioner for Human Rights. In it she recommended the preparation of a new treaty that, if adopted, would reduce states' reporting obligations to the periodic submission of a single document on their fulfilment of their obligations under all the treaties they had ratified. The new treaty would replace the existing six treaty-monitoring bodies with two bodies, one for examining state reports and the other for dealing with individual communications and inter-state complaints (should any of these ever arise). Implementation of this proposal would enable states to move back towards the original proposal to translate the Universal Declaration of Human Rights into a single treaty, before the split into two covenants supplemented by specialized conventions. However, there is no sign that states would be willing to accept a change that would entail closer oversight of the manner in which they fulfil their treaty obligations.

The adoption of the ICERD was the outcome of a specific initiative to respond to a priority of the early 1960s. It has been made into an instrument of much greater scope and potential than was contemplated at the time of its creation, and has become part of the wider system for the protection of human rights. While this gives it additional strength, it means that any proposals for improved implementation will have to be part of a more general reform.

By August 2001, 157 states had become parties to the Convention and thirty-three of them had made declarations to permit the Committee to consider communications under Article 14. The World

Conference in that year could have been an opportunity for them to review the operation of the Convention and remedy some of the deficiencies. It was difficult for states to take advantage of this opportunity because so many of them had other objectives to pursue and because very few diplomats take any interest in the treaty monitoring as a whole. Most of them are directed by their governments to prioritize their states' bilateral relations with the reporting system.

Problems ahead

The Convention, and human rights law generally, can be seen as part of a movement to transfer certain kinds of problem resolution from the sphere of politics to the sphere of law, or to extend the rule of law. The speed of the movement depends upon the degree to which states can be confident that the text of a treaty, with any reservations to it, expresses the powers they are willing to cede, and nothing more, and can trust any treaty body to discharge its duties in the way states envisage.

The interpretation of a treaty is subject to a conception of its object and purpose. CERD has never explicitly discussed the object and purpose of the Convention under which it has been established, or attempted to relate its view on this matter to the principle of the sovereign equality of states. Though there have been some minor variations in practice, it has interpreted that principle as obliging it to make available equal time for the consideration of each state report, regardless of whether it is a big state or a very small one, a state that it supposes to have many problems of racial discrimination, or one with very few. In my view, the object and purpose of the Convention is one of protecting a right to be free from the kinds of discrimination defined in Article 1.1. This is a significant conclusion, because there is a tension between the Convention's end and the means, which is that of an inter-state contract. If the object is that of protection, the states parties and the Committee should recognize that people in some localities have a greater need of protection than people elsewhere. In some states there are more people to be protected, while in some states individuals run a greater risk of suffering these kinds of discrimination. The question of the Convention's object and purpose should be clarified because it has implications for the conduct of Committee business. The consideration of the implementation of the Convention in some countries requires significantly greater time and a more proactive search for additional information on the extent to which victims' rights are protected in practice. Under Article 2.1(d) a state party undertakes to bring racial discrimination to an end 'by all appropriate means, including legislation as required by circumstances'. A monitoring body should examine the circumstances as carefully as it examines the legislation. It has to call on both legal expertise and expertise in social research.

The concept of discrimination is relatively new. Its origins lie in Aristotle's discussion of justice and his argument that 'equals are entitled to equal things'. This is expressed in the proposition that the unlike treatment of like things, or persons, is unjust. The first of three steps is the comparison of like things or persons. Is it discriminatory to reserve the priesthood to persons of a particular gender? If discrimination is simply the unequal treatment of a person because that person belongs in, or is believed to belong in, a particular class of persons, to refuse entry to the priesthood on grounds of gender is discriminatory. Some, however, would maintain that there is a significant difference between a priest and a lay person; they are not comparable classes. The second step is to ascertain whether or not such a limitation infringes a specific law, one that may prohibit less favourable treatment on specified grounds and in specified circumstances, such as in fields of public but not private life. An occupational limitation may be lawful in one country and unlawful in another. Whether the reservation of the priesthood to a particular gender is morally justified gives rise to a third question, one that is involved with the argument about whether priests and lay people are comparable classes of person.

By enacting a particular law, a legislature determines what are to be considered like things or persons. Courts may then be able to extrapolate from that law, and from earlier applications of it in the courts, in a manner that applies the law to categories of persons that were not in contemplation when the law was drafted. Thus, under the ECHR, courts have found homosexuals and heterosexuals to be like persons for certain particular purposes even though they may not be for others (Banton, 1994: 82–9).

Moving problem resolution from the sphere of politics to that of law also depends upon a capacity to refine the issues in a manner that makes them susceptible of legal determination. Criminal cases, for example, are usually initiated by a prosecutor who has concluded that a certain action has breached a particular provision of the criminal code. The accused is usually represented by a lawyer who has been told the nature of the evidence against his or her client, and who may notify the prosecutor of any defence that is likely to be advanced. As a result, the issue, or issues, are clearly defined before the court is convened. If, during the proceedings, either side strays from the issue, the judge will correct the deviation. When CERD, acting under Article 14 of the Convention, and in private session, considers individual complaints, its proceedings resemble those of a court. When, acting under Article 9 of the Convention, it considers state reports, the issues may be less well defined; some members may introduce what others consider irrelevancies, but it is much more difficult than in any court to correct this. Diplomatic practice, being based on the sovereign equality of states, has brought about a situation in UN bodies in which, if challenged, a speaker can always advance a justification, even if specious, for an attempt to redefine the issue. An attempt to rule such a speaker out of order may consume much scarce time to little effect.

The difficulty of agreeing upon the issue for consideration may be exemplified by circumstances in Zimbabwe. When the state's fourth report was considered by CERD in March 2000 only the first signs of tension between the government and the supreme court were being publicized. The situation in Zimbabwe rapidly developed into one in which undisciplined groups of men claiming to be veterans of the war of independence used violence to seize farms and lands in the possession of white settlers. The police took no action. On the face of things, it seemed clear that the government was failing to protect the rights of the white farmers to personal security, to equal treatment before tribunals, and to ownership of property under Articles 5 (a), (b) and (d)(v) of the Convention. Had this been discussed in Committee, some members would surely have queried whether the white farmers were lawful owners of land unlawfully taken from African owners perhaps a century earlier. It would have been difficult for Committee members to decide, especially in the limited time available and without hearing witnesses, what were the issues and what was the order of priority for their determination. The present treaty body system is not constructed in a way suitable for taking decisions on such matters.

In 1985, when considering the case of *Abdulaziz, Cables and Balkandali*, the European Court of Human Rights distinguished discrimination from differentiation. It held that differential treatment may be permitted where:

1   there is a reasonable and objective justification;
2   the differential treatment is in pursuit of a legitimate aim; and
3   there is proportionality between the effects of the measures and the objectives.

Such a distinction has been echoed in statements from some UN bodies (Bossuyt, 2000: para. 52); it defines discrimination as necessarily unlawful and differentiation as lawful. There is a third term, distinction, which is used when it has not yet been determined whether a differential treatment may or may not be justified. Though this attempt at clarification is not without its difficulties, it may be helpful in dealing with troublesome cases, such as those that arise from policies designed to prevent residential segregation. If a person, of whatever colour or ethnic origin, is denied housing in a particular locality because there are already too many persons of that colour or ethnic origin resident there, that person is treated less favourably than someone of different colour or ethnic origin. If the law does not permit exceptions to a simple definition of racial discrimination the result may be increased segregation, which in turn can lead to increased discrimination. Other problems can arise with respect to immigration legislation. A class of persons distinguished by ethnic origin and other features can be treated less favourably. If a person belonging in this class complains of discrimination but no evidence can be adduced that a person with all the other features except that particular ethnic origin has been treated more favourably, it may be impossible for a tribunal to decide that the complainant's rights have been violated. The determination of discrimination hangs upon evidence of less favourable treatment and therefore requires a comparison. The Convention's conception of discrimination is based upon a definition developed to combat discrimination in the workplace, where comparison is relatively easily achieved. When comparison is not possible the concept cannot be applied. The problems of applying the Convention in new circumstances will therefore require imagination and legal expertise in the years to come.

Because it is an inter-state contract, the Convention necessarily concentrates upon the responsibilities of states. This suited the atmosphere in the General Assembly at a time when delegates from the Eastern bloc, and from authoritarian regimes everywhere, talked as if states should be all-powerful. Kwame Nkrumah had advised his fellow Africans: 'Seek ye first the political kingdom and all things shall be added unto you.' Therefore it is not surprising that the text of the Convention took little account of the part of civil society in preventing racial discrimination. It was acknowledged only in Article 2.1(*e*), according to which: 'Each State Party undertakes to encourage, where appropriate, integrationist multi-racial organisations and movements and other means of eliminating barriers between races, and to discourage anything which tends to strengthen racial division.' This implies that the object of the Convention goes beyond the elimination of racial division and can support the view that the full enjoyment of human rights without distinction as to race must ultimately overcome the idea that humans belong in races. This conclusion has particular relevance to circumstances in the USA, discussed in chapter 6.

Article 8 of the Convention states that CERD shall consist of 'eighteen experts of high moral standing and acknowledged impartiality'. Who qualifies as an expert and what does he or she have to be expert in? Since the Convention is a legal document that has to be understood in the light of treaty law and the reasoning of international tribunals, expertise in international law is essential. During their service on the Committee its members learn much about the problems faced by particular states and about the relative success of different methods of tackling them. In this way they build up practical knowledge and acquire a distinctive kind of expertise that should be of value in advising states about the measures that may be appropriate to their problems. Lawyers have occupational blind spots, so this kind of knowledge and the personal experience of individual members can be useful to the Committee. Since the time at which the Convention was drafted much has been learned, both nationally and internationally, about the causes of racial discrimination. To take but two examples, much has been learned about the ways of measuring and monitoring the incidence of discrimination. Equally, it is now better understood that residential segregation, though attributable to differences of income and other factors independent of ethnic origin, can transmit disadvantage and be a cause of racial discrimination. This kind of expertise has somehow to be fed into the treaty-monitoring process.

The previous chapter referred to the way in which the first world conference against racism in 1978 was spoiled by the priority given to rhetoric on the political problems of Palestine. Delegations that took one side in the dispute were able to secure a majority vote by soliciting the support of states in other regions that had no immediate interest in the matters at stake. As subsequent events have shown, there can be progress in resolving such a dispute only when the parties, plus other states with an interest in the region, negotiate a solution. Since many human rights issues have powerful political dimensions, regional human rights treaties and institutions have a part to play distinct from international and national institutions. Chapter 7 will outline those in Europe, but it should be noted here that the European Commission Against Racism and Intolerance (ECRI) functions like CERD in reporting on states' fulfilment of their obligations. ECRI's members are appointed by the governments of states belonging to the COE. Selected members visit each country in turn, meet with representatives of relevant authorities, and engage in a confidential dialogue with them before issuing their report. They have more time for their work than members of CERD, greater resources, and stronger political support. This will enable the Commission to secure greater state compliance.

Other regional institutions are gradually gaining authority, notably those established by the Organization of American States, like the Inter-American Indian Institute. An American Declaration on the Rights of Indigenous Peoples is under active consideration. The Inter-American Commission on Human Rights issues country reports and receives complaints of violations of the Inter-American Convention on Human Rights. The Inter-American Court of Human Rights has ruled upon the mass deportations of Haitians from the Dominican Republic, which involved what many regard as elements of racial discrimination. In a landmark judgement of September 2001, the Court affirmed the existence of indigenous peoples' collective rights to their land, resources and environment, by declaring that the Mayagna Community of Awas Tingni's rights to property and judicial protection were violated by the government of Nicaragua when it granted concessions to a foreign company to fell trees on the Community's traditional land without consulting them or securing their consent. The government was found to have violated its obligations under international law to give effect to its duties under the American Convention on Human Rights. The Court ordered the government to demarcate and recognize the title of the Mayagna and other communities to their traditional lands, to submit biannual reports on measures taken to comply with the Court's decision, and to pay compensation and legal costs.

The Organization of African Unity in 1981 adopted the African Charter of Human and Peoples' Rights that provided for the establishment of a Commission and a Court of the same name. African states are beginning to submit periodic reports to the Commission, to send high-powered delegations to speak for them when necessary, and to take heed of its conclusions. As the states of the Asia-Pacific region constitute the largest and most diverse of the UN's regional groups it is little wonder if they have greater difficulty in agreeing upon common action. Nevertheless, they are moving in the same direction, helped by the UN's strategy for strengthening national capacities for the promotion and protection of human rights. Regional institutions should be free from some of the inter-regional disputes that can constrain collective action in the UN.

5

Australia Arraigned

Australia had good reason to ratify the Convention in 1975. The racially discriminatory component of its immigration policy had been widely deplored; as its controversial features had recently been removed, the Commonwealth government may have wished to demonstrate the improvement in its record. It was also sensitive to criticisms of the treatment of Aboriginal Australians, for which the state governments were partly responsible, and may have seen this as an opportunity to publicize Commonwealth policy.

In 1900 the colonial governments in Australia had come together to create a federation. The states retained most of their existing powers, including law enforcement, health, education and responsibility for Aboriginal affairs, ceding to the Commonwealth government responsibility for immigration and defence. In 1788, when British settlement started, the Aboriginal population seems to have been around one million. By the 1930s there were about 70,000 Aborigines (including persons of partly Aboriginal ancestry). They had long been presumed to be a 'dying race' and this presumption had been used to justify many actions of a genocidal character (like the poisoning of their watering holes). In the first two-thirds of the twentieth century Aboriginal Australians were not citizens of Australia, were not entitled to vote, and were not counted in the census.

White Australia

The settler population at the time of federation was 3,765,000, a small number for so huge a territory. In the latter part of the nineteenth century large numbers of free Chinese had entered Australia to seek their fortunes in the goldfields. Larger numbers of Chinese and Melanesians were recruited as indentured labourers and employed under conditions so harsh that critics were justified in charging that they would have been treated better had they been slaves. White hostility towards Asians was intense, so that despite their desire for cheap labour the newly federated states agreed on a 'white Australia' immigration policy.

From the time of first settlement there were officials and settlers who believed that the Aborigines were the true owners of Australia and maintained, despite popular hostility, that it was wrong to force them to work for the settlers (Reynolds, 1998). What part did ideas of race play in the processes by which many whites came to believe that Aborigines could make no moral claims upon them? In the early part of the nineteenth century the settlers described the Aborigines as savages and as 'brutes'. When the settlers began, a little later, to describe the Aborigines as a race or races, there were no echoes of contemporary European racial theories. For example, in 1880 a Queenslander wrote to a newspaper: 'Is there room for both of us here? No. Then the sooner . . . we clear the weak useless race away the better.' This was a concept of race as lineage. Only at the very end of the century, when non-European workers were perceived as offering competition with Queensland workers, did references to their racial characteristics (in the sense of race as species) become frequent (Markus, 1979:259).

The assumption that Aborigines were a dying race was used to justify systematic brutalities in Queensland and Western Australia. It was also the rationale for the removal of Aboriginal children from their parents by deceit or force. A government inquiry into what was popularly known as 'the stolen generation' reported in 1997 on the racially discriminatory procedures whereby indigenous children were made wards of state. Over the period 1910–70 between one in three and one in ten indigenous children were forcibly removed from their families. Some were exploited by those responsible for their care. The inquiry found that from about 1946 many of these laws and practices were in breach of the international prohibition of genocide, though this finding was not upheld by the High Court. The Commonwealth government made available funds for facilitating family reunion and assisting indigenous people to cope with the stresses caused by separation, but denied that monetary compensation would be appropriate since, *inter alia*, the practices were at the time sanctioned by law and were intended to assist the people they affected. The government's refusal to apologize for the practices was a major disappointment to indigenous Australians.

Though significantly weakened during the 1960s, the white Australia immigration policy lasted until 1973. Domestic political considerations obliged Australian governments to defend it. Thus when international criticism of South Africa intensified after the Sharpeville Massacre in 1960 the Australian prime minister insisted that the apartheid issue lay within the field of domestic jurisdiction. As he saw it, 'I was defending my own country, its sovereign rights and its future.' He must have had in mind both the white Australia policy and the status of Aboriginal Australians. In 1961 a member of the Australian Federal Council for Aboriginal Advancement wrote to President Nkrumah of Ghana asking that the position of Aborigines in Australia be placed on the agenda of the next meeting of Commonwealth prime ministers. The same lady had a letter published in the London *Times* drawing a parallel with apartheid. Perhaps in part because Australian diplomats worked hard on the issue, the threat to Australia's reputation never materialized, though the awareness of foreign criticism encouraged reformist tendencies and complemented domestic pressure for change (Clark, 1997).

In 1967 Australian citizens voted in a referendum to empower the Commonwealth to legislate for 'the people of any race for whom it is necessary to make special laws'. In the following year, Aboriginals became citizens. Their numbers are now increasing at double the rate of the rest of the population, partly because of a higher birth rate, partly because children of mixed ethnic origin are regarded, and accepted, as Aboriginal (in a fashion that is reminiscent of the 'one-drop' rule in the USA), and partly because it has become more acceptable for Australians of mixed ancestry to identify with their Aboriginal ancestry. Another important change was that in 1975, having obtained the agreement of the states, the Commonwealth government ratified the ICERD and gave effect to its obligations as a state party by enacting the Racial Discrimination Act. This sets the only national standard of non-discrimination in Australian law, since the constitution includes no prohibition of racial discrimination. The Act binds the Commonwealth government and has prevented state governments within the Commonwealth from acting in ways incompatible with its standard.

Native title

The 1975 Act had implications for other litigation brought by Aboriginal Australians. Some stockmen in the Cape York Peninsula had entered into a contract to purchase property, but the transfer of the lease had been vetoed by the government of Queensland, which declared the property a national park. In 1982 the High Court of Australia held that the action of the Queensland government contravened the 1975 Act. In the same year, 1982, Eddie Mabo and some other residents of Murray Island in the Torres Strait filed a claim to ownership of their land under 'native title', as a right independent of the system of land tenure introduced by the British. The government of Queensland attempted to invalidate this by passing the Queensland Coast Island Declaratory Act. On appeal, the High Court held in 1988 that if, under state law, a right is denied to people of one racial group, or limited by comparison with other racial groups, then by virtue of the 1975 Act, those people shall enjoy that right to the full extent. The Queensland law would have extinguished rights under the law of the islands while leaving intact rights based on Queensland law. This part of the case became known as 'Mabo No 1'.

The substance of Mabo's claim was upheld in a High Court judgement in 1992, commonly known as 'Mabo No 2'. The decision established that pre-existing land rights survived the extension of British sovereignty over Australia and may still survive in the present provided that (1) the relevant native group maintains sufficient ties with the land in question, and (2) the title has not been extinguished as a consequence of valid governmental action. In line with decisions in other common law jurisdictions, the court held that: 'the exercise of a power to extinguish native title must reveal a clear and plain intention to do so, whether the action had been taken by the Legislature or the Executive.' Where this standard had not been met, native title to land had subsisted from the pre-colonial period. The decision was of far-reaching effect. It cast doubt on the validity of all government grants of land since 1975, because they had been based on the supposition that the land belonged to the government and none other. Aboriginal representatives agreed to give up potential claims on pastoral leases granted after 1975 if the federal government would agree that any pastoral leases currently held or acquired by Aboriginal people in the future could be converted to native title if the Mabo principles applied to them. Mining leases would be validated without extinguishing native title. These and other matters became part of what was called a social justice and reconciliation package. A new Native Title Act was then enacted in 1993.

Another decision of the High Court in the case of *Wik v. Queensland* in 1996 established that native title had subsisted in further unanticipated circumstances, leading the government to introduce a second amending act. Unlike its predecessor, the new government was unable to secure the assent of Aboriginal representatives to its draft second act. Learning that there was, or had been, a major dispute over the measure, and handicapped by the government's tenth periodic report having been overdue since October 1994, CERD in August 1998 requested the government to provide it with information on the changes. The Native Title Amendment Act had in fact been passed the previous month, its final form having been influenced by the negotiations needed to secure a majority of one vote in the upper legislative chamber. The reply from the government was considered in 1999 and led the Committee, in decision 2(54), to express concern:

> over the compatibility of the Native Title Act, as currently amended, with the State party's international obligations under the Convention. While the original Native Title Act recognises and seeks to protect indigenous title, provisions that extinguish or impair the exercise of indigenous title rights and interests pervade the amended Act. While the original 1993 Native Title was delicately balanced between the rights of indigenous and non-indigenous title-holders, the amended Act appears to create legal certainty for Governments and third parties at the expense of indigenous title.

The Committee went on to identify four specific discriminatory provisions and to make some other comments. It stated: 'the Committee urges the State party to suspend implementation of the 1998 amendments and reopen discussions with the representatives of the Aboriginal and Torres Strait Islander peoples with a view to finding solutions acceptable to the indigenous peoples and which would comply with Australia's obligations under the Convention.'

The attorney-general of Australia, in a press statement, declared: 'The Committee's comments are an insult to Australia', and the government embarked upon an unprecedented diplomatic offensive to persuade members of CERD that their conclusions were unbalanced. About this time members received from organizations and individuals in Australia many documents and letters critical of the government's actions. Some of them were from supporters of a campaign 'Australians say No to racist laws', showing that for some, at least, the issue was perceived as racial. Annex VIII to the Committee's report for 1999 publishes the comments of the government of Australia on decision 2(54). The most important comments concerned the measures for extinguishing native title. After studying those comments the Committee, in decision 2(55), reaffirmed the decisions concerning Australia that it had taken at its previous session.

The combined tenth, eleventh and twelfth periodic reports of Australia were considered in March 2000. CERD then expressed concern over 'the absence from Australian law of any entrenched guarantee against racial discrimination that would override subsequent law of the Commonwealth, states and territories'. It reiterated its recommendation that the Commonwealth government 'undertake appropriate measures to ensure the consistent application of the provisions of the Convention, in accordance with Article 27 of the Vienna Convention on the Law of Treaties, at all levels of government'. Expressing concern over 'the continuing risk of further impairment of the rights of Australia's indigenous communities', the Committee reaffirmed its previous decisions and reiterated 'its recommendation that the State party ensure effective participation by indigenous communities in decisions affecting their land rights, as required under article 5(c) of the Convention and General Recommendation XXIII of the Committee, which stresses the importance of the "informed consent" of indigenous peoples'.

CERD noted that a Parliamentary Joint Committee was conducting an inquiry into 'the Consistency of the Native Title Amendment Act with Australia's international obligations under the Convention on the Elimination of All Forms of Racial Discrimination' and requested copies of the report when ready. Resolution of the issue of compatibility is of vital importance for the Convention's future and for governmental policy in Australia. The report, made available to the Committee the following August, showed only that the Committee had split on party lines. There was no progress on substantive issues.

In 2001 the Australian government welcomed the findings of the study by Professor Bayefsky that was referred to in the previous chapter, observing that it underscored the urgent need for the reform of the treaty bodies to make them work more effectively. The report had stated that: 'Political bias is sometimes evident in the differential depth of treatment of some states (in the absence of corresponding justification in terms of human rights conditions).' In a media release, the minister for foreign affairs claimed, incorrectly, that: 'Professor Bayefsky observes that political bias is most evident in the CERD's concluding observations.' He went on to state that variations in accuracy of concluding observations 'often reflected a poor knowledge of the country in question and the excessive influence exerted on committees by external sources'. The foreign minister tried to represent the report as supporting his government's resentment of criticism from CERD.

Equal treatment

A public scandal broke out over information about the disproportionately high proportion of Aboriginal persons who died while
held in police custody or in prison. A Royal Commission reported
in 1991 that Aboriginals were imprisoned at a rate twenty-nine
times that of the general community and that the major cause of this
was their disadvantaged and unequal position in Australian society.
In its ninth report the government informed CERD that the Commission found that those who had died had not lost their
lives as a result of unlawful violence or brutality. Rather were
they 'victims of entrenched and institutionalised racism and
discrimination'.

In March 2000 CERD examined new periodic reports and received additional information from NGOs about the disparate
effect upon Aboriginal people of mandatory sentencing laws. Examples were described, like that of the homeless Aboriginal man who
took a towel from a clothes line; because it was his third minor property offence he was imprisoned for one year. An indigenous
mother was sentenced to fourteen days' imprisonment for receiving a stolen $2.50 can of beer. A 15-year-old boy from a remote
island hanged himself in a detention centre while serving a twenty-
eight-day sentence for stealing a small quantity of stationery and
minor criminal damage. There were many others. CERD noted
'with grave concern that the rate of incarceration of indigenous
people is disproportionately high compared with the general population'. It also expressed 'its concern about the minimum mandatory sentencing schemes with regard to minor property offences
enacted in Western Australia and in particular in the Northern Territory', especially in their effect upon juveniles, and questioned the
compatibility of these laws with the state party's obligations. With
reference to housing, employment and education programmes, it
stated that it 'remains seriously concerned about the extent of the
dramatic inequality still experienced by an indigenous population
that represents only 2.1 per cent of the total population of an industrialized state'.

Both the UN Committee on the Rights of the Child and the
Human Rights Committee also commented critically on the com-
patibility of the minimum mandatory sentencing laws with the
Convention on the Rights of the Child and the ICCPR.

The Government submitted comments on the CERD's concluding observations on the periodic reports (covering both the native
title and the other issues), stating that it rejected the observations.

The government's comments can be found in the Committee's report for 2000.

A multicultural society

The name 'multiculturalism', used to identify a political policy, was brought from Canada to Australia in 1973 and employed as an umbrella term for a set of measures intended to rectify the social and economic disadvantages of immigrants. A former chairman of the Australian Ethnic Affairs Council attributed it to 'an on the spot decision by a politician who assumed that Canadian multicultural-ism – no more than a by-product of the official policy of bilingual-ism and biculturalism of an earlier era – would be a suitable designation for a range of programs the introduction of which he rightly considered was long overdue' (Zubryzcki, 1995:5). It came to be seen as a justification for campaigns designed to secure the votes of non-English-speaking immigrants, something for the benefit of minorities and not for Australians as a nation. So at the end of 1999 the government announced a new agenda based on four principles:

> *Civic duty*: all Australians are obliged to support the basic structure and principles of Australian society – our Constitution, democratic institutions and values – which guarantee us our freedom and equal-ity and enable diversity in our society to flourish;
>   *Cultural respect*: subject to the law, the right to express one's own culture and beliefs involves a reciprocal obligation to accept the right of others to do the same;
>   *Social equity*: all Australians are entitled to equity of treatment and opportunity enabling them to contribute to the social, political and economic life of Australia, free from discrimination on the grounds of race, culture, religion, language, location, gender or place of birth;
>   *Productive diversity*: the significant cultural, social and economic dividends which arise from the diversity of our population should be maximised for the benefit of all Australians.

The celebration of national harmony day on 21 March was intro-duced to coincide with the UN international day for the elimination of racial discrimination.

In the Australian case, 'multiculturalism' is not a systematic political philosophy but simply a convenient designation for a set of policies adopted to respond to a rapidly changing demographic and social situation. Three Article 14 communications alleging breaches of Convention obligations by the Australian government have been considered by CERD. They all related to relations be-tween persons of European descent, not to persons of Aboriginal descent. In case 6/95 CERD found no violation by the state, but suggested that where more than one kind of recourse procedure is available, a simplification of procedures might reduce delay. In case 8/1996 also CERD found that the facts disclosed no violation but recommended that steps be taken to make the procedures more transparent and speedier. The third case was declared inadmissible, as its author had failed to exhaust the domestic remedies available to him.

Unfinished business

In some countries an exchange of views between the government and CERD, and the treaty body's report on its examination of the state report, pass without attracting any public attention at all. It has been different in Australia since 1998 because the issues involv-ing CERD were matters of dispute in national party politics. The government in office at that time may have been taken aback to learn that there was an international dimension to problems it had been regarding as domestic business. The opposition may have wel-comed the opportunity to use UN criticism as a stick with which to beat its opponents. The indigenous peoples may have been relieved to find that international law helped compensate for their weakness when votes came to be counted. But 1998 was only a new turn in a longer tale. Disputes over native title to land and over justice for Aboriginal people have a two-hundred-year history in Australia. The scandal of Aboriginal deaths in custody presented an issue to which the national political and legal institutions eventually responded. Subjecting such matters to international oversight has had a cautionary effect upon those who exercise power and obliged all parties to view them in the light of principles applying through-out the UN.

The uncertainty about whether Australia has met its obligations under the ICERD is likely to continue until new elections lead to a change in the policies of the government. CERD has no power to request the International Court of Justice to give an advisory opinion on the issues and it did not recommend the General Assembly to make such a request. Another state party could invoke Article 22 of the ICERD to do so, but that would be regarded as a hostile move and Australia has no enemies that would take such a step.

Ideas about racial differences have played, and continue to play, a part in the relations between Aboriginal peoples and the majority, but discrimination is only part of a larger picture of disadvantage. Human rights law, specifying economic, social, cultural, civil and political rights, can bear on the whole range of unequal development and ensure that the racial element is not overemphasized. Given the great inequalities in Australia, the cultivation of an anti-racist racism would not promote racial equality. If an anti-racist movement is to be truly international it has to adopt a broader perspective when considering the disadvantages suffered by indigenous peoples.

6

The USA Enlists

Few countries calculate the costs and benefits of treaty-making as carefully as the USA. Whereas in the United Kingdom the treaty-making power is within the prerogative of the crown, in the United States it resides with the president 'with the advice and consent of the senate' and the concurrence of two-thirds of the senators. Although the ICERD was signed by Ambassador Goldberg in 1966 during the Johnson presidency, it was not submitted for the Senate's consideration until 1978 when Jimmy Carter was president. Democratic administrations, like those of Johnson, Carter and Clinton, have been more favourably disposed towards the ratification of human rights treaties than Republican administrations. Indeed, John Foster Dulles, secretary of state under Eisenhower, declared that he would never send any human rights treaty to the Senate for ratification. Whether the Senate would take action on the president's submission might depend upon the priority given to it by the chairman of its Foreign Relations Committee. Because of the Senate's seniority rule, this office has often been occupied by a Southerner holding conservative views on matters to do with race.

Why ratify?

Before World War II the Chinese and Japanese governments had criticized US immigration policy, and the treatment of their nationals. With the founding of the UN and the USA's assumption of a leading part in world affairs, criticism of the US record in respect of racial discrimination came from countries all over the globe, often in very sharp terms (Lauren, 1996:199–208, 218–19).

Other countries disliked lectures from the US about the evils of communism when the US was so palpably undemocratic over racial issues in its own territory. External criticism had a significant influence, first, upon the domestic policies of federal administrations, and then, second, upon their attitude towards the international anti-racist movement.

President Eisenhower, who had opposed desegregation of the armed forces in 1948, was reluctant to override states' rights; he refused to endorse the Supreme Court's momentous (and unanimous) 1954 *Brown* decision on school desegregation, and declared racial issues to be 'matters of the heart, not of legislation'. Yet he was forced to mobilize federal troops to protect the nine black pupils attending Little Rock High School. His presidency saw the creation of the 1957 Civil Rights Commission, a body that was disturbed by the negative consequences of domestic racism upon the government's global ambitions. With the independence of former colonies in Asia, and the imminent independence of many more in Africa, many overseas representatives important to those ambitions were travelling to the USA and meeting humiliations in segregated airport facilities or along route 40 between New York and Washington. The resulting pressure upon and from the Department of State was enough to overcome the resistance of Southern legislators to the executive's proposals for domestic reform, advanced from the late 1960s (Layton, 2000). Then, as the civil rights movement gathered momentum and rogue elements in the white population were permitted to attack demonstrators, negative publicity overseas ballooned. For example, in 1963 the USSR broadcast 1,420 news items regarding racial conflict in Birmingham, Alabama, as proof that capitalism and racism went hand in hand (Thernstrom and Thernstrom, 1997:137–8). The USA was losing the propaganda Cold War.

President Carter made human rights one of his priorities. The Bureau of Democracy, Human Rights and Labor within the Department of State began the publication of a series of annual *Country Reports on Human Rights Practices* in which US diplomats reported on events on each country. These have become progressively more comprehensive and reliable, but in the 1980s they were far from even-handed; they suppressed negative evidence concerning governments that the US supported. Predictably, this aroused resentment, and, coupled with the failure of successive administrations to ratify UN human rights treaties, gave rise to the charge that the US saw human rights as being for export only.

When, in 1994, the Senate eventually conducted hearings on the proposed ratification of the ICERD, the assistant secretary of state for democracy, human rights and labor told the Senate that ratification was essential for several reasons:

> First, by ratifying the Convention, we will be better able to hold other signatories to their commitments. We need no longer fear that in doing so we would be playing into the hands of geopolitical adversaries. Instead, we can use the Convention as a reference point in our bilateral dealings with states, and we will strengthen our position in multilateral gatherings.
>
> Second, we could be a more effective part of the discussion now taking place over evolving international norms in the world. If we are not fully and actively engaged in this debate, then others will be setting the international community's agenda on race discrimination. One forum for the discussion is the Committee on the Elimination of Racial Discrimination, where we cannot currently participate because we have not ratified the Convention.
>
> Third, and this would be part of our effort to inject new American energy and purpose into the UN human rights system, which, until now, has frankly not been as consistent as we have hoped . . .
>
> Once we have ratified the Convention, our participation in the work of the Committee will give us a greater opportunity to share our own hard-won and historically proven experience in promoting tolerance and ending discrimination with other countries, and especially with the world's newly democratic nations.
>
> In conclusion, Mr. Chairman, we have much to gain from ratifying the Convention.

From this it can be seen that one of the State Department's objectives was to secure the election to CERD of a US national. This they accomplished in 1998, although the US had not then submitted its Initial Report (due in 1995), which to some will have appeared decidedly cheeky and to others simply a manifestation of diplomatic muscle.

In November 1994 President Clinton forwarded notification of US ratification of the ICERD, accompanied by a statement that the Senate's advice and consent was subject, *inter alia*, to the following reservations:

> (1) That the Constitution and laws of the United States contain extensive protections of individual freedom of speech, expression and association. Accordingly, the United States does not accept any obligation under this Convention, in particular under Articles 4 and 7, to restrict those rights, through the adoption of legislation or any other measures, to the extent to which they are protected by the Constitution and laws of the United States.
>
> (2) That the Constitution and laws of the United States establish extensive protections against discrimination, reaching significant

areas of non-governmental activity. Individual privacy and freedom from governmental interference in private conduct, however, are also recognized as among the fundamental values which shape our free and democratic society. The United States understands that the identification of the rights protected under the Convention by reference in Article 1 to fields of 'public life' reflects a similar distinction between spheres of public conduct that are customarily the subject of governmental regulation, and to spheres of private conduct that are not. To the extent, however, that the Convention calls for a broader regulation of private conduct, the United States does not accept any obligation under this Convention to enact legislation or take other measures under paragraph (1) of Article 2, subparagraphs (1)(c) and (d) of Article 2, Article 3 and Article 5 with respect to private conduct except as mandated by the Constitution and laws of the United States.

Article 20 of the Convention provides that a reservation incompatible with the object and purpose of the Convention shall not be permitted; it shall be considered incompatible if at least two-thirds of the states parties object to it. The Human Rights Committee, which monitors implementation of the ICCPR, has issued its General Comment 24 on reservations (CCPR/C/21/rev.1/Add.6), in which it maintains that human rights treaties are not a web of inter-state exchanges of mutual obligations. The principle of inter-state reciprocity has no place in the endowment of human rights, so that the absence of protest by states cannot imply that a reservation is compatible with a Convention. It therefore falls to the treaty-monitoring body to determine whether reservations like those of the United States are acceptable. It elaborates on the criteria to be employed. The ninth meeting of persons chairing the human rights treaty bodies reported its belief that the capacity of a monitoring body to perform its function of determining the scope of the provisions of a relevant convention cannot be performed effectively if it is precluded from exercising a similar function in relation to reservations. The then chairman of the US Senate's Committee on Foreign Relations, Senator Jesse Helms, took strong exception to the Human Rights Committee's General Comment on reservations to human rights treaties and tried to prevent the executive from reporting further until the Committee had revoked it and accepted the views of the United States about the validity of reservations (Grant, 2000:323).

In ratifying the Convention, the US also declared 'that the provisions of the Convention are not self-executing'. This had no effect on the international obligations of the US or on its relations with other states parties, but it precluded the assertion of

Convention-based rights by private parties litigating in US courts. Similar reservations qualified US ratification of the ICCPR and the Convention Against Torture. They show that while the US is willing to report to a monitoring body on its activities in these three fields it would not be willing to amend its constitution were that to be found inadequate to protect any of the rights listed in the treaties. US enlistment is half-hearted and not in full conformity with international law. A parallel example was provided in the case of *Breard*, a Paraguayan national who had been systematically denied consular access rights, contrary to the 1963 Vienna Convention on Consular Relations. Unlike the human rights treaties the Vienna Convention is self-executing, but the US Supreme Court declined to apply international treaty law and refused a request for delay from the International Court of Justice (Grant, 2000:318). The US conception of rights recalls Edmund Burke's conception (mentioned in chapter 3) of rights as the fruits of a struggle waged by the ancestors of the present generation that have been transmitted as the patrimony of the nation, rather than the 1789 French conception of universal rights as attributes of the human individual.

Ethnogenesis

The historical experiences of a country condition the population's conception of itself, of its constituent groups, and of the nature of racial discrimination. This is particularly apposite to the case of the USA, where the black–white distinction has taken a unique form. The peculiarity of the US structure of group relations is not always appreciated within the country. To the contrary, those socialized within its borders sometimes expect other countries to conform to their model.

The Fourteenth Amendment to the constitution of the USA, adopted in 1868 after the Civil War, began with the affirmation that: 'All persons born or naturalized in the United States, and subject to the jurisdiction thereof, are citizens of the United States and of the State wherein they reside. No State shall make or enforce any law which shall abridge privileges or immunities of citizens.' This could have been the foundation for the building of a non-racial society. There were moves in this direction, particularly in the programme for the reconstruction of Southern states, but this came to an end in 1877 and did not attempt any reconstruction of society in the Northern states. Under President Johnson, nearly a century later, there was a so-called 'second reconstruction', but by that time hope of a non-racial society had faded and the reforms only reinforced the bi-racial structure of society.

In the aftermath of the Civil War urban blacks and urban whites 'moved in a common social world, spoke a common language, shared a common culture, and interacted personally on a regular basis. In the north, especially, leading African American citizens often enjoyed relations of considerable trust, respect, and friendship with whites of similar social standing' (Massey and Denton, 1993:17–18). Before 1900 blacks and whites lived side by side in the cities of the USA. After that date everything changed as industrialization led to the construction of new residential suburbs inhabited by people of roughly similar incomes away from their places of employment, and as many blacks moved from farms to cities. Southern blacks were sometimes used by Northern employers as strikebreakers. The communal riots that erupted in the wake of massive black immigration provided an impetus to the formation of ghettoes. The National Association of Real Estate Brokers exerted an important influence. From 1924 to 1950 it held, as part of its code of ethics, that: 'a Realtor should never be instrumental in introducing into a neighborhood . . . members of any race or nationality . . . whose presence will clearly be detrimental to property values in that neighborhood'. According to an authoritative study of what the authors (Massey and Denton, 1993:2, 26–37) call *American Apartheid*:

> No group in the history of the United States has ever experienced the high level of residential segregation that has been imposed on blacks in large American cities for the past fifty years. This extreme racial isolation did not just happen; it was manufactured by whites through a series of self-conscious actions and purposeful institutional arrangements that continue today . . . Because of racial segregation a significant share of black America is condemned to experience a social environment where poverty and joblessness are the norm, where a majority of children are born out of wedlock, where most families are on welfare, where educational failure prevails, and where social and physical deterioration abound . . . Segregation created the structural conditions for the emergence of an oppositional culture that devalues work, schooling and marriage and that stresses attitudes and behaviors that are antithetical and often hostile to success in the larger economy.

The black response to the racial discrimination suffered in so many fields of social life was to build a supportive community of a unique character. Myrdal (1944:927) wrote of 'The Negro

Community as a Pathological Form of an American Community'. The pathology was on the white side of the colour line, for it was the whites that had failed to make a reality of the Fourteenth Amendment. Without intending to do so, the USA had created a new people, now over thirty million strong, that had some of the characteristics of a nation but who could not become a nation-state. Eighteen years after Myrdal another author (Singer, 1962) perceptively identified this process of people-building as ethnogenesis. Though it relied upon racial categorization in social life it was something more positive in the lives of its members. As blacks became a political force their leaders demanded recognition in many connections, notably in wanting constituency boundaries drawn along lines that would maximize the black vote.

A bi-racial society was built upon what is sometimes called the 'one drop' rule, the assumption that anyone with an ascertainable African ancestry counted as black. Native Americans found themselves in an anomalous position. In some parts of the South local custom allowed them to use the facilities reserved to whites, in other parts they counted as black. Local communities might be able to cope with such anomalies but they are troublesome for national statistics. The decennial population census has to utilize categories that are generally understood and can produce reliable results. At the same time, the way in which they identify themselves in the census is psychologically important to many individuals. In the census of 1 April 2000, question 5 asked 'Is this person Spanish/ Hispanic/Latino?' Those answering 'yes' could then identify themselves by national origin. Question 6 asked 'What is this person's race? Mark one or more races to indicate what this person considers himself/herself to be.' It offered the alternatives White, Black, American Indian, Asian Indian, Chinese, Filipino, Korean, etc., followed by 'Some other race'.

The new US system of classification does not satisfy those who maintain that its distinction between race and ethnicity is false, or the many people who want to be able to identify themselves as 'multiracial' (Vermeulen, 1999). However, it accords with the Convention and its requirement in Article 2.1(*e*) that states discourage anything that tends to strengthen racial division. In its General Recommendation VIII CERD has stated that, after having considered reports from states parties about the ways in which individuals were identified as members of racial and ethnic groups, 'it is of the opinion that such identification shall, if no justification exists to the contrary, be based on self-identification by the individual concerned'.

The initial/third report

The Clinton administration submitted the first US report almost five years late, at the end of September 2000. It is possible that submission was delayed until just before the November presidential election from fear of partisan misrepresentation of its character. In the event it fell to the new administration of President George W. Bush to send a delegation led by the assistant attorney-general to present to the Committee what had become the combined initial, second and third periodic reports of the USA. It is simplest to refer to it as the initial report.

Approximately the first quarter of the 104-page document is of a general nature, setting out relevant information about the US. The next quarter describes the legal means by which racial discrimination is prohibited and the reservations to US ratification. The second half then considers the state's implementation of its obligations, article by article. As a whole, the first report is an impressive statement of the action taken by the federal government with a candid acknowledgement of the need for further action. Whether enough had been done to discharge the obligations falling on a state party was not easily determined because the action had to be assessed with reference to the prevailing incidence of discrimination. US experience was also relevant to the question of the unintended, and sometimes undesired, consequences of governmental action. It has been maintained (e.g., Sowell, 1984) that in some circumstances governmental intervention has done more harm than good. Indeed, at one point Daniel Patrick Moynihan (later Senator Moynihan) advised President Nixon on the merits of a policy of 'benign neglect', enforcing the laws against discrimination but limiting governmental intervention.

CERD's 2001 report to the General Assembly about the US report followed the structure used by all the treaty bodies in being divided into an introduction, a section on factors impeding implementation of the Convention, a section noting positive aspects, and then its concerns and recommendations. This discussion will take the main Convention articles in turn, commenting on what the government had to say, and summarizing the Committee's views as to how well it was fulfilling its obligations.

The Committee began by welcoming the comprehensiveness of the report, its preparation in consultation with NGOs, and the professionalism that the delegation brought to the dialogue. It had noted that, in US law, treaties have a legal status equivalent to federal statutes. This means that a recent statute can take priority over an earlier treaty obligation, whereas under international law subsequent statutes must comply with treaty obligations. (A comparable situation arose in the United Kingdom in the 1992 case in which a duty under the subsequent Education Act took priority over Cleveland County Council's obligation to avoid racial discrimination.) The Committee expressed concern that in this way treaty obligations could be overridden and about the far-reaching nature of the US reservations. It emphasized that, whatever the relations between the federal government and other national institutions, it was the federal government that had accepted obligations under the Convention and was therefore responsible for their implementation throughout its territory.

In connection with Article 2.1(*d*), CERD had to consider whether the means utilized in the USA were appropriate to fulfil the obligations that had been assumed. The report stated in para. 71(b) that enforcement had been inadequate due to underfunding, but mentioned no criteria for determining the degree of underfunding. This should be of concern to CERD. By the standards of smaller and poorer states, the federal resources devoted to anti-discrimination are considerable. For example, the Civil Rights Division in the Department of Justice had 432 full-time staff in 1980, and 521, not all of whom were full-time, in 1991. The Office of Civil Rights within the Department of Education had a staff of 1,314 in 1980, but following the presidential election of that year the budget of this office declined by one-third (Goering, 1994). At one time the Office of Management and Budget used to prepare an analysis of resource allocation as a basis on which the federal government could set targets for the various agencies, institute arrangements for inspection, and have the outcome reported to the legislature. This had lapsed.

Social research suggests that policies that rely upon members of the general public to report incidents of suspected discrimination are of limited effectiveness. Too many Americans, of all groups, underestimate the incidence of discrimination, believe it would be dangerous to report instances, or do not know enough about the remedies available. This places a greater responsibility on governmental bodies to initiate proactive programmes. More could be done to develop independent measures of the incidence of discrimination in given fields at, say, five-year intervals, and to devise benchmarks against which to assess progress. So the failure of CERD to press the US delegation on the monitoring of resource allocation was unfortunate.

The second part of Article 2 authorizes what is commonly called affirmative action. It states that states parties *shall* undertake special measures when the circumstances so warrant, so the initial report was not entirely correct when in para. 249 it claimed that decisions as to race-based affirmative action programmes are at the discretion of the state party. A decision about whether or not the circumstances warrant special measures may not be arbitrary; it must relate to the circumstances objectively considered. The Article stipulates that special measures may not be maintained after their objectives have been attained. CERD therefore emphasized 'that the adoption of special measures by States parties, when the circumstances so warrant, such as in the case of persistent disparities, is an obligation'. Had they gone into the detail of group circumstances, Committee members might have noted that by the late 1960s Japanese-Americans and Chinese-Americans had attained levels of income and education equivalent to the European-origin white population. Immigrants from India have been notably successful in securing well-paid employment. According to one expert (Patterson, 1997:193):

> It is ridiculous that all persons of so-called Hispanic ancestry are considered disadvantaged minorities. The only Hispanics who should qualify for affirmative action are Puerto Ricans, of any generation, and Mexican-Americans of second or later generations. First-generation persons of African ancestry from Africa, the Caribbean, and elsewhere should also be excluded from affirmative action recruitment, although they may be considered where diversity – a secondary goal – is the objective, as should under-represented Euro-Americans. Like Mexican-Americans, their children and later generations should be eligible in the light of the persistence of racist discrimination in America. In addition, all Asians except Chinese-Americans descended from pre-1923 immigrants should be immediately excluded from all affirmative action considerations.

CERD did not pursue these questions.

The initial report referred in para. 262 to some special measures on behalf of Native Americans, but otherwise provided little information about the application of Article 2.2 to the circumstances of indigenous peoples. The Report of the President's Advisory Board, *One America in the 21st Century*, stated on p. 39:

> On virtually every indicator of social or economic progress, the indigenous people of this Nation continue to suffer disproportionately in relation to any other group. They have the lowest family incomes, the lowest percentage of people ages 25 to 34 who receive a college degree, the highest unemployment rates, the highest percentage of people living below the poverty level, the highest accidental death rate and the highest suicide rate.

CERD asked for more detail on such disparities in the next report and noted with concern that treaties signed between the government and Native American tribes could be abrogated unilaterally by Congress, and that there were plans for the expansion of mining and nuclear waste storage on the land of an indigenous people, and for other activities contrary to their wishes. It called attention to its General Recommendation XXIII, which stresses the importance of the 'informed consent' of indigenous communities and that they should receive compensation for any losses they suffer. Behind these observations lay a concern about the legal status of indigenous peoples in the USA as 'domestic dependent nations'. One committee member recalled that Australia had recently repudiated an analogous doctrine of guardianship in favour of a policy of indigenous self-determination within the national framework. He thought it would be welcome were the USA to move in a similar direction.

With respect to Article 3, the initial report in para. 282 stated that state-sponsored segregation had been prohibited and that the Civil Rights Acts had extended the reach of this prohibition to many private relationships and activities. The report did not note that CERD, in its General Recommendation XIX, had maintained that the article prohibits all forms of segregation, not just state-sponsored segregation; it noted that a condition of partial segregation might arise as an unintended by-product of the actions of private persons; it had invited states parties to monitor all trends that can give rise to racial segregation, to work for the eradication of any negative consequences that ensue, and to describe any such action in their periodic reports. Following up this concern, CERD could have noted that the position in the US, though still serious, is improving. Segregation may be measured by indices that calculate the percentage of blacks that would have to leave the neighbourhood in order to achieve an even distribution. Applying this measure to census tracts, the average index for Northern cities was 84.5 in 1970; it fell to 80.1 in 1980 and 77.8 in 1990; in Southern cities the indices for the same three years were 75.3, 68.3 and 66.5. There are other ways of measuring residential segregation. In social surveys over the years 1964–94 the percentage of blacks replying that members of the other group lived in the same neighbourhood as they did rose from 66 to 83, and for whites from 20 to 61. While discrimination was the prime cause of ghetto creation there are now other causes of residential inequalities. In 1990, 60 per cent of African-Americans stated a preference for a neighbourhood that was half black and half white. Such a preference is not easily met in a city with as large a black population as Detroit, or in one where most of the population is white. Members of minorities often prefer to live in clusters. Nevertheless, the persistence of black ghettoes has a causal influence upon the persistence of criminal behaviour and drug abuse. It contributes to racial inequality and to white fears of blacks, and makes it more difficult to attain racial justice and equality of opportunity (Massey and Denton, 1993: 2, 8; Thernstrom and Thernstrom, 1997: 213–30).

Preliminary analysis of the results of the 2000 census has shown that over the preceding decade segregation increased in many Northern cities. The flight from the central areas that led to the creation of white suburbs has now produced largely black suburbs as well. Black–white contact among school-age children has also diminished. This highlights the importance of federal government action to make it easier for those seeking housing to exercise their preferences as to neighbourhood racial mix.

The section of the initial report dealing with Article 4 and the prohibition of incitement to racial hatred was relatively brief, partly because the US had entered a reservation to cover those obligations under this article that it does not acknowledge. CERD mentioned its particular concern about the bearing of the reservation upon the implementation of this article, reiterating its earlier statements that the prohibition of the expression of racial hatred is compatible with the right to freedom of opinion and expression, given that a citizen's exercise of this right carries special duties and responsibilities among which the obligation not to disseminate racist ideas is of particular importance. The US government does not agree. One Committee member insisted that even if the Supreme Court had found the intimidatory practice of cross-burning to be compatible with the first amendment to the US constitution, such an action must generate the sort of tension that was to be prevented. Among the many states parties to the Convention the USA is at the furthest extreme in protecting freedom of expression, even at the expense of the right to be protected from discrimination. Other countries have been more ready to take repressive action, but on present evidence it is difficult to conclude that either policy has been more successful in eradicating racial prejudices.

The initial report had much to say on the implementation of Article 5. CERD expressed concerns about persistent disparities in the enjoyment of the rights to adequate housing, equal opportunities for education and employment, and access to public and private health care. With respect to only two of the many sections of this article did it go into any greater detail, namely those on the administration of criminal justice and on voting.

In connection with the administration of criminal justice, covered by para. 5(*a*), the report acknowledged the shocking disparity in incarceration rates, blacks being nearly eight times more likely to be imprisoned than whites. Some of the causes of the disparity are proximate causes, lying within the area of responsibility of the Department of Justice. Some federal actions addressing proximate causes were described. Blacks were disproportionately more likely to be sentenced to death and executed than members of other groups. The report concentrated on facts rather than causes, leaving the reader to conclude that if discrimination was a cause of the disparity, it started to operate from an early stage in the process. Persons who have grown up in highly disadvantageous circumstances are more likely to commit capital crimes. Some of the causes of the disparity in incarceration rates are ulterior causes, lying outside the criminal justice system. If the black rate were reduced so that it equalled the white rate, millions of dollars would be saved. The money cannot now be diverted to combating the causes of criminality, but neither can the incidence of racial discrimination be much reduced without such action.

CERD noted 'with concern the incidents of police violence and brutality, including cases of deaths as a result of excessive use of force by law enforcement officials, which particularly affects minority groups and foreigners'. It recommended improved training of the police and 'that firm action is taken to punish racially motivated violence and ensure the access of victims to effective legal remedies'. It noted with concern 'that the majority of federal, state and local prison and jail inmates in the State party are members of ethnic or national minorities, and that the incarceration rate is particularly high with regard to African-Americans and Hispanics'. The Committee recommended firm action to secure equality of treatment and ensure that disparities were not the result of the disadvantaged position of these groups. It urged the government 'to ensure, possibly by imposing a moratorium, that no death penalty is imposed as a result of racial bias on the part of prosecutors, judges, juries and lawyers' or as a result of the disadvantaged position of the convicted persons.

In connection with the right to security of person (para. 5(b)), the Committee might have inquired whether there was any disparity between the rates at which blacks, whites, Hispanics, etc., were the victims of crime, and whether members of some groups enjoyed less security of person than others.

In connection with the right to vote (para. 5(c)), the report in para. 337 stated that the Department of Justice brought suits to challenge discriminatory voting practices. The state representative added that counsel had been appointed to prosecute violations of electoral law and that the budget of the relevant section had been increased by

22 per cent. Committee members might nevertheless have asked whether the Department had brought a sufficient number of suits, and about action on recommendations on this subject from the US Civil Rights Commission. CERD, perhaps recalling what happened in Florida in the presidential election of 2000, expressed concern about the political disfranchisement of a large segment of the ethnic minority population by denying them the right to vote through 'disfranchising laws and practices based on the commission of more than a certain number of criminal offences, and also sometimes by preventing them from voting even after completion of their sentences'.

The scope of Article 5(*c*) also governs 'redistricting'. The US Census has reported that in the ten-year period up to April 2000 the population increased by 13 per cent to 281,422,000, thirty-five million being blacks. To apportion equally the 435 seats in the House of Representatives it will be necessary to transfer twelve house seats, affecting eighteen states, by a process known as redistricting. Electoral boundaries will be redrawn by states, in many cases subject to the oversight of the Department of Justice in accordance with the Voting Rights Act. When boundaries have been redrawn in a manner that unfairly reduces the chances of the election of a black representative, they have been declared unlawful by the federal courts. There have also been instances in which boundaries have been drawn in a bizarre manner designed to increase the chance that a black representative will be elected. This can affect the balance between the main parties; in the 1992 and 1994 elections the Democrats lost about ten congressional seats to the Republicans because of minority redistricting. An authoritative and recent study maintains that redistricting illustrates the racial divide in the USA. 'Supreme Court justices, members of Congress, political pundits and the nation's leading voting rights experts look at the same set of facts and reach diametrically opposed positions. One side looks at the evidence and sees apartheid, balkanisation, polarisation, and disenfranchisement; the other sees integration, diversity, harmony, and empowerment' (Cannon, 1999:xi). The political problem parallels that in some other countries in which elections to the legislature are based on single-member constituencies and the constituency parties nearly always select male candidates. In such systems it is very difficult to find lawful means for ensuring that the legislature includes an equitable number of females and members of ethnic minority ancestry. The same study noted that governmental action over civil rights has sometimes had unintended and undesired effects. The 'busing' of schoolchildren had increased segregation, while 'affirmative action' caused a backlash that deepened racial division. The redistricting that has created 'black majority' districts, however, has tended to reduce racial divisions. Contrary to the fears of the Supreme Court in the 1993 case of *Shaw v. Reno*, the representatives from such districts have not represented the interests of only a section of their constituencies. There are now plenty of districts in which black politicians represent white voters, and vice versa.

In connection with the right to employment (para. 5(*e*)(*i*)), the report in para. 354 detailed the number of complaints recorded annually. It would have been interesting to hear how they relate to the estimated incidence of discrimination. Four experimental studies of employment discrimination in the USA parallel the ILO model for situation testing. They indicated that black job applicants experience racial discrimination in 19.4 per cent of applications; Hispanic applicants experience discrimination in 33.2 per cent of applications (Bendick, 1996:38). It is argued that the studies used in the ILO report were based on the experience of job applicants in the market for private employment in Washington and that this gives a misleading impression because in that city minority applicants may enjoy a preference when seeking jobs in the public sector. There has also been a study in Denver that found that the apparently less favourable treatment of black job applicants was not significantly greater than that against whites (Thernstrom and Thernstrom, 1997:447–9). Further research is needed before any definite conclusion can be reached about actual rates of discrimination in employment.

In connection with the right to housing (para. 5(*e*)(*iii*)), the report in para. 184 mentioned a new national housing discrimination study; its findings may well prove to be very important. The 1989 study found that on average black and Hispanic customers were not supplied with information about 25 per cent of the available housing units; they were steered towards particular localities in a fashion that tended to maintain segregation. When applying for mortgages their applications were rejected twice as often as those of comparable whites (Yinger, 1995). A definitive evaluation of the Federal Experimental Housing Alliance Program demonstrated that because low-income African-Americans lived in segregated neighbourhoods they were unaware of the better housing opportunities in nearby suburbs; they were cut off not only from information about housing opportunities but also from job opportunities. The Gautreaux programme in Chicago has demonstrated the practicability of schemes to help families to move to suburbs where there are more jobs, and in so doing to promote residential and educational integration. Congress allocated roughly $80 million for

Moving to Opportunity for Fair Housing, an initiative that is likely to produce further evidence that this kind of programme can substantially improve the lives of poor black and Hispanic public-housing residents.

In connection with health and social services (para. 5(*e*)(*iv*)), helpful data were provided in paras 376–88 of the report. Higher morbidity and mortality rates put any group at a disadvantage in competition with others. They contribute to the construction of an unfavourable image of the group that in turn leads to discrimination. Social services like food stamps, housing subsidies, aid to families with dependent children, and Medicaid have done much to reduce racial disadvantage, but, once again, the adequacy of such provisions has to be assessed by reference to the need for them. Children in lower-class African-American families suffer a high level of disadvantage; as teenagers they are more likely to drop out of school, are three times more likely to be incarcerated, and the females are much more likely to become teenage mothers. Racial discrimination is only one of the causes of this disadvantage, and sometimes only a distant one, but this is an interactive relationship; disadvantage can be a cause of discrimination in the next generation. The report has little to say about the health of indigenous peoples. Committee members know from other state reports that indigenous peoples are often demoralized by what has befallen them. Their relatively poor health and, sometimes, a high incidence of alcoholism reflect this, but the symptoms of malaise cannot be remedied by health measures alone.

CERD has not so far given consideration to the seventh and eighth words in the heading to Article 5(e), namely *in particular*. They can be read as implying that there may be economic, social and cultural rights requiring protection additional to those listed in sub-paragraphs (i) to (vi) and therefore support the claim that sub-paragraph (iv) on the right to health should be read broadly to cover what is sometimes called environmental racism, that is, governmentally sanctioned actions that damage the environment in ways that impair the well-being of indigenous peoples and of local communities distinguished by race or ethnic origin. This may be taken up on another occasion.

In connection with the right to education (para. 5(*e*)(*v*)), the initial report includes some very helpful historical passages, but does not recount the remarkable history of educational segregation and desegregation. The Supreme Court's unanimous 1954 judgement in *Brown v. Board of Education* did not hold that the US constitution was colour blind, only that: 'segregation ... has a tendency to retard the educational and mental development of Negro children ...

Separate educational facilities are inherently unequal.' The school-children in the case were being denied equal protection in the terms of the Fourteenth Amendment. Twelve years later, because the affected localities were slow to desegregate, the Department of Education, Health, and Welfare issued a circular stating that districts would be ineligible for federal funding without evidence of substantial desegregation as measured by the percentage of minority children who were attending majority-white schools. That required use of a racial standard that, at the time, was unlawful, but that became lawful in 1968 by the decision of the Supreme Court in *Green v. School Board of New Kent County* (see Thernstrom and Thernstrom, 1997:317–22). It seems fairly clear that the USA carried affirmative action in education to lengths that were incompatible with Article 2.2. It had signed the Convention in 1966 and therefore was obliged to refrain from acts that would defeat the object and purpose of the treaty, but this was overlooked in the controversies about school desegregation.

The initial report recognized differences in educational attainment associated with differences in ethnic origin (paras 407–11). While these are not necessarily attributable to racial discrimination they nevertheless tend to strengthen racial divisions. Though the gap in reading skills between blacks and whites fell between 1980 and 1988, it then increased so that in 1994 blacks aged 17 could on average read no better than the typical white child who was one month past his or her thirteenth birthday. Blacks in the twelfth grade could deal with scientific problems at the level of whites in the sixth grade and write about as well as white children in the eighth grade. The authors of *America in Black and White* (Thernstrom and Thernstrom, 1997:357–9) can find no convincing explanation for this retrogression.

Article 6 of the Convention governs the availability of effective remedies. In the USA many of these are provided at levels other than the federal, which complicates the tasks of reporting and examining. Questions remain about the extent to which the remedies in the USA are effective, and on the length of time needed for someone with a grievance to obtain redress.

Under Article 7 states parties undertake to propagate the principles of UN human rights instruments. The USA is famous for the attention paid in schools to teaching about the US constitution and for the way that the values enshrined in the constitution have been used in unifying a population of diverse origins. It should not be difficult to extend this teaching to explain the universality of human rights law. On ratification, the federal government accepted new obligations to propagate the purposes and principles of the

UN Charter, the Universal Declaration of Human Rights and the ICERD, but the report did not describe the way in which they were being implemented.

A full examination of the extent to which the USA fulfils its obligations under the Convention would be a major task, requiring expertise in both law and social research. A treaty body like CERD has to work under severe constraints of time and information. Its members cannot be experts in all the relevant fields. After the state delegation has replied to members' questions one member of the Committee has a few days in which to draft a set of concluding observations, receive comments from the other seventeen members, and try to prepare a document that will be accepted when it is brought formally before the Committee. Often several drafts will be needed; there may be problems of translation and there are sometimes disagreements about whether it is appropriate to take up certain issues. There can be obstacles that would not be perceived by an outsider. For example, in 1998 it was difficult to secure agreement within the Committee on a set of concluding observations on the report of Israel. The summary record of the 1,272nd meeting shows that after their adoption one member declared that, despite his reluctance to undermine a decision reached by consensus, he would have voted against them had they been put to a vote because he thought that Israel was being treated leniently. Another member associated himself with this statement. An outside observer would not know that neither of these members had come forward with specific proposals during the earlier informal discussions on successive drafts.

A language of diversity

The anti-racist movement in the USA has based its arguments on the country's constitution. It has also been acutely sensitive to the naming of groups. The Report of the President's Advisory Board, *One America in the 21st Century*, which has been referred to earlier, concluded that the country needed 'a new language of diversity'. It noted that: 'most Americans have learned that it is inappropriate to use the terms "Colored" or "Negro" to refer to blacks or "Oriental" to refer to Asian Pacific Americans', and that many Americans of Asian Indian descent were uncomfortable if they were placed in this last category (Franklin, 1998:55).

According to the report, one motor for change will be the increased number of marriages between people who are classified differently in the census. The 1990:

data for people ages 25 to 34 indicate that almost 32 percent of native-born Hispanic husbands and 31 percent of native-born Hispanic wives had white spouses. Thirty-six percent of native-born Asian Pacific men married white women, and 45 percent of Asian Pacific women espoused white men. A majority of American Indian and Native Alaska men and women married white spouses and had the highest rates of intermarriage. In the 25-to-34 age group, 8 percent of black men and 4 percent of black women married individuals of another race. The percentage of whites intermarrying was smaller than that of blacks.

The use of the word *intermarriage* in this setting is inappropriate in that it reinforces the assumption that the parties to such a marriage belong naturally in distinct groups. *Multiracial* (sometimes favoured by people of mixed ancestry) is no better, while the expression *mixed-race* is particularly unfortunate in implying that there are pure races. It is regrettable that the Franklin report did not explain how the popular use of *race* as a category recycles obsolete ideas and can contribute to anti-racist racism among both whites and blacks. The chief source of the Board's difficulty lay in their top-down approach of trying to describe the sort of society that the US was becoming (Goering, 2001:481). It could have been avoided had they started from the rights of individuals (under the constitution of the USA and the treaties it has ratified) and, working from the bottom upwards, analysed the obstacles that prevent individuals from enjoying these rights without discrimination. Forms of self-identification will be more and more important as the old categories dissolve.

An approach from human rights would not solve all these problems but in present circumstances it offers the most promising way of escaping from the trap that lies in the vocabulary of race. As noted earlier, there are two separate UN covenants for the protection of human rights: one specifies economic, social and cultural rights; the other, civil and political rights. In the USA civil and political rights are protected in the constitution; economic, social and cultural rights are protected by other laws, but the protection is less comprehensive and the government has, for example, disputed whether there is any right to housing (which makes the reference to a right to housing in Article 5(*e*)(*iii*) the more important). A strategy for consolidating 'One America in the 21st Century' that started from human rights could both build upon and extend the well-established concern for constitutional rights. Unequal development poses problems of inequality between groups within a country as well as between countries. These problems are compounded by the ways in which inequality is transmitted from one generation to the next, so that 'the right of everyone, without distinction as to race, colour, or national or ethnic origin, to equality before the law' in the enjoyment of economic and social rights has a particular significance for the USA.

7

Britain in Europe

Human rights standards are set at three levels. Those at the national level are expected to be no lower than those at the regional level, while those at that level are expected to be no lower than the international standards. Sometimes the national protections are the highest, and the national remedies quickest and most effective. It can be similar with anti-racist movements.

National anti-racist movements in many European countries are sustained by memories of Nazi doctrine, but their strength is closely associated with the history and character of immigration from countries outside Europe.

European institutions

The governments of West European countries founded the COE in 1949 'to achieve a greater unity . . . for the purpose of safeguarding and realising the ideals and principles which are their common heritage'. Its statute required every member state to 'accept the principles of the rule of law and of the enjoyment by all persons within its jurisdiction of human rights and fundamental freedoms'. In the following year the Council adopted the European Convention on Human Rights and Fundamental Freedoms that included, as Article 14, a prohibition of racial discrimination. In 1952 some of the same countries joined in the creation of common institutions for the regulation of the coal, steel and atomic energy industries, and then later for establishing a common market. In 1993, following upon the Maastricht Treaty, these countries formed the European Union (EU). The Conference on Security and Co-operation in Europe, convened on a proposal from the USSR in Helsinki in 1972–5, adopted a Final Act that included declarations about co-operation in humanitarian fields. It led to the establishment in 1994 of the OSCE. There are therefore three chief regional organizations. The OSCE is the largest, including among its fifty-three member states the USA, Canada, the Russian Federation, and states of the former USSR stretching to Uzbekistan and Tajikistan; it has a special orientation to security. The COE, with forty-two member states, is much concerned with human rights. The EU, with fifteen members, is starting to construct a constitution of its own with a common citizenship in order to supplement its orientation towards economic relations (Weiler, 1999). There is some overlap in the activities of the three bodies.

Those states to the East that, since the fall of the Berlin Wall in 1989, have sought the economic benefits of closer association with the West have to meet standards set in these institutions. Initially, the newly independent Baltic states planned to make the conferment of citizenship dependent upon passing language tests at a level that would have been extremely difficult for members of their Russian-speaking minorities to reach. As a result of negotiations with the OSCE high commissioner for national minorities, these requirements were modified. More recently, the OSCE has taken special interest in discrimination against members of the Roma minorities. Croatia's application to join the COE was held up for a time because of concerns about its treatment of its Serb minority, while Turkey's candidacy for membership of the EU is questioned on human rights grounds.

Within the COE, the European Committee on Migration has for some years been promoting common policies. In October 1993 the heads of state and government of the member states adopted the Vienna Declaration, which included a decision to launch a European Youth Campaign to mobilize the public against racism. Of greater long-term significance, it set up an expert committee that has since taken the name European Commission Against Racism and Intolerance (ECRI). The Commission's programme provides for the periodic examination of national legislation and policy, drawing attention to any changes needed to ensure that a member state fulfils its obligations under various Council instruments. As mentioned on pp. 86–7, ECRI's members prepare 'country reports', of increasing detail and authority, on the implementation of their legal obligations by the forty-two COE member states, thus including, for example, Moldova, Russia, Turkey and Ukraine. At the same 1993 summit in Vienna the member states agreed the Framework Convention for the Protection of Minorities that came into force in 1998. It draws on relevant texts of the OSCE and the UN to create a framework for the legislation and practice of member states. An advisory committee of independent experts is selected by the Committee of Ministers from candidates proposed by states, examines state reports, and then reports to the ministers on the measures taken to implement the Convention. This action received added impetus from the abuses of human rights associated with the break-up of the Federal Republic of Yugoslavia that started in 1991.

Article 14 of the ECHR conferred a protection against racial discrimination only with respect to 'the rights and freedoms set forth in this Convention'. This meant that anyone seeking to demonstrate a violation of the article had to establish that one or more of his or her rights under Articles 2 to 13 had not been protected *and* that this failure was on the ground of discrimination. If a violation of one of the earlier articles could be substantiated, a possible violation of Article 14 was of lesser significance. Articles 2 to 13 set forth civil and political rights, not economic, social and cultural rights, so for fifty years the European Convention was narrower in scope than the human rights conventions later agreed by the UN. In 2000 it was brought into line with the international standard for twenty-five of the Council's states when they adopted Protocol 12 to the Convention. This declares that: 'The enjoyment of any right set forth by law shall be secured without discrimination on any ground such as sex, race, colour, language, religion, political or other opinion, national or social origin, association with a national minority, property, birth, or other status.' The new protocol is free-standing, extending the protection to any right recognized in a country's laws, including economic, social and cultural rights. (Independently, the European Court of Human Rights has concluded that if states, without an objective and reasonable justification, fail to treat differently persons whose situations are significantly different, this can lead to a violation of Article 14 – *Thlimmenos v. Greece*, application 00034369/97.)

Within the EU, a committee of the European Parliament presented a report on the rise of fascism and racism in Europe in 1985 and another similar one in 1991. Three years later the European Council established a Consultative Commission on Racism and Xenophobia that recommended amendment of the Treaty of Rome to permit the Council of Ministers to issue directives about racial discrimination for enforcement in national courts. The European Court of Justice would then be able to ensure that the directives were uniformly applied, and it could enforce action against racial discrimination as it had already done for sex discrimination. This objective was attained in 2000 when the Council adopted a Directive implementing the principle of equal treatment between persons irrespective of racial or ethnic origin. It stated that:

direct discrimination shall be taken to occur when one person is treated less favourably than another is, has been or would be treated in a comparable situation on grounds of racial or ethnic origin; indirect discrimination shall be taken to occur when an apparently neutral provision, criterion or practice would put persons of a racial or ethnic origin at a particular disadvantage compared with other persons, unless that provision, criterion or practice is objectively justified by a legitimate aim and the means of attaining that aim are appropriate and necessary.

The Race Directive is supplemented by an Employment Directive prohibiting discrimination in employment and vocational training.

The EU designated 1997 as the European Year Against Racism. Having to devise a plan for the Year was a new task for the Commission, which may help explain why the scheme that resulted was simple-minded. 'Key decision-makers' were invited to 'commit themselves to the fight against racism' as if moral dedication was the chief requirement for combating racial discrimination. A total of 4.7 million euros was spent, mainly on supporting projects in member states. A high proportion of these seem to have been directed to the easy problems, for example, those involving children, which doubtless encouraged a warm glow of solidarity. Relatively few confronted the causes of racial discrimination and hatred, or tackled the more difficult problems (such as those presented by disaffected youth, particularly among the ethnic majorities). The obligations of states under international law were virtually ignored.

The year 1998 saw the establishment, in Vienna, of the European Union Monitoring Centre on Racism and Xenophobia. It is intended to be a manager of knowledge, a clearing house and a bridge-builder, which will submit to the Union and its member states 'objective, reliable and comparable' information on 'racist, xenophobic and anti-Semitic phenomena in the EU'. Early in 2001 it published in the Eurobarometer series the findings of a survey of attitudes towards minority groups in the fifteen member states. The EU has not yet found a way to co-ordinate its anti-racism activities with those of the COE and UN. Overlapping is wasteful.

Immigration

Post-war economic recovery and expansion had similar consequences for migration into all West European countries. The general pattern was first to recruit migrant workers from neighbouring countries and then to look to more distant sources. Because of their colonial connections, Britain, the Netherlands and France admitted non-European workers earliest. Elsewhere the recruitment of non-European workers did not start until the late 1960s, and then, because of the deep recession that followed the oil price shock of 1973, all primary immigration was brought to a halt. Later it resumed for the more southern countries. The initial immigration of work-seekers was followed by the phase of family reunification, as allowed for by the increasingly strict controls. To evade these controls, more persons whose motivations were primarily economic have presented themselves as political refugees seeking asylum.

Immigration into the countries of Western Europe is certain to continue because their inhabitants are living longer and the age structure is changing. The numbers of persons in employment is insufficient to maintain the pension payments, health and social services at the levels to which voters have become accustomed. As birth rates are unlikely to increase, this will generate pressure for increasing the age of retirement and for the use of migrant or immigrant labour.

Migrant workers plan to return to their countries of origin whereas immigrants plan to settle. This distinction is sometimes obscured because many who enter as migrant workers become sojourners; these are persons who talk of going back but postpone their return and, without having planned it, become settlers. Migrant workers are a source of labour complementary to native labour. They take the jobs native workers do not want, and in this way the job market becomes ethnically segregated, especially if the newcomers specialize in a particular kind of work (like the Chinese in the restaurant trade). Some migrant workers travel independently, but Germany entered into contracts with Turkey in order to regulate the admission of guest workers, while Swiss and Austrian policies have likewise assumed that foreign workers are only temporary residents. Governments may be unable to prevent migrant workers becoming settlers. Continuing immigration is encouraged when employers have an interest in employing foreign workers as complementary labour, particularly foreigners who have no permit to work and are therefore outside the rules that protect the interests of native workers. In Belgium, for example, employers have had to pay into the social security system almost as much as they paid in wages. If they engaged illegal workers they might be able to avoid these additional costs.

If the newcomers settle, there is a second phase in which the immigrants fan out and compete with native labour. Their labour becomes substitutable for, instead of complementary to, that of the native workers. The settlers may have to struggle to get recalcitrant members of the majority to accept that they have become permanent residents. It is easier for them to do this when their population has stabilized and is no longer increased by new immigration. In this phase they continue to seek many of their ends by individual action, but they may conclude that they have a better chance of attaining other goals if they join together in collective action, embarking on a process of implicit inter-group bargaining with members of the ethnic majority. One pattern is for measures to promote equality of opportunity to be devised by a political elite within the ethnic majority and later to receive electoral support from minorities.

Integration has tended to be slower when the immigrants have differed significantly from the majority population in skin colour, religion and cultural distinctiveness. When, in a Eurobarometer survey of attitudes in 1988, respondents were asked: 'When you think about people of another race, whom do you think of?', respondents in ten of the twelve countries cited black people in first place, indicating greatest distance. The French cited 'Arabs' first, while the British cited 'Indians'.

Integration may result from individual action independent of state policy, but, as they have found themselves moving into the phase of settlement, most West European states have formulated policies that they describe as promoting national integration. These often legitimate the maintenance of distinctive minority religious and cultural observances, and if the ethnic majority comes to accept this as appropriate to the national society, the perception of cultural distance is reduced. The concept of national integration rests on a mathematical metaphor, assuming that the social processes of group interaction can be likened to the arithmetical processes of making up a whole number. Anyone who uses it should specify the integer, the whole number, into which the fractions are being combined. A person can be well integrated into a local group without being so well integrated into a national society, because local groups are sometimes in conflict with national societies. Until there are satisfactory ways of measuring the degrees to which members of ethnic *majorities* are integrated into their national societies it will not be possible to measure the integration of members of minorities. Even were such measures available it would be difficult to draw cross-national comparisons because the highly explicit modes of integration into the French republic, for example, are very different from the less articulated modes by which immigrants can become British. Despite the conceptual problems, the idea of integration will continue to be used in policy discussion because there is no alternative expression that is not open to even greater objections.

It may be helpful to try to express the argument mathematically, by holding that the degree of integration of non-European groups in different European countries is a function of the number of years for which they have been settled, multiplied by an index of their economic and social dispersal throughout the society, and divided by the perceived cultural distance between natives and the descendants of immigrants. An index of economic and social dispersal would include measures of the percentage of persons of immigrant origin elected to the legislature, appointed as judges, as police officers, and to influential social positions generally, as well as their representation in various other occupations and their residential dispersal.

Three main processes determine social dispersal. First, immigrants change as they enter the receiving country's system of social stratification, either climbing up through it or being incorporated into a particular part of it; second, the majority changes either to make room for them in part of the system or to resist their entry; third, much of the change is the result of interaction between members of the majority and of the minorities within particular institutions, and is channelled by them. The goals of individuals may change, or they may adopt other means to attain their goals.

There have been many similarities between West European countries in their responses to suggestions of racial discrimination against immigrants. Like the first countries to report under the UN convention, many Europeans have tended to regard racial discrimination as something that occurred elsewhere, in South Africa or the USA, but not in their neighbourhood. When asked about ethnic discrimination, officials and employers have often replied in words that in Britain have become a cliché: 'We have no problem here.' In a letter to a newspaper (*Guardian*, 18 June 1998; see also Wrench, 2000:276) John Wrench wrote:

> I have been attending conferences on racism for years and have been told quite firmly by academics and officials in each country that racism could not possibly exist there. For example:
> - There is no racism towards migrants in Spain because it has been a country of emigration and understands the problems of immigrants.
> - Racism is not a normal part of Italian culture because Italian fascism, unlike German fascism, was never anti-Semitic, and Italy had the largest communist party in Europe, reflecting a culture of international brotherhood.
> - Germany had been the most institutionally racist state in Europe under the Nazis and, therefore, racism was removed when the Nazi state was abolished.

- Racism is absent from French culture because the 1789 revolution institutionalised 'liberty, equality and fraternity' into French society.
- Sweden has never been a colonial power ruling over non-white peoples.
- The Dutch operated a more benevolent form of colonialism, illustrated by a high rate of intermarriage between Dutch and ex-colonial peoples.
- Portugal was the first country to open up new lands with its voyages of discovery to Africa and India, thus exposing the Portuguese people to non-Europeans earlier than other countries.

In no European country has it been in the interest of political parties to counter such ideas. Whereas they have been able to gain many votes by promising to introduce legislation against discrimination on grounds of sex, by promising legislation against discrimination on racial grounds they stood to lose far more votes than they could gain. Much has depended upon the effectiveness of pressure groups able to influence the political elite. These have usually been to the left of the political centre and Jewish intellectuals have often played prominent roles. They have been more concerned than others to try to account for group hostility. Through their history of persecution they have learned what I once called the Jewish lesson: that if they are to enjoy their right to a separate identity as a minority, they must support the claims of other minorities to a similar right (Banton, 1985:15).

Despite the similarities in the different countries' responses to complaints of racism, there have been many striking differences. Some have been associated with the characteristics of the immigrant groups; others with the receiving countries' laws regarding nationality and conceptions of national community. Popular support for anti-racist measures has depended upon how much members of the ethnic majority know about the minorities and the incidence of discrimination against them. In this connection social research, and the willingness of the mass media to publicize its findings, has been an important variable.

An initial comparison of the stages reached by different West European states in the process of integrating non-European immigrants suggests that five groups may be distinguished: British, Nordic, French, German and Italian. Britain has been able to exert most control over immigration, and has progressed furthest towards integration. As this state was the pioneer in developing what in chapter 3 was called Thesis One, it is justifiable to describe British policies at greater length than those that have so far been put in place by other European states. Those in the Italian group have been least able to control immigration and are the most inclined to see it as presenting the short-term problems of migrant labour. National anti-racist movements in Europe have often begun by criticizing governmental policies concerning immigration and asylum, pointing out that policies written in neutral terms are often implemented in a racially discriminatory manner. Only later have these movements campaigned against the discrimination experienced by settled migrants. Once they start to address discrimination within the national society they have to criticize many institutions and employers and to risk evoking resentment and hostility. In reviewing policies it is well to bear in mind that the best chances for superseding the language of race lie in correcting the emphasis it confers upon physical differences so as to keep their significance proportionate to other differences, like those of national origin, religion, language, culture and place in processes of settlement and integration.

National variations

The relatively early industrialization of Britain entailed a correspondingly early transfer of population to the cities. Though Britain continued to attract labour from the rural areas of Ireland and was steadily increasing female employment, by the 1950s its employers had to look to labour from outside Europe. Residents in the New Commonwealth countries (particularly those of the West Indies, India and Pakistan), like those in the old Commonwealth (Canada, Australia and New Zealand), were British nationals, and were therefore not subject to the immigration controls upon alien workers. The non-European minorities admitted to Britain were distinguished by their appearance but not by their nationality (as in other European countries), though Britain, uniquely, later created distinctions of citizenship among persons possessing the same nationality. Persons who in part or whole are of non-European ethnic origin now constitute about 10 per cent of the population of Britain.

The British, though deeply divided on class lines, have seen themselves as a *historical* community. People enjoy the rights of British subjects that Edmund Burke, reacting against the French idea of universal human rights, represented as a national patrimony from their forefathers. The sense of a national community has been weakened by three special characteristics. First, the identity 'British subject' is vague. Whereas in Germany citizenship has been an identity reinforcing an ethnic self-conception, in Britain the category 'citizen' has been multiethnic and multiracial. Second, for many people what matter are the national identities English, Welsh, Scottish, and Irish in the Province of Northern Ireland, not the shared identity 'citizen of the United Kingdom'. Third, because of geography, history and the continuity of language, the UK has in some respects an open frontier vis-à-vis the United States of America. Afro-Caribbeans have shared in some of the ideological movements of African-Americans. They have imported into Britain assumptions about the nature of race as a social construct and a black identity that have been fashioned by experience in North America. These complicate the sense of national community in the UK in ways that differentiate it from comparable conceptions in France and Germany and mean that the British have a less cohesive image of their society and of civil duties.

The first parliamentary proposal for anti-discrimination legislation, with the title 'Colour Bar Bill', was introduced in 1951 by a private member without government support, and it therefore made no progress. Then in September 1958 the Labour Party published a statement entitled *Racial Discrimination* in which it declared: 'the next Labour Government will . . . introduce legislation which will outlaw discrimination in public places'. When in 1965 it gave effect to this promise its bill was entitled not 'Racial Discrimination Bill' but 'Race Relations Bill'. Nowhere in the Bill or its explanatory memorandum was the word *relations* used. The title was unfortunate since it suggested that each individual could be assigned to a race, and that relations between persons of different race were necessarily different from relations between persons of the same race. This attracted no comment at the time, though there had been some hesitation over the title 'Institute of Race Relations' when a body with this name was established in London in 1958 to study relations in Commonwealth countries overseas.

Enactment of the Race Relations Bill was made easier by the Labour government's decision to maintain the 1962 legislation limiting Commonwealth immigration. A Labour MP, Roy Hattersley, contended that: 'without integration, limitation is inexcusable; without limitation, integration is impossible.' For him, there was not one racial issue, but at least two issues. This was important because many on the political left then insisted that 'race' constituted a single issue and that the changes to the immigration law were motivated by racism. Chapter 1 described some of the senses in which the word race was used before World War II, so it is relevant to note here that by the 1960s the word was often used as a label for immigration as a political issue.

The title 'Race Relations' was repeated for the Acts of 1968 and 1976, though no one proposed to call the 1976 Sex Discrimination

Act a Sex Relations Act. Events within the United Nations seem to have had little influence upon domestic policy in the 1960s. Roy Jenkins, when home secretary from 1965 to 1967, was not aware of the ICERD 'as being in any way a major factor in the preparation of the legislation in 1966 and 1967. I think we would certainly have done what we did without the Convention' (personal communication, 14 April 1986). Many legislators did not believe that racial discrimination was a significant problem, so research was undertaken in which three testers, an Englishman, a Hungarian and a West Indian, applied for the same jobs, housing, car insurance, and certain other services. This was an early example of what the ILO later called practice-testing and what in the USA is often called audit. The results revealed racial discrimination to be more widespread than anyone (including members of the minorities) had believed. The research findings played a vital part in creating a climate of opinion in which parliament could extend the existing legislation.

The 1968 Act established a Race Relations Board with responsibilities for implementation of its anti-discriminatory provisions and a separate body to promote 'harmonious community relations', which it chose to call the Community Relations Commission. The implication that it was better to avoid the idiom of race for the promotional side of official policy had much to commend it, so when new proposals in a 1975 white paper disclosed the government's intention to set up a Race Relations Commission I wrote to the home secretary (who was once again Mr Jenkins) to maintain that the expression 'community relations' was preferable. The Home Secretary replied:

> The Standing Committee . . . recognised, as I had, that there are objections to the use of the term 'race' in this context. But I believe that it has become firmly established in public usage. I believe that a title for the new Commission which did not include this or a related term would place it under a significant handicap in establishing its position with the public at large . . . There is, I recognise, a great danger in encouraging the belief that the differences between the minority communities and the rest of the population are in any relevant sense biological. But the Race Relations Bill is designed to counter the mistaken beliefs and actions of ordinary men and women for whom race (in no academic sense) along with colour and national origins, has become a basis for invidious distinctions. I believe that the balance of advantage lies in facing this squarely by talking of race relations and racial discrimination. To call the new body dealing specifically with these new matters by a more general (or euphemistic) title, would, I believe, only mislead. (personal communication, 9 July 1976)

The 1976 Act established the new body with the name Commission for Racial Equality.

In the 1960s the policy impetus came from an activist section of the white elite operating mainly through governmentally sponsored councils. With the growth of a New Commonwealth settler population, leadership of the anti-racist movement gradually diversified. In the same period a new language of race and culture came into use. I (Banton, 1970:29) noted that in several countries 'policies implying the unequal treatment of ethnic groups are more and more defended on political and cultural rather than on pseudo-biological grounds'. People who considered themselves anti-racist, seeking to get away from a vocabulary based in biology, also started to stress cultural differences even in situations (such as those involving Euro-Americans and African-Americans) in which the differences were minute relative to the culture that both parties shared.

Incitement to racial hatred is an offence against public order and has to result in criminal proceedings, but in drafting the 1976 Race Relations Act the UK government proposed that complaints of racial discrimination in working life would be dealt with under labour law, using civil rather than criminal procedures. The former have many advantages. The state assumes the role of a neutral arbiter, the dispute usually being between an employer and an employee. The parties often settle their dispute privately so that it does not need to come before a tribunal, but, if it should, the complainant has to prove his or her case according to the balance of probabilities, not according to the higher criminal law standard of proof beyond reasonable doubt. Countries that rely on the criminal law to deal with allegations of racial discrimination at work find it much less effective. The Nordic countries and Germany have traditionally seen labour disputes as a matter for negotiation between the 'social parties', the employers and the trade unions. Since immigrant workers often are not union members, or join a union only after obtaining a job, this approach too has been less effective than that adopted in Britain.

The press in Britain is also distinctive. Journalists in most countries have little understanding of the nature of UN and other international bodies, but in Britain they seem more ready than elsewhere to criticize such bodies without having first informed themselves about their mandates or ascertaining exactly what conclusions they have reached. For example, in 2001 ECRI reported that in the UK problems of racism and xenophobia were 'particularly acute' with respect to asylum-seekers and refugees. It expressed regret that the tone and presentation of the asylum issue had been influenced for the worse by some sections of the media and some political statements. Some of the press reaction to this report rehearsed the very sensationalism that was being criticized. The ECRI secretariat in Strasbourg was then assailed by email from the UK that varied from abuse to injunctions to 'mind your own business'. The population in no other country has reacted in this way. It is evidence of a streak of isolationism and of a hostility towards arrangements for European co-operation that is untroubled by ignorance of the facts.

Turning to other European countries, it should be noted that Ireland did not attract immigrants until the 1990s and, that although there was much well-documented discrimination against Travellers (or Roma), the government was very slow to legislate against it. The first non-European immigrants to the Netherlands were from formerly colonial territories in South-East Asia, followed by Surinamese, Spaniards, Italians, Turks, Moroccans and a further wave of Surinamese. Official policies resembled those in Britain. From 1974 immigration was restricted and assisted repatriation was attempted, but in the 1980s this was replaced by a policy of promoting integration, and to this end certain ethnic minority groups were given official recognition. An active anti-racist movement gathered momentum. A comprehensive Equal Treatment law was enacted in 1994 and from this time there was pressure on settlers to follow classes in the Dutch language and to benefit from vocational training, together with other integration-promoting measures.

Primary immigration into Denmark and Sweden from non-EU countries, initially from Yugoslavia, started about 1967 and continued until 1971. The immigration of non-Nordics to Norway started later and all three countries have accepted relatively many refugees. Finland, too, started in the 1970s to receive refugees (initially from Chile, and then Somali asylum-seekers in 1990). Neither Finland nor Iceland has attracted economic migrants from outside Europe. In Sweden more than 10 per cent of the population is now of foreign birth. Government policy has since the 1970s assumed that the immigrants are or will become settlers and has committed substantial resources to assisting integration. Settled immigrants were entitled to vote in local elections and it was not difficult for them to obtain Swedish nationality provided they surrendered their existing nationality (this proviso was lifted in 2001). In the mid-1990s vigorous national anti-racist movements mobilized in Denmark and Norway, stimulated by the growth of neo-Nazism in those countries, as in Sweden. In all three countries the laws against racial discrimination had been ineffective but, stimulated partly by the observations of CERD, major improvements were effected. In Sweden in 1996 there was a shift in order to expect immigrants to do more for themselves. In 1997 Denmark formulated a comprehensive policy on integration based upon reciprocity and the recognition that immigrants have both rights and duties; the cultural right of the individual was to be respected. In the same year Norway declared that its policy was to promote equal participation, noting at the same time that integration and equality required co-operation throughout society. The Nordic governments have avoided use of the vocabulary of race, preferring to designate immigrants by ethnic and national origin.

From 1946 the French government recruited workers from Italy, Spain and Portugal and up to 1972 allowed uncontrolled immigration from Algeria (which became independent in 1962). Subsequent policies intended to restrict immigration have been of limited effect. In 1990, 7.4 per cent of the total population had been born abroad as non-citizens, a third of them having become French citizens. About one in five of the total population had at least one immigrant parent or grandparent.

In these respects French experience has not been very different from that of Britain and the Netherlands, but the French have approached questions of racial discrimination, like other political questions, from a distinctive standpoint. In 1789 the French created a secular republic based on a constitution articulating distinctive values. Over the next one hundred years they built a nation, a *political* community, giving institutional expression to these values. In 1991 the Constitutional Council decided that the legislature could not refer to *le peuple corse*, even as part of the French nation, because this would admit a distinction based upon ethnic origin contrary to Article 2 of the constitution. If Corsicans, Bretons and Basques cannot be recognized as minorities, neither can immigrants from North Africa. An official commission, the Haut Conseil à l'Intégration, at one time (1993:35–6) affirmed its conviction that the French conception of integration had to conform to a logic of equality and not to a logic of minorities. It was founded on 'the equality of individuals before the law, whatever their origins, their race, their religion . . . to the exclusion of any institutional recognition of minorities. In Western Europe this conception is shared with countries like Germany and Belgium, whereas the Netherlands and the United Kingdom for the most part pursue a policy of minorities.' Whether the Conseil properly understood Dutch and British attitudes is open to question, but in France the legal logic of equality has prevailed over the practical evidence of inequality and has not been shaken by the persistent strain of anti-Semitism. Since

France is a secular republic, there is no law against blasphemy and the publication of Salman Rushdie's *The Satanic Verses* could not cause the same agitation as in Britain.

The French have worried about maintaining the size of their population and (unlike the Germans) have been ready to confer their nationality upon anyone born or schooled in their country, on the assumption that anyone who has experienced this socialization will accept republican principles. New citizens could retain the nationality of some other country, though in recent times doubt has been cast on the loyalties of men who chose to serve their period of conscription in the Algerian army. The prime concern is with anything that threatens republican doctrine, so when girls have come to school wearing an Islamic scarf their action has been seen as a challenge to the school's mission to induct pupils into the political community. The French conception of racism is of sentiments and actions that threaten this idea of France as a political community. This explains why the French law against racism has been used to prosecute the authors of ideologically suspect statements while nearly all actions of racial discrimination in employment and housing have gone unpunished. National NGOs, like the SOS Racisme and the Mouvement contre le Racisme et pour l'Amitié entre les Peuples, have not utilized the opportunity to draw attention to such deficiencies when their government's reports have been examined by CERD.

Addressing the evidence of inequalities associated with immigration and malintegration, the French have used the metaphors of inclusion/exclusion and of *insertion*. That they are not always kept distinct can be seen from a passage in the Final Report of the Commissariat Royal à la Politique des Immigrés in Belgium (1993:51) (a country that has established a central institution rather like the Commission for Racial Equality in London). The passage runs:

> From the beginning the Royal Commission has argued for an insertion midway between assimilation and segregation. The propositions advanced in all its reports have been inspired by a concept of integration which rests simultaneously on:
> 1. an idea of 'insertion' that meets the following criteria:
>   a. assimilation wherever public order requires it,
>   b. the consequential and thorough promotion of an insertion in conformity with the fundamental principles supporting the culture of the receiving country and of a progressive character with respect to 'modernity', 'emancipation' and 'pluralism' in the sense given to these by a modern Western state, and

    c.   unequivocal respect in other fields for cultural diversity as a
        reciprocal enrichment;
2.   the structural involvement of minorities in the activities and
    objects of the public authorities.
It should be noted that this concept of integration applies not only
to immigrants but also to Belgians, who ought also to respect this
constitutional order, for example in its recognition of minority rights,
and that they too are required to respect the same fundamental social
principles, though they do not always do so.

The word 'assimilation' is used here not in the English dictionary
sense of 'becoming similar', but to identify a policy that provides
for change by members of the immigrant minority without corresponding change by members of the majority, something that for
the English speaker is suggested by 'insertion'. The Belgian author
treats 'integration' and 'insertion' as synonymous, whereas in the
English-speaking world the policy she recommends would be
regarded as one of integration.

The economic growth of the Federal Republic of Germany ('West
Germany') in the 1950s was fed by the immigration of ethnic
Germans from the East, but with the construction of the Berlin wall
in 1961, and the sealing of the frontier, the influx was halted. Thereafter immigration was characterized by a much higher degree of
state control than had been the case in either Britain or France. In
1961 the federal government concluded the first of several agreements with the government of Turkey. The migrants were called
Gastarbeiter, guest workers, indicating that they were expected to
return when they were no longer wanted. In 1997, 9.1 per cent of
employees registered for social security were of foreign birth.

German perceptions of the problems associated with immigration have been powerfully affected by their history. Germans felt
themselves to be a people, a *volk*, before they were able to come
together in 1871 as members of a state. They were an *ethnic* community, and continue to see themselves in this way, starting from a
conception of *Volkszugehörigkeit*, or ethnic belonging. They have
accepted as fellow-Germans all those descended from people who
lived on what counted as German soil in 1913, plus persons of
German origin whose ancestors were invited to settle in the Volga
river valley in 1762 but who no longer spoke German. To become
German by naturalization an applicant must renounce any other
citizenship, because no one can be allowed to identify with a second
ethnic community unless he or she belongs to a legally recognized
minority. Only a group of citizens of the same origin and living in
the same area can be accounted a minority, so there are just three;
the Danish minority, the Sorbs in Dresden and Cottbus, and the Sinti

and Roma; additionally, the Friesians are entitled to use their own language. Representatives of the state maintain that Germany is not a country of immigration, though there are problems when *Gastarbeiter* decide to remain. Most children of Turkish immigrants are and will remain Turkish nationals.

Many Germans have found it difficult to come to terms with their country's recent past, summarized in the expression *Vergangenheits-bewältigung*. They are uncomfortable with the expression *Rassismus* because it is so strongly associated with the Nazi era and prefer to speak of *Fremdenfeindlichkeit*, which is usually translated as xeno-phobia. The attacks on asylum-seekers in the years 1992–3 aroused a strong counter-reaction among the general population. Between 1992 and 2000 ten associations with extreme right-wing objectives were banned, a kind of measure that would be impossible in many other European countries. German NGOs have not yet submitted to CERD views alternative to those of the government.

In the late 1970s Italy switched from being a migrant-sending to a migrant-receiving country. Most of the immigrants came from North Africa and from countries in Asia (like the Philippines) with a labour surplus. There were similar switches in Spain, Portugal and Greece a few years later. Supply-driven clandestine immigration has continued wherever borders are difficult to police, as across the Mediterranean to Italy and Spain, and from Albania into Italy and Greece. Anti-racist movements in these countries are comparatively weak and have as yet done little to draw UN attention to their per-ceptions of the problems. According to one authority, state institu-tions and national identity in Italy are less powerful than in other industrialized countries so there is less organization of either the protection of immigrants or of hostility towards their presence (Martucelli, 1994:215–33).

Ethnic monitoring

The European Conference Against Racism, preparatory to the UN World Conference, included among its conclusions a paragraph 25 on monitoring, which read:

> The European Conference strongly recommends monitoring all poli-cies and programmes aimed at combating racial discrimination in order to assess their effectiveness in assisting targeted groups. All data should be broken down by sex and age, and information should include issues of multiple discrimination. Such statistical data may be complemented by public opinion surveys and also targeted surveys to ascertain the experience and perception of discrimination and racism from the point of view of potential complainants.

It may therefore be helpful to summarize British experience in connection with ethnic monitoring.

The post-war period in Britain was one of housing shortage, with considerable competition between persons wishing to be allocated municipally owned flats and houses. There was reason to believe that the criteria for allocation were sometimes applied in a racially discriminatory manner. In 1968 an official inquiry emphasized the importance to managers of keeping records of the ethnic origins of would-be tenants in order to ensure that they were treated fairly. Official records, as in the census, were at this time often based upon birthplace, a form of record keeping that became less useful with the growth of the British-born population of immigrant origin. Then the police developed a racial identity code for purposes of identification. Proposals were advanced for 'ethnic monitoring' in employment, but there was much unease about the kinds of category to be used for the classification of individuals and in the national census, particularly when they referred to racial identity and used simple oppositions like black/white. Data on ethnic origin were collected in the census of 1991. Then in the census of 2001 for England and Wales, persons were required to answer the question: 'What is your ethnic group?' It offered possible replies divided into five sections, each sub-divided, as follows:

A. White: British, Irish, or Any other White background;
B. Mixed: White and Black Caribbean, White and Black African, White and Asian, Any other Mixed background;
C. Asian or Asian British: Indian, Pakistani, Bangladeshi, Any other Asian background;
D. Black or Black British: Caribbean, African, Any other Black background;
E. Chinese or other ethnic group: Chinese, Any other.

Persons selecting an 'any other' response were asked to please supply an indication of their cultural background. Unlike the corresponding question in the 1991 census, this did not use the word 'race'. In the next census, due in 2011, the wording may have to change again because popular conceptions of identity are altering all the time.

In its recognition that many people are of mixed ethnic origin and that many wish to specify which components are important to them, this formulation allows freedom of choice. The British government does not assign individuals to ethnic groups; it does not impose quotas, but believes that, if it is to monitor progress, it must take account of how people see themselves, and of differences in their experience of life.

The Criminal Justice Act of 1991 included a section 95 stating that: 'The Secretary of State shall each year publish such information as he considers expedient for the purpose of . . . facilitating the performance by [persons engaged in the administration of criminal justice] of their duty to avoid discriminating against any persons on the ground of race or sex or any other improper ground.' As a result statistics are published indicating the frequency with which police stop on the street, and possibly search, black, Asian and other non-white persons by comparison with the frequency with which whites are stopped. There are similar comparative figures about numbers of arrests, cautions, convictions, probation orders and imprisonment. They show the extent to which minority people are disproportionately the victims of crimes of different kinds, whether they were racially motivated, and the number of 'racial incidents'.

No European government has found it easy to secure legislative support for measures that many members of the ethnic majority are likely to see as being in the interest of minorities rather than of themselves. An interesting case study of the political management of such an issue has been provided by the Labour government that assumed office in Westminster in 1997. There had been much public concern over the racially motivated murder of a black student called Stephen Lawrence in 1993. A representative of the Labour Party had promised that if they were to form the government after the election of 1997 they would establish an official inquiry. This they did.

At the time of the murder the police were required to record the occurrence of any racial incident, defined as 'any incident in which it appears to the reporting or investigating officer that the complaint involves an element of racial motivation, or any incident which includes an allegation of racial motivation made by any person'. The recording of such incidents was important to the implementation of official policy against racial attacks and for prosecution purposes. The Court of Appeal had declared that: 'it cannot be too strongly emphasised that where there is a racial element in an offence of violence, that is a gravely aggravating feature', which should attract a harsher sentence.

The requirement to record racial incidents did not harmonize with the customary working practices of police officers. One of the detectives questioned by the Inquiry explained that while he accepted that it counted as a racial attack because such an allegation had been made, the motivation had not been established. The suspects in the case had earlier attacked whites and Stephen Lawrence might have been attacked simply because he was in the wrong place at the wrong time. Other police witnesses also insisted that the motives behind the attack might not have been racial and that their task was to solve a murder, not to speculate about such matters (for a description of some of their responses to questions see Cathcart, 1999:347–60). One of Her Majesty's Inspectors of Constabulary (Home Office personnel responsible for inspecting police forces) confirmed the impression formed by the Inquiry that the definition was poorly understood by many officers. The main reason for this may have been inadequate training. From reports under the ICERD it is apparent that in very many, perhaps most, European countries, police officers, prosecutors and even judges have been unwilling to recognize the racial motivation of offences as a distinctive motivation that can be regarded as an aggravating circumstance when considering the imposition of punishment. The British police are not alone in this.

After proceedings that attracted much publicity, *The Stephen Lawrence Inquiry* (1999:313–14), chaired by Sir William Macpherson, reported:

> We believe that the use of the words 'racial' or 'racially motivated' are in themselves inaccurate and confusing, because we all belong to one human race, regardless of our colour, culture or ethnic origin. When referring to crime or incidents involving racism we believe 'racist' to be the appropriate adjective. Our recommendation is that the universally recognised definition should be:
> 'A racist incident is any incident which is perceived to be racist by the victim or any other person.'

If the statement that we all belong to one human race is an argument against use of the word 'racial' it is also an argument against use of the word 'racist'. The Inquiry might have believed that the latter was the appropriate word but they should have explained why in their view others should so regard it. Why should they have considered that 'the emphasis upon motivation was potentially confusing' since anyone who has to administer the criminal law needs to be able to deal with questions of intent and recklessness? That they should have thought that the 'apparent priority of the views of investigating or reporting officers was unhelpful' in the definition of a racial incident was also strange. Any reconsideration of the definition would have been more helpful had it distinguished between initial recording and a conclusion as to motivation presented to the Crown Prosecution Service. In the Crime and Disorder Act the government introduced specific new offences of racially aggravated violence, harassment and criminal damage that came into effect in 1998. Prosecutions under the Act have to prove that the offending behaviour was racially motivated, not that they were motivated by racism, so the use of this latter word in the definition of an incident increases rather than diminishes confusion.

The 1985 definition was designed to facilitate the recording of a particular kind of incident but it had not been applied to the Lawrence murder in the way intended. The murdered boy's parents were outraged by the refusal of some police officers to acknowledge the racial motive. Critics of police practice wanted a definition that, in addition to assisting in the recording of incidents, would signify their special character as aggravating what was already presumed to be criminal. The change from 'racial' to 'racist' was therefore attractive for reasons that were political, even if not political in any party sense.

The report of the inquiry (1999:20) stated: 'we have not heard evidence of overt racism or discrimination, unless it can be said that the use of inappropriate expressions such as "coloured" or "Negro" fall into that category', but concluded that the original police investigation into the murder 'was marred by a combination of professional incompetence, institutional racism and a failure of leadership by senior officers'. Public attention centred upon the second of these failings and the language used (on which see Cathcart, 1999:359, 412–13). The report defined two of its key terms as follows:

'Racism' in general terms consists of conduct or words or practices which advantage or disadvantage people because of their colour, culture or ethnic origin. In its more subtle form it is as damaging as in its overt form.

'Institutional Racism' consists of the collective failure of an organisation to provide an appropriate and professional service to people because of their colour, culture or ethnic origin. It can be seen or detected in processes, attitudes and behaviour which amount to discrimination through unwitting prejudice, ignorance, thoughtlessness, and racist stereotyping which disadvantage ethnic minority people.

These are definitions for political purposes, not social science purposes. They helped the report create a new climate of opinion. Nearly all of the seventy recommendations it made to the government were immediately accepted. In the view of the report: 'if racism is to be eliminated from our society there must be a co-ordinated effort to prevent its growth. This needs to go well beyond the police services.' It added: 'it is incumbent upon every institution to examine their policies and practices to guard against disadvantaging any section of our communities.' It has since been cited as an authority in support of proposed changes in other institutions.

On pp. 35–6, I described the change in the meaning given to the word racism at the end of the 1960s. The distinctions between the ideological, psychological and behavioural dimensions of a complex were lost and the one word racism was used to designate all three. Discrimination has a fairly precise meaning in both law and social science. To prove that someone has acted on racial grounds is difficult, but to accuse that person of racism by imputing thoughts or attitudes to him or her is easy, especially for a body like a high-powered official committee of inquiry. This is what happened in the Macpherson report (Dennis et al., 2000); but without its accusation of institutional racism the report could not have achieved its effect. With the support of the home secretary, it succeeded in moving the case for action against racial discrimination and disadvantage to the head of the political agenda and in shaking the complacency of some bureaucratic institutions that are resistant to change. This was a major achievement even if its methods were crude. Level-headed commentators read the report's findings as unequivocal and as proving that the London police service was riddled with racism. To this extent, the report was another noble lie.

Before coming into office the Labour Party had developed plans for a comprehensive anti-racism programme. The new home secretary was ready to exploit his opportunity. He capitalized upon the public sentiment generated by the report to push through extensive measures for ethnic monitoring and to instruct those responsible for the inspection of public bodies to monitor their progress towards the targets he set. The targets were calculated to ensure that the proportions of persons of different ethnic origin at the different levels in public institutions matched the proportions of those people in the area of recruitment. This programme was set out in an action plan relying on four principles: partnership and involvement; policing diversity; recognizing and rewarding success; and raising standards and promoting professional competence. A statutory duty to promote good race relations and equality of opportunity has since been imposed on every public body.

The British government will not wish its targets for the employment of ethnic minority workers to be pursued with the rigidity of some court-imposed racial quotas in the US, but the targets are bound, at least on occasion, to have similar effects. Consciousness of racial differences will be increased and it will often be asked whether a particular job applicant will count as helping an institution towards its target. Inevitably, some will receive more favourable treatment on racial grounds, and to this extent the policy will encourage a short-term form of 'anti-racist racism' in order to attain a long-term goal of diminishing racial consciousness.

To combat discrimination the Macpherson report and the Race Equality Plan endorse measures that will increase consciousness of racial differences. The language of human rights cannot at present offer any alternative course, but it is well to recognize the difficulty and utilize any opportunities that may arise in the future to formulate issues in a better way. The government's race equality plan parallels the adoption of the Human Rights Act 1998, by which the UK incorporated into domestic law the ECHR. The UK has yet to adopt Protocol 12 to the Convention, expanding the scope of Article 14 to make it free-standing instead of being accessory to Articles 2 to 12, but this is of less significance now that the EU Race Directive has extended the scope of EU law. By providing a protection against discrimination on grounds of religion, the Directive has filled what many saw as a gap in the protection of human rights on the British mainland (Northern Ireland having been covered earlier).

Reflections

The question of ethnic monitoring illustrates the value of regional human rights law and policy as supplementing UN action, because African and Asian governments would never accept any recommendation that ethnic monitoring be adopted for their countries. African governments, in particular, would say that in their countries ethnic loyalties and antagonisms threaten their national unity. To seek ethnic data in a national census would be to invite attempts to inflate the size of groups in order to build a better case for resource allocation. An increase in ethnic consciousness could only militate against the national consciousness these governments wish to cultivate.

Within European countries, the position is different, but there are few indications at present of any willingness on the part of other governments to take the British road. The British form of monitoring would be ideologically unacceptable in France, where, in any case, majority prejudice against North Africans, 'Arabs', is stronger than that against black Africans, and where Muslims are seen as threatening a secular republic. In many other European countries the different ethnic minorities are too varied to sustain division into simple categories like 'black' and 'Asian', so country of birth will continue as the chief criterion of difference. Yet as more children are born in the country of settlement to households with one or two foreign-born parents, classification by country of birth will be unable to provide a reliable measure of the effectiveness of equal opportunities programmes.

Racial discrimination is often triggered by the social significance vested in differences of appearance. Skin colour, in particular, can be taken as a sign of an individual's social class position. In contemporary Europe there is a danger that dark-skinned people will be trapped at the bottom of the social scale and that disadvantage will be transmitted from one generation to the next. The USA provides examples of how skin colour can become an all-important criterion and of how disadvantage can be inherited. Experience there and elsewhere shows that while laws against discrimination and anti-racist campaigns are needed, they are both blunt instruments. There are many circumstances in which a discriminatory motive may be mixed with other motives, and be relatively weak, but still strong enough to be decisive. Laws and public education therefore need to be complemented by measures of the outcomes, in particular, of who gets the jobs. If programmes are to be devised to counter this possibility they will require sophisticated population data. The blunt instruments will need to be complemented by ethnic monitoring.

National governments in most European countries are reluctant to introduce ethnic monitoring and the internal pressures in its favour are still weak. Recommendations from European institutions can be important and oversight of the effectiveness of national anti-discrimination programmes can more easily be achieved at the regional than at the global level. Any such recommendations are more likely to be acceptable if they present ethnic monitoring as part of a wider protection against all forms of discrimination. In Britain in some recent years the number of cases under the Sex Discrimination Act initiated by males has exceeded the number initiated by females; the act is seen as protecting both sexes. If proposals for monitoring are presented in the terms of Thesis One, they will appeal to the largest possible constituency. The thesis of racial inequality and the antithesis of increased racial consciousness will then have been synthesized in the institutions for the protection of human rights, and Europe, thanks to its more favourable circumstances, will have advanced further along this path than the United States.

8

The Third World Conference

In December 1997 the General Assembly decided to convene a
World Conference, specifying that its main objectives were to: (1)
'review progress in the fight against racism and racial discrimination, xenophobia and related intolerance'; (2) 'consider ways and
means to better ensure the application of existing standards and the
implementation of existing instruments'; (3) 'increase the level of
awareness about the scourges of racism'; (4) 'formulate concrete recommendations on increasing the effectiveness of the UN in these
connections'; (5) 'review the factors leading to racism'; (6) 'formulate concrete recommendations to further action-oriented national,
regional and international measures'; (7) 'draw up concrete recommendations for ensuring that the UN has the necessary resources
for its actions'. The Conference was to be 'action-oriented and focus
on practical measures . . . taking into full consideration the existing
human rights instruments'.

The General Assembly's decision was based upon a recommendation from the CHR. The leader of the Norwegian delegation to
the Commission had told an Oslo newspaper in April that he and
other leaders of Western delegations doubted the purpose of such
a gigantic conference. They questioned whether the UN in its difficult economic situation should spend money in this way when
a special session of the General Assembly might suffice. Other
Western diplomats were said not to hide their view that the proposal was quite misguided, but, not wishing to give the impression
that they believed racism to be unimportant, they had insisted that
they had nothing against a review of the campaign.

Why did many non-Western states favour the convening of a
conference? It could be said that the programmes for the first two

decades had included conferences and that therefore the third should also. But what had those conferences achieved? Some states may have considered that they had been worthwhile, though many of them may have been states that made little contribution to their financing (for many UN activities the attendance of delegations from poor states and by NGOs depends upon subventions). It could be honestly maintained that a special session of the General Assembly, if properly prepared, could conduct just as good a review far more economically. The reasons for wanting a conference will have been varied, but it is probable that underlying them will have been the reaction to unequal development. The relative wealth of Western countries and the relative poverty of African countries influences attitudes in so many circumstances, even if unconsciously. Westerners are suspected of believing themselves superior, not always with justification. Rational differences of opinion about such questions as how best to promote economic growth or to combat racial prejudice cannot always be separated from a consciousness of physical differences and from the suspicion that Western views are racially motivated. Unsurprisingly, those who feel that they have been victimized wish to correct the balance. Thus the pressure for a World Conference may have sprung in part from a desire to reproach the West for what is seen as one of its greatest failings.

Recognition of this psychological dimension may have encouraged Western states to join the consensus in favour of a conference. They may have concluded that if a substantial majority favoured such a proposal it would be better for them to participate in the movement and to try to influence it than to remain on the sidelines. Moreover they may themselves have regarded racial discrimination as an evil and have seen this as an opportunity to publicize what they were contributing to the struggle against it.

Alternatives

If there was to be a review, how might it best be conducted? An answer had to depend upon the conception of the evil that was to be combated. According to the first of the two theses described at the end of chapter 3, racial discrimination is a crime-like form of behaviour resembling other forms of discrimination prohibited under Article 26 of the ICCPR. According to the second thesis, racial discrimination is a manifestation of a social pathology, often called racism, that is characteristic of certain forms of society, as implied by the preambular paragraphs of the ICERD.

Someone conducting a review from the standpoint of Thesis One might have maintained that the most effective measures would be those taken by states to implement the Convention within their own jurisdictions. A review had therefore to start from a consideration of the willingness of states to accept and fulfil obligations under the ICERD, from an assessment of how well the monitoring body, CERD, discharged its duties, and the attention that states parties, individually and collectively, paid to its recommendations. In present circumstances the UN is not capable of carrying out such a review. It would be too difficult to organize. The foreign policies of the various states are oriented towards other priorities; they insist on preserving their independence of action and resist attempts to tighten international supervision of the extent to which they discharge their treaty obligations. This in turn limits the extent to which any world conference can be truly action-oriented and focus on practical measures.

As the discussion of the three decades in chapter 3 has shown, many states prefer to see racial discrimination as a matter for their foreign policies, and wish to minimize opportunities for other states to criticize their domestic policies. They close their eyes to the Article 26 conception of racial discrimination as crime-like, a normal feature of society to be expected wherever humans are distinguished by race or ethnic origin. They prefer the Thesis Two conception because it enables them to assert that racism is a pathology of Western society that is absent from their country or their region.

Drafting

The climax of a UN World Conference is the adoption of a Declaration and Programme of Action. The General Assembly appointed the high commissioner for human rights as secretary-general of the Conference and invited her to draw up a draft Declaration and Programme of Action for its consideration. This was to be based on the regional preparatory meetings and expert seminars, and on the suggestions of UN member states, specialized agencies, treaty bodies and concerned NGOs. Experience shows that drafting has to begin about a year in advance, with preparatory meetings following the regional ones, so that a relatively small amount is left to be decided at the conference itself. If, as in 1978, a significant number of states oppose the final proposals, they do not contribute to the growth of international law, so it is important to provide for preliminary discussion and compromises.

The preparatory committee appointed by the CHR held its first session in May 2000, when it drew up a provisional agenda for the Conference. It adopted, by consensus, five themes for consideration:

1   Sources, causes, forms and contemporary manifestations of racism, racial discrimination, xenophobia and related intolerance.
2   Victims of racism, racial discrimination, xenophobia and related intolerance.
3   Measures of prevention, education and protection aimed at the eradication of racism, racial discrimination, xenophobia and related intolerance at the national, regional and international levels.
4   Provision of effective remedies, recourse, redress, [compensatory]* and other measures at the national, regional and international levels.
5   Strategies to achieve full and effective equality, including international cooperation and enhancement of the United Nations and other international mechanisms in combating racism, racial discrimination, xenophobia and related intolerance, and follow-up.
*Delegations of the Western Group and some others accepted point 4 with the word 'compensatory' in square brackets on the basis that, in this context, and in the light of further discussions, they had the right to revisit this point.

By selecting these themes the delegations moved away from the General Assembly decision; they did not provide for a systematic review of progress and, in particular, of the application of existing standards and instruments; they postponed the difficult task of formulating the concrete recommendations for which the Assembly called. By giving priority to 'manifestations of racism' and the experience of victims they downgraded the intention that the conference should be 'action-oriented and focus on practical measures'. Nevertheless, the five themes were the basis for the planning of the four regional conferences: those of the European states in Strasbourg in October 2000, of the American states in Santiago the following December, of the African states in Dakar in January, and of the Asian states in Tehran in February. The reports from the four conferences may be compared in order to note the variations in their assumptions about the nature of racism, racial discrimination, xenophobia and related intolerance (particularly that in their own regions) and the attention paid to generalities suited to the Declaration relative to specific proposals for the Programme of Action. From the perspective of Thesis One, the proposals for the Programme of Action are the more important. Once that has been settled, the Declaration can set out its rationale and situate it in a vision of how UN policy can develop. From the perspective of Thesis Two, the Declaration is the more important. Its function is seen as the formulation of principles that are to be given expression in the Programme of Action. The difficulty is that it is states that have to implement any Programme and their commitment to action is far from certain.

The report from the European Conference began with nine paragraphs explaining the context in which the conference was convened. One of them welcomed ethnic diversity as a source of social and economic vitality; another expressed the conference's belief 'that all States must acknowledge the suffering caused by slavery and colonialism. It further believes all States must reject ethnic and religious cleansing and genocide, in Europe and in other regions of the world, and work together to prevent their recurrence . . . the Holocaust must never be forgotten'. A further paragraph recognized thirteen particular problems, starting with 'the "everyday" discrimination that exists in employment, housing, education, services and so on', listing the persistence of racial discrimination both inside and outside state institutions, widespread persecution of Roma, and the proliferation of violence inspired by politically extremist groups; it ended with the observation that most of these problems were experienced in other regions also.

The document then listed sixty conclusions and recommendations of a practical character relating to national, regional and international levels. As the Conference had been convened by the COE, it had much to say about developments at the regional level, including those for the protection of national minorities, which had been made more urgent by the ethnic conflicts in the Balkans. Implicit in the text was an assumption that racism, racial discrimination, xenophobia and related intolerance were universal problems to be addressed by action to prevent discrimination between individuals as well as by governmental policies. The recommendations called upon participating states to promote the social inclusion of migrants, to monitor implementation of their own policies, and to ensure that their treatment of asylum-seekers was fully in accord with the 1951 Convention relating to the status of refugees.

The report of the Conference of the Americas included nineteen preambular paragraphs and seventy-six proposals for the Declaration. They concentrated on the American region, recognizing and admitting 'that conquest, colonialism, slavery and other forms of servitude were a source of racism', and that 'in the Americas the victims of racism, racial discrimination, xenophobia and related intolerance are the indigenous peoples, peoples of African descent, migrants and other ethnic, racial, cultural and linguistic groups or minorities affected by these scourges.' They highlighted possible action to protect the rights and interests of indigenous peoples.

Other paragraphs urged states to collect statistics on the situation of groups that were the victims of racial discrimination and on racially motivated crimes. Three paragraphs were subject to reservations on the part of Canada and the United States. Concerning references to the transatlantic slave trade, these two states maintained that it was inappropriate to apply a modern conception of international law to acts that took place centuries previously. (Canada and the USA are part of the West European and Other Group for electoral purposes at the UN but the preparatory conferences were organized on the basis of geographical regions.)

The Conference of the Americas agreed 148 draft paragraphs for the Programme of Action. One urged 'States to officially recognise the identity and rights of indigenous peoples and to adopt, *in agreement with them*, the administrative, legislative and judicial measures necessary to promote, protect and guarantee the exercise of their human rights and fundamental freedoms' (italics added). It was complemented by support for the planned American Declaration on the rights of indigenous peoples. Other paragraphs urged states 'to collect, compile, and disseminate data on the situation of groups which are victims of discrimination' and to 'request States which practised and benefited from the trans-Atlantic slave trade and the system of enslavement of Africans to initiate a constructive dialogue with people of African descent in order to identify and implement measures for ethnic and moral satisfaction and any others that may be agreed'. Canada and the United States objected to a paragraph calling for action to widen the scope of existing international instruments, maintaining that any such call was premature without the prior undertaking of an examination of the need for and scope of any new instrument.

The report from the African Conference included ten preambular paragraphs and thirty-four draft paragraphs for the Declaration. They included expression of a conviction that 'a victim-oriented approach to victims of racial discrimination at both the national and the international level' was needed. The Conference wanted protection of the victims' right to reparation and access to justice 'in the light of their vulnerable situation'. Some paragraphs may have been intended as a tacit reference to the genocide in Rwanda, unquestionably an example of racial discrimination, but the reference was minimal. These paragraphs stated that: 'external interference, mainly linked to the exploitation of minerals and the arms trade, an unfavourable international economic development and foreign debt are the main contributing factors in the spread of conflicts and instability in Africa.' They recalled 'the historical fact' that the racial discrimination suffered by 'the African continent and Diaspora' in the slave trade and colonial rule was 'essentially motivated by economic objectives and competition between colonial powers', for which they wanted 'an explicit apology'. One paragraph referred to racial discrimination against migrant workers 'practiced in certain countries' in terms suggesting that it was directed against Europe, ignoring the discrimination against immigrant workers in African countries.

The African Conference agreed twenty-four paragraphs containing proposals for the Programme of Action. They recommended an international compensation scheme for victims of the slave trade, a development reparation fund, and two proposals for following up the conclusions of the World Conference. One was to be the appointment of a unit of five eminent persons from the different regions to supervise implementation of what had been agreed. The other was to be 'an international mechanism' to gather information about 'racial acts', maintain a website, and provide support to victims. How this would relate to the work of CERD was not explained, though states were advised to improve their arrangements for implementing this body's recommendations.

The report from the Asian Conference included twenty-nine preambular paragraphs and fifty-eight draft paragraphs for the projected Declaration. Some related to the situation in Palestine but these were not integrated into the conception of racism, racial discrimination, xenophobia and related intolerance, the prime sources of which were said to be colonialism and slavery. One paragraph rejected 'the concept of regional fortresses, bolstered by political and economic accords amongst some developed countries, that generate a climate in which foreigners are readily discriminated against'. On Palestine, the Asian states 'affirmed that a foreign occupation founded on settlements, its laws based on racial discrimination . . . constitute . . . a crime against humanity, a form of genocide and a serious threat to international peace and security'. They reemphasized the responsibility to provide international protection for the Palestinian people. Another paragraph recognized the increase in international migration and stressed that: 'policies towards such migration from the South to the North should not be based on discrimination', but failed to acknowledge that there is as much migration between Asian countries as from South to North, and that there is discrimination against migrants within Asian countries. Nor did the report acknowledge discrimination based upon descent within Asian societies, although delegations will have been aware of moves to publicize at the World Conference evidence of caste-based discrimination against Dalits in India and Burakumin in Japan. There was no reference to racially motivated violence within the region (as was exemplified by the attacks on ethnic Chinese in Indonesia at the time of the currency crisis).

The Asian Conference agreed forty-two paragraphs concerning proposals for the Programme of Action. Nearly all of them began by recommending that the conference should 'urge states', 'encourage states' or 'request states' to take action. Nothing was said about improving state compliance with obligations under the ICERD. Exhortation apart, the only practical measure envisaged was that the Conference should call upon the General Assembly 'to undertake a comprehensive review of the implementation of the Declaration and Plan of Action'.

The African and Asian regional conferences started work on the basis of texts drawn up in Geneva by diplomats of their respective groups. A fairly familiar pattern was becoming evident: some states, or their representatives, either do not understand the relevance of the human rights treaties or lack confidence in legal measures designed to bind all participating states equally in the attainment of common objectives. They prefer the political route to the legal one. As indicated in chapter 3, the political route derives its authority from the UN Charter and has the advantage of imposing certain minimum obligations on all UN member states. The legal route derives its authority from treaty obligations, which are more extensive, while their fulfilment is monitored by a treaty body far more effectively than the political institutions, like the CHR, can monitor Charter obligations. The World Conference offered an opportunity to reinforce the authority and activity of the ICERD and its monitoring body, yet some diplomats, meeting in Geneva (of all places!), were either blind to this or chose to evade it.

The report from the European Conference was action-oriented, proposing practical measures. The other regional Conference reports were more hortatory in tone. None of them took proper account of the provisions in the ICERD or included any suggestions for more effective implementation. The African regional Conference was opened by the president of Senegal, who appealed to Africans to address ethnic conflicts in their own continent. Migrant workers from Burkina Faso, he said, were treated worse in Ivory Coast than black men in Europe. He maintained that it would be wrong to build an anti-racist racism and described the demand for reparations as childish. His remarks evoked the looting of Senegalese shops in the capital of Ivory Coast but passed unheeded by the conference delegates. The Africa editor of *The Economist* (Dowden, 2001) described the call for reparations as an attempt to play on Western feelings of guilt and on ignorance of history. The image of whites capturing Africans for enslavement was false. The slave business, from capture to sale on the coast, was in the hands of Africans and the trade began when surplus slaves were sold in exchange for manufactured goods. The Europeans built forts along the coast for protection from other Europeans, not from Africans. Any compensation should be paid by the perpetrators, that is, by 'the African kingdoms, such as the Ashante in Ghana, who captured and sold them'. The record of African governments in using aid money to bring progress to their peoples was not a good one. 'They have stolen quite a lot of it.' For the foreseeable future, he wrote, Africa is an agricultural exporting region. 'If we want to help Africa, a little bit of well-targeted aid will be helpful, but it is far more important to give Africa the chance to earn its living in a fair marketplace.' Western governments that subsidized their own farmers should stop insisting that African governments cut subsidies on food and force their farmers to pay the full costs of fuel, fertilizer and transport. This debate about slavery then took another turn when, shortly afterwards, there was extensive publicity about the numbers of children who, in West Africa, were sold into slavery on the plantations in other West African countries.

Any positions that states adopt in the drafting process are influenced by estimations of the positions likely to be taken by others. A delegation may well remain silent during discussion of issues that are not very important to it in the hope that its views will be shown more respect when it indicates that it is obliged to intervene. A delegation that believes the whole enterprise of a World Conference on racism to be misguided, or that reacts against what it perceives as hostility or stupidity on the part of other delegations, may feel quiet satisfaction when time is spent debating inessentials. A Declaration that is short and coherent has a greater impact than one that is lengthy and verbose, so a cynically disposed delegation will not object if, to please particular interest groups, a draft text is continually expanded to incorporate marginal issues and thereby loses bite.

In parallel with each regional conference of state representatives there was an NGO forum that drafted its own recommendations. NGOs also held a preparatory consultation in Geneva in January. The priority given to consideration of 'Sources [of] . . . contemporary manifestations of racism' was heartily endorsed by many NGOs that wished to put the blame for contemporary discrimination upon colonialism and the transatlantic slave trade of the eighteenth and early nineteenth centuries. A representative of the International League for Human Rights recognized this stress and attempted to correct it when explaining:

We wish to emphasise that the roots of aggressive nationalism and ethnocentrism flourishing in Russia differ from the roots of racism caused by the colonial past, slavery and the slave trade in other countries. Rather, these manifestations of racism are connected to Russia's imperial past, a persistent xenophobia, enmity and intolerance of 'other' culture, other ways of life, and those who differ from the customary language, beliefs and traditions. The growth of these phenomena in our region in recent years has led to serious and massive violations of human rights, hatred, discrimination, and persecution targeted at specific groups such as representatives of the peoples of the Caucasian region of Russia.

Any attempt to determine the sources of racism in Rwanda, Indonesia, or the occupied territories of Palestine, or of that directed against Roma in Europe, was bound to be controversial. Neither an assembly of diplomats nor a meeting of NGO representatives is qualified to identify such sources. Historians and social scientists who have specialized in the study of such matters might agree on many of the relevant facts but would be unable to agree upon the allocation of responsibility for the abuses. Discussion of sources can only detract from the desire to be action-oriented and to focus on practical measures.

In March there was a meeting of a working group appointed by the Commission's preparatory committee. This considered a secretariat draft synthesizing the proposals for the Declaration so far received, paying most attention to those supported from more than one region. The draft consisted of a forty-two-paragraph draft Declaration and a 108-paragraph draft Programme of Action. Proposed actions at the national level occupied eighty-nine paragraphs, divided into sections on policies, education, prevention, the Internet, the media, poverty, youth, women, children, disadvantaged groups, migration, asylum, minorities, Roma, indigenous issues, remedies and impunity. Proposed actions at the regional level took only two paragraphs, while those at the international level needed sixteen. Some delegates complained that their special interests were not fairly reflected, as when one from Syria queried why anti-Semitism and the Holocaust should be mentioned five times but Islamophobia and anti-Arab racism only once. Many of the delegations from Arab and Muslim states (even Iraq) wanted mention of military occupation listed as an arena of extreme racism. Nothing in the proposals emanating from the regional conferences suggested any tightening of the oversight of state action. Nor did anything survive from the European and American proposals for monitoring government policies and for collecting better statistics.

The preparatory committee met for a second time in May. Its session was attended by representatives of 136 member states, Palestine, twenty-one UN and inter-governmental institutions (including the ILO, UNESCO, World Bank, World Health Organization (WHO), and the Red Cross), two national human rights institutions and 185 NGOs. It began by considering NGO requests for accreditation, but, finding that it could make little progress on some requests, planned to postpone the issue while allowing interim accreditation. The Asian group agreed to postponement but not to interim accreditation. A day of procedural wrangling ensued. Eventually all the requests were approved except for one from a Chinese and one from a Sri Lankan NGO. A group of Latin American NGOs circulated a protest expressing 'profound preoccupation that one week has passed and no substantive advance has been achieved' and denouncing 'the unproductive form that characterised the work and the interminable delays in the treatment of substantive questions . . . which seems conceived to make the Conference fail'. The preparatory committee had drafts with over 600 paragraphs of text to negotiate; it succeeded in agreeing twenty-five. There seemed little prospect of agreement upon two sections of the draft Declaration; one concerned the claim to reparations, to which countries like Britain, the US and Canada were firmly opposed. Some states thought the demand for reparations so much in their interest that they were willing, indeed apparently eager, to use the issue to force the Western states to withdraw from the Conference. The other hotly disputed section of the draft was that including references to racial discrimination against Palestinians in the Middle East. Further meetings were arranged to consider these passages, plus a third preparatory committee at the beginning of August, but as time passed it looked as if some states might prefer a symbolic victory at the conference at the expense of an effective Programme of Action. In late July the US government therefore invited representatives from some twenty-eight countries to a meeting at which it explained its objections to these references in the prevailing draft, adding that it would await the outcome of the third preparatory committee before deciding whether to be represented at the World Conference.

The second preparatory committee was also an opportunity for bargaining among NGOs. Organizations lobbying for inclusion in the Declaration and Programme of Action of passages relating to the Dalits and caste discrimination were promised support from African NGOs if they would support the African demand for reparations, while NGOs sympathetic to the position of the Indian government were willing to trade their support in return for the exclusion of references to caste.

Durban 2001

The third preparatory committee was unable to resolve the most contentious issues. Negotiations on them continued throughout the Conference. The participants included 2,300 representatives from 163 countries, including sixteen heads of state, fifty-eight foreign ministers and forty-four ministers. Nearly 4,000 representatives of NGOs and over 1,100 media personnel were registered. In all some 18,000 passes were issued. Most Western states postponed any decision about whether they would be represented by their foreign ministers, and, dissatisfied with the lack of progress over the draft texts, eventually sent junior ministers.

In June the high commissioner had established an 'Eminent Persons Group' of twenty-one, including Jimmy Carter and Mikhail Gorbachev, and with Nelson Mandela as president. The African states had recommended that such a group might follow up implementation of the Declaration and Programme of Action by states. It was announced just before the Conference that one of its members, the chief rabbi of Britain, was withdrawing his support for the group and the Conference because the final draft of the Declaration 'demeans Jewish suffering by referring to the Nazi Holocaust with a lower case "h", compares Zionism to racism and condemns Israel's policy towards Palestinians'.

State representatives met in the main Conference. NGOs held a parallel forum alongside in marquees erected in the cricket stadium. There were emotional parades with many sorts of banner, including 'landlessness = racism' and 'Muslim lesbians against racism'. At fringe meetings there were angry confrontations at which both Israeli and Jewish representatives were subject to racial abuse and physical harassment. The NGO forum was organized on the basis of some twenty-six to thirty groups or caucuses that drafted sections for the NGO Declaration and proposed Programme of Action. Some of these were special interest groups that tried to bring their concerns within the scope of the Conference and its reference to 'related intolerance'. The groups included: Africans and African Descendants, Slave Trade and Slavery, Reparations, Antisemitism, Asians and Asian Descendants, Caste, Criminal Justice, Disabilities, Education, Ethnic and National Minorities, Environmental Racism, Gender, Globalisation, Hate Crimes, Health, Indigenous Peoples, Labour, Migrants, Palestinians, Refugees, Religious Intolerance, Roma, Sexual Orientation, Young People, the Girl Child, and Trafficking in Persons.

The work of the caucuses was influenced by their composition. Groups that had been able to raise their own funds or were supported by friendly governments were represented in strength, like the Palestinians and the Dalits. Others, like the Kurds, had relatively few representatives. EU contributions were used to support participation from developing countries. The UK government contributed financial support to the NGO Forum and the Youth Forum as well as to the main conference; it funded the participation of community and NGO representatives. However, governmental support was not always altruistic. NGOs from some non-European countries complained of opposition from NGOs that were organized by the governments they wished to criticize.

The NGO Declaration was a document of 193 paragraphs. Its direction was set in paragraph 8 of the preamble, which, in line with Thesis Two, started: 'Recognising that racism, racial discrimination, genocide, slavery, xenophobia and related intolerances are based on an ideological construct that assigns a certain group of persons a position of political, economic and social power over others through notions of racial superiority, colour, identity, dominance, purity, and majority status'.

The expansive conception of their remit was illustrated by paragraph 28's recognition of 'environmental racism as a form of racial discrimination which refers to exploitation and depletion of natural resources and any environmental policy, practice, action or inaction that intentionally or unintentionally disproportionately harms the health, eco-systems, and livelihood of nations, communities or groups, or individuals, and in particular the poor'. Paragraph 38 was equally expansive in 'recognising homophobia as a particular form of discrimination and a form of multiple discrimination that makes gay, lesbian, bisexual and transgendered persons even more vulnerable to all forms of violence, including hate crimes and racialised violence'.

The NGO representatives declared:

> We extend our solidarity to the struggle for self-determination for people of Palestine, West Sumatra, Aceh-Sumatra, Bougainville, Nagaland, Assam, Meghalaya, Manipur, Tripura, North Cyprus, and other states and indigenous communities including the Kurdish people, the indigenous people in the north east of India and in the north east of Sri Lanka, in Tibet, Kashmir, Bhutan, Mindanao and the non-independent countries of the Caribbean like Puerto Rico.

Elsewhere they expressed their concern for other groups, including the Uyghur people of East Turkestan. They stated that the development of Africa had been greatly impeded by the slave trade, slavery and colonialism, which were crimes against humanity; they demanded that the USA, Canada and those European and Arab nations that had benefited from the transatlantic slave trade establish a compensatory mechanism.

The NGOs' proposed Programme of Action began by reiterating the conception of racism, racial discrimination and xenophobia as acting entities that: 'mutate, re-invent and continue to manifest themselves in contemporary societies'. It went on to call, *inter alia*, for the restructuring of the UN Security Council, the supervision of transnational corporations, the abolition of the death penalty, the representation of persons with disabilities in the decision-making process of states at all levels, and protection of the fundamental rights of all people to clean air, land, water, food and safe and decent housing. It asserted that: 'any qualification of the right of Indigenous Peoples to self-determination is racist' and recommended: 'Repeal those laws that criminalise consensual same-sex relations.' It did not consider whether any of these problems might be tackled more effectively by regional institutions. Some seventy NGOs, headed by groups from Eastern Europe, distanced themselves from the text adopted.

The Declaration

The Conference opened on a Friday. The following Monday, despairing over the prospective condemnation of Israel, the USA and Israel withdrew their delegations. The African group, having been lobbied hard by African-American single issue campaigners, stiffened their demand for specific apologies from named European countries. The atmosphere soured. The concerns of many victim groups were lost in the acrimony over Israel and over reparations. In the political negotiations the African group had overplayed its hand; it had either to settle for what it could get or go away without an agreement. In the end, the Conference had to be reconvened a day after it had officially finished so that a Declaration and a Programme of Action could be formally adopted.

Following the UN's established pattern, the Declaration was divided into preambular and operative paragraphs (UN, A/CONF.189/12). The preamble consisted of thirty-eight unnumbered paragraphs setting out the background. A section entitled 'General Issues' preceded five sections recapitulating the agreed themes. Thus the first was 'Sources, Causes, Forms and Contemporary Manifestations of Racism, Racial Discrimination, Xenophobia and Related Intolerance'; it included the following paragraphs on what had been a contentious issue:

13. We acknowledge that slavery and the slave trade, including the transatlantic slave trade, were appalling tragedies in the history of humanity not only because of their abhorrent barbarism but also in terms of their magnitude, organised nature and especially their negation of the essence of the victims and further acknowledge that slavery and the slave trade are crimes against humanity and should always have been so, especially the transatlantic slave trade, and are among the major sources and manifestations of racism, racial discrimination, xenophobia and related intolerance, and that Africans and peoples of African descent, Asians and peoples of Asian descent and indigenous peoples were victims of these acts and continue to be victims of their consequences;

14. We recognize that colonialism has led to racism, racial discrimination, xenophobia and related intolerance, and that Africans and peoples of African descent, and peoples of Asian descent and indigenous peoples were victims of colonialism and continue to be victims of its consequences. We acknowledge the suffering caused by colonialism and affirm that, wherever and whenever it occurred, it must be condemned and its reoccurrence prevented. We further regret that the effects and persistence of these structures and practices have been among the factors contributing to lasting social and economic inequalities in many parts of the world today;

21. We express our deep concern that socio-economic development is being hampered by widespread internal conflicts which are due, among other causes, to gross violations of human rights, including those arising from racism, racial discrimination, xenophobia and related intolerance, and from lack of democratic, inclusive and participatory governance;

22. We express our concern that in some States political and legal structures or institutions, some of which were inherited and persist today, do not correspond to the multi-ethnic, pluricultural and plurilingual characteristics of the population and, in many cases, constitute an important factor of discrimination in the exclusion of indigenous peoples;

23. We fully recognize the rights of indigenous peoples consistent with the principles of sovereignty and territorial integrity of States, and therefore stress the need to adopt the appropriate constitutional, administrative, legislative and judicial measures, including those derived from applicable international instruments;

24. We declare that the use of the term 'indigenous peoples' in the Declaration and Programme of Action of the World Con-

ference against Racism, Racial Discrimination, Xenophobia and Related Intolerance is in the context of, and without prejudice to the outcome of, ongoing international negotiations on texts that specifically deal with this issue, and cannot be construed as having any implications as to rights under international law;

29. We strongly condemn the fact that slavery and slavery-like practices still exist today in parts of the world and urge States to take immediate measures as a matter of priority to end such practices, which constitute flagrant violations of human rights.

The second section, on victims, included:

42. We emphasize that, in order for indigenous peoples to freely express their own identity and exercise their rights, they should be free from all forms of discrimination, which necessarily entails respect for their human rights and fundamental freedoms. Efforts are now being made to secure universal recognition for those rights in the negotiations on the draft declaration on the rights of indigenous peoples, including the following: to call themselves by their own names; to participate freely and on an equal footing in their country's political, economic, social and cultural development; to maintain their own forms of organization, lifestyles, cultures and traditions; to maintain and use their own languages; to maintain their own economic structures in the areas where they live; to take part in the development of their educational systems and programmes; to manage their lands and natural resources, including hunting and fishing rights; and to have access to justice on a basis of equality;

43. We also recognize the special relationship that indigenous peoples have with the land as the basis for their spiritual, physical and cultural existence and encourage States, wherever possible, to ensure that indigenous peoples are able to retain ownership of their lands and of those natural resources to which they are entitled under domestic law;

44. We welcome the decision to create the Permanent Forum for Indigenous Issues within the United Nations system, giving concrete expression to major objectives of the International Decade of the World's Indigenous People and the Vienna Programme of Action;

45. We welcome the appointment by the United Nations of the Special Rapporteur on the situation of human rights and fundamental freedoms of indigenous people and express our commitment to cooperate with the Special Rapporteur;

58. We recall that the Holocaust must never be forgotten;

63. We are concerned about the plight of the Palestinian people under foreign occupation. We recognize the inalienable right of the Palestinian people to self-determination and to the establishment of an independent state and recognize the right to security for all States in the region, including Israel, and call upon all States to support the peace process and bring it to an early conclusion;

68. We recognize with deep concern the ongoing manifestations of racism, racial discrimination, xenophobia and related intolerance, including violence, against Roma/Gypsies/Sinti/Travellers and recognize the need to develop effective policies and implementation mechanisms for their full achievement of equality.

The third section, on measures of prevention, included:

77. We affirm that universal adherence to and full implementation of the International Convention on the Elimination of All Forms of Racial Discrimination are of paramount importance for promoting equality and non-discrimination in the world;

79. We firmly believe that the obstacles to overcoming racial discrimination and achieving racial equality mainly lie in the lack of political will, weak legislation and lack of implementation strategies and concrete action by States, as well as the prevalence of racist attitudes and negative stereotyping;

89. We note with regret that certain media, by promoting false images and negative stereotypes of vulnerable groups and individuals, particularly of migrants and refugees, have contributed to the spread of xenophobic and racist sentiments among the public and in some cases have encouraged violence by racist individuals and groups;

90. We recognize the positive contribution that the exercise of the right to freedom of expression, particularly by the media and new technologies, including the Internet, and full respect for the freedom to seek, receive and impart information can make to the fight against racism, racial discrimination, xenophobia and related intolerance; we reiterate the need to respect the editorial independence and autonomy of the media in this regard;

91. We express deep concern about the use of new information technologies, such as the Internet, for purposes contrary to respect for human values, equality, non-discrimination, respect for others and tolerance, including to propagate racism, racial hatred, xenophobia, racial discrimination and related intolerance, and that, particularly, children and youth having access to this material could be negatively influenced by it.

The fourth section, on remedies, included:

99. We acknowledge and profoundly regret the massive human sufferings and the tragic plight of millions of men, women and children caused by slavery, slave trade, transatlantic slave trade, apartheid, colonialism and genocide and call upon States concerned to honour the memory of victims of past tragedies and affirm that wherever and whenever these occurred they must be condemned and their reoccurrence prevented. We regret that these practices and structures, political, socio-economic and cultural, have led to racism, racial discrimination, xenophobia and related intolerance;

100. We acknowledge and profoundly regret the untold suffering and evils inflicted on millions of men, women and children as a result of slavery, slave trade, transatlantic slave trade, apartheid, genocide and past tragedies. We further note that some States have taken the initiative to apologize and have paid reparation where appropriate, for grave and massive violations committed;

101. With a view to closing those dark chapters of History and as a means of reconciliation and healing, the Conference invites the international community and its members to honour the memory of victims of these tragedies. We further note that some have taken the initiative of regretting or expressing remorse or presenting apologies, and calls on all those who have not yet contributed to restoring the dignity of the victims to find appropriate ways to do so and, to this end, we appreciate those countries that have done so.

The fifth section, on strategies, included:

118. We welcome the catalytic role that non-governmental organisations play in promoting human rights education and raising awareness about racism, racial discrimination, xenophobia and related intolerance. They can also play an important role in raising awareness of such issues in the relevant bodies of the United Nations, based upon their national, regional or international experiences. Bearing in mind the difficulties they face, we commit ourselves to creating an atmosphere conducive to the effective functioning of non-governmental human rights organisations.

The Declaration was not forward-looking. In so far as it commented on past events it should surely have referred to the ethnically based genocide in Rwanda, which led to the slaughter of about a million people. Its paragraphs on the rights of indigenous peoples lay foundations for further improvements, but the innocuous nature of most of the remainder recalls the old Latin tag about the mountain going into labour and giving birth to a mouse. The declaration omitted much that some groups had wished it to feature. For example, until a late stage it included, in draft paragraph 109, a resolve 'to ensure that all necessary constitutional, legislative and administrative measures, including appropriate forms of affirmative action, are in place to prohibit and redress discrimination on the basis of work and descent'. This was directed against discrimination based on caste and the kind of discrimination suffered by the Burakumin in Japan. To progress, it needed the sponsorship of a state. India exerted heavy diplomatic pressure upon those states that at one time or another undertook sponsorship; it then secured support for amendments that would have weakened the paragraph so much that its supporters allowed it to be dropped.

The Programme of Action

The Programme of Action is not what might be expected from a document with such a title. It does not say who is to do what, when and how. It follows the five themes, but of the 219 paragraphs, some of them long, all but forty-four are addressed to states, and are mostly hortatory. It looks as if, in order to satisfy particular delegations, material was included even when it duplicated other passages. A good editor, if permitted, could have reduced the document to a quarter of its length.

A systematic Programme would have paused over the first theme, the sources of racism, because any proposal for remedy must rest on a diagnosis of the condition to be remedied. The text provides none. There are simply two paragraphs urging states to co-operate and to end enslavement. The section on victims pleads for action on behalf of Africans and people of African descent, for the protection of the rights of indigenous peoples, migrants, refugees, those subject to trafficking in persons, Roma, people of Asian descent, minorities and disabled persons; it urges states to guarantee the equal right of all children to the immediate registration of birth, to recognize that sexual violence has been used as a weapon of war, and to end impunity for abusers of human rights.

The section on prevention constitutes almost half the Programme of Action and includes much that would have been better placed in the Declaration. It urges states to reinforce existing international human rights standards and conventions and to establish commissions to oversee their implementation. It commends affirmative action and the UNESCO Slave Route Project. It urges states to act against discrimination in the workplace and in health care and to promote equal participation in decision-making. It underlines the responsibility of politicians. While welcoming the positive contribution of new communications technologies, it calls for action to prevent the dissemination of racism on the Internet. Many of these paragraphs fail to take account of the variations in circumstances between developed and undeveloped states. For example, the proposals for the collection of statistics to monitor action against racism are quite beyond the capacities of many states.

The section on remedies first focuses on the reduction of inequality in development and then stresses the significance of the availability to victims of legal remedies for racial discrimination. Like many earlier passages it traverses the ground covered by CERD in monitoring implementation of the Convention without recognizing the duplication. The final section, on strategies, urges states to support, or establish, regional institutions to combat racism. To follow up its recommendations the Conference proposes that the chairman of the CHR nominate five independent experts, one from each region, to report annually on their implementation. There is no consideration of how this would avoid duplication of the work of the special rapporteur on racism and xenophobia or of CERD. If the proposal is implemented it will lead to a diversion of scarce resources that could have been used to reinforce the monitoring of the implementation of treaty obligations.

The core of any UN Programme of Action has, necessarily, to be the action against racial discrimination; action against xenophobia and related intolerance can be seen as additional to this central element. In evaluating the various Conference proposals, it is necessary to ask what implementation of them would entail that is not already covered by implementation of the ICERD. The answer must depend upon the practicalities. For example, one of the first paragraphs:

4. Urges States to facilitate the participation of people of African descent in all political, economic, social and cultural aspects of society and in the advancement and economic development of their countries, and to promote a greater knowledge of and respect for their heritage and culture.

The ICERD is an inter-state contract. States need to know what obligations they assume when they ratify it. New obligations have to be compatible with existing ones, such as the obligations not to treat people unequally on account of their ethnic origin. Who is to decide, and how, whether a state has facilitated the desired participation of people of African descent and promoted respect for their heritage? If account is taken of the practicalities, it must be concluded that the Programme of Action adds relatively little to the scope of the Convention.

A systematic Programme would have begun by reviewing what has been learned about the elimination of racial discrimination since the Convention came into force in 1969. Have the states parties at their meetings done all that they should? Could CERD's fulfilment of its obligations be improved? What resources are needed for a treaty body to function optimally? A review must surely conclude that the task requires a division of labour involving action at different levels. At the international level, the mandate of the special rapporteur of the CHR should complement the work of CERD and not overlap with it. Contributions should be solicited from the specialized agencies to ensure that the programme is comprehensive. At the regional level, additional institutions are needed to complement the international ones, because the experience accumulated in the struggle against racial discrimination is now too diverse for a single international committee to master. On the basis of its examination of one country's report, CERD can advise a state on the kinds of policy it thinks desirable, but a regional body like ECRI may be able to call upon more detailed knowledge of local circumstances. At the national level action must fulfil international and regional obligations.

A proper division of labour would also have to cover the various fields of social life. To attain the General Assembly's fourth objective (p. 142), those charged to increase the effectiveness of UN activities needed to engage in dialogue with the UN's specialized agencies. In the case of the ILO, they needed to examine the research described in chapter 3 (pp. 57–8) and discuss with those responsible the best ways of extending it to other countries and of moving forward from it. Comparable discussions with the WHO, the International Organization for Migration and the UN Research Institute for Social Development would be needed.

The effects of residential segregation are of special concern in Western countries, but they are relevant to other regions also. In many cities there is a physical separation between the localities in which the rich people live and those where the poor are housed. This separation excludes the poorer people from many facilities. Migrants to the cities settle in the poorest localities, so that differences of colour and ethnic origin are compounded with differences of social class. The Habitat Agenda adopted at the UN Conference on Human Settlements in 1996 highlighted the priority due to the avoidance of discrimination in settlement patterns but failed to underline the way in which patterns of inequality, once established, can then be a major cause of the transmission of inequality from one generation to the next. Habitat, as a UN agency, should have been encouraged to give these problems greater priority in connection with the avoidance of racial discrimination. Experimental research into what happens to would-be house purchasers or those seeking to rent apartments could be modelled on the ILO research into discrimination in the workplace.

The discussions with UNESCO should have been intensive because there are so many distinct problems to consider. Article 7 of the ICERD requires states parties to adopt immediate and effective measures to combat racial prejudices but it is a matter of common observation in Western countries that pupils can attend schools that follow an appropriate curriculum but nevertheless in their adolescent years adopt the prejudices of the surrounding community. UNESCO could have been requested to synthesize knowledge about how to reduce prejudice. Sometimes the most important educational measures are not those in schools but are training programmes for persons in particular occupations, such as law enforcement officials. Policies to combat racist ideology need to identify and address the reasons why certain kinds of person are attracted to such doctrines and movements. Within such programmes, it can be helpful to publicize examples of good practice and to draw up codes of practice. UNESCO's mandate also relates to the mass media and to sport, both fields of social life important to action against racial discrimination.

The Declaration and Programme of Action do not reflect the contribution of social science over the preceding half-century to the understanding of the nature of racial discrimination and of the more effective means for combating it. It was UNESCO's responsibility, in collaboration with bodies like the International Sociological Association, to feed this knowledge into the preparatory process. The attempt should have been made, even though it might well have been disregarded by state delegations. When delegations are clear what they want, and have sufficient support, they will override reasonable objections. For example, the Declaration at the 1983 world conference began with the paragraph: 'All human beings are born equal in dignity and rights. Any doctrine of racial superiority is, therefore, scientifically false.' The first sentence states a moral principle; the second attempts to derive from it a factual conclusion, which is logically impossible. Political considerations took precedence.

The Programme adopted in Durban was too generalized. A systematic Programme would have allowed for the great differences between countries related to the stages of their development, their political conditions and their environments. Oversight of its implementation would have been best delegated to an expert body able to take account of circumstances. The International Convention requires that CERD consist of eighteen experts; those who serve on such a body acquire over the years a knowledge of the problems that is much deeper than that of the diplomats who represent their governments when drafting texts for a World Conference. A Programme of Action should have synthesized the knowledge acquired in the course of monitoring implementation of the Convention and that built up by persons who have made a specialized study of the issues.

Reservations

Before the adoption of the draft Declaration and the draft Programme of Action, statements and reservations by participating states were entered into the record. Those made by the representatives of Canada and Syria were expressed in the strongest terms.

The representative of Canada declared:

> We are not satisfied with this Conference. Not enough time has been dedicated to advancing its objectives, that is, developing forward-looking, action-oriented strategies to eradicate the many forms of discrimination that exist today. Instead, too much time has been spent on an issue that does not belong here. Canada is still here today only because we wanted to have our voice decry the attempts at this Conference to de-legitimize the State of Israel and to dishonour the history and suffering of the Jewish people. We believe, and we have said in the clearest possible terms, that it was inappropriate – wrong – to address the Palestinian–Israel conflict in this forum. That is why the Canadian delegation registers its strongest objections and disassociates itself integrally from all text in this document directly or indirectly relating to the situation in the Middle East. We state emphatically that this text is *ultra vires*; it is outside the jurisdiction and mandate of this Conference . . . it is an unhelpful and irresponsible intrusion by this Conference into one of the world's most dangerous conflicts.
>
> Canada regrets that the World Conference has not been able to acknowledge that there is a close, sometimes inseparable relationship between discrimination based on religion and language and that which is based on racism and xenophobia. . . . Furthermore, it is Canada's understanding that under international law there is no right to a remedy for historical acts that were not illegal at the time at which they occurred.

Australia made a statement along similar lines; it objected that the language used to condemn colonialism should have been the same as that used to condemn apartheid and genocide. New Zealand associated itself with this objection, maintaining that only where colonialism had been founded on racist attitudes and practices could it have been a source of racism.

The representative of the Syrian Arab Republic stated that:

> Syria wished for clearer wording, especially on the Middle East – and I am speaking here about practices, not a political solution for the Middle East and Israel, because from the beginning I agreed with those colleagues who said that we were not here to find a solution – and although the Conference is not part of a peace process for the Arab–Israeli conflict, we should not forget that racist practices are being carried out in the occupied Palestinian and Arab territories.

The speaker continued:

> the Holocaust was a horrible thing, regardless of where it happened. But we must remind our European friends who are very sensitive about the Holocaust that the Holocaust happened in Europe, and was committed mostly by Europeans. To generalize it, as though the Europeans want to distribute their sense of guilt throughout the whole world, is a mistake. Let us be morally courageous enough to tell the truth: what do they mean by, 'We recall that the Holocaust must never be forgotten'? It should not be forgotten by the people who made it, who created it, who did it. We were not party to it, we have never been a party to it and we will never be a party to it, and that is why we do not accept this general term here. We would like it to be very concise and very specific and not to be applied to every nation on earth.

Iran complained that:

> all efforts made by members of the Organization of the Islamic Conference to justly address the causes of the oppressed Palestinian people were rendered futile in the atmosphere of intimidation, threat and ultimatum . . . the Islamic Republic of Iran would like to disassociate itself from all paragraphs pertaining to the Palestinian and Middle East issue as appear in the final documents . . . the suffering of the Palestinian people and their legitimate rights, which have been vastly and grossly violated by the occupying racist power in the course of the past 50 years, have not been given proper and due consideration.

Equally, the delegation of Iraq declared 'that it is neither a party to, nor bound by the consensus concerning the paragraphs relating to the Middle East'. With reference to the mention of anti-Semitism, Qatar observed that: 'the Member States of the Organization of the Islamic Conference stress the fact that the overwhelming majority of Semites are Arabs'.

The representatives of several Latin American countries made statements concerning the rights of indigenous peoples, while Switzerland stated:

> The World Conference has been a valuable learning experience and we wish to thank the host country, South Africa, for its enormous dedication. We have thus come to realize how important it is for many countries to retain the word and the idea of race. This can be explained by their history, which is unique and therefore different from our painful experience in Europe. The exclusively negative connotation of the word 'race' is connected with the racist and biological concepts of the last few centuries, particularly those of the Nazi period. Hence, in this context, we should emphasize that we see race as a social construct. In any event, race must never be used as a justification for discriminatory practices or to advocate ideologies of racial superiority. Switzerland therefore associates itself with the statement made in the Main Committee by the representative of Belgium on behalf of the European Union concerning the words 'race' and 'racial'.

(This is mentioned at p. 7 above.)

At the closing meeting, Kenya, speaking on behalf of the African Group, answered Western objections by observing that the Judgement of Nuremberg in 1946 'made it clear that crimes against humanity are not time bound'. Shortly afterwards the representative of Belgium, speaking on behalf of the EU plus Bulgaria, Cyprus, Czech Republic, Estonia, Hungary, Latvia, Lithuania, Malta, Poland, Romania, Slovakia, Slovenia and Turkey, insisted that:

> The Declaration and the Programme of Action are political, not legal documents. These documents cannot impose obligations, or liability, or a right to compensation, on anyone. Nor are they intended to do so. In particular, nothing in the Declaration or the Programme of Action can affect the general legal principle which precludes the retrospective application of international law in matters of State responsibility. Furthermore, the European Union has joined consensus in a reference to measures to halt and reverse the lasting consequences of certain practices of the past. This should not be understood as the acceptance of any liability for these practices, nor does it imply a change in the principles of international development cooperation, partnership and solidarity.

A calamity

If the First World Conference was a disaster, the Third was a calamity that has damaged the reputation of the UN and has set back the prospect for international co-operation in this field. The First and Second Conferences were diplomatic assemblies in Geneva. The Third was a bigger affair from which more was expected. Some governments consulted carefully with national NGOs and funded their participation in the NGO meetings at which men and women committed to conflicting conceptions of the anti-racist cause contended with one another. The publicity was so much greater than that for the previous conferences that the disappointment must be the more serious.

Of the seven main objectives decided by the General Assembly, the Conference attained only the third, 'to increase the level of awareness about the scourges of racism'. Domestic political considerations explain only in small part why so many governments treated the Conference as a political arena in which they attempted to impose additional responsibilities on other states without accepting any themselves. They overestimated what they could achieve by taking the political route and (in part because they know too little about them) underestimated the long-term gains to be obtained by improving the application of the standards and instruments to which the General Assembly's second objective referred. The NGOs as a group might have helped correct this had they publicized the benefits to be obtained from better oversight of treaty obligations, but most of them also preferred to pursue political agendas. All governments should have learned from the previous conferences that a majority vote is worth little when a Conference has no power to enforce its decisions. In evaluating voting patterns it has to be remembered that forty-four member states have populations of under one million. Some are client states whose votes can be bought by the promise of development aid. The governments arguing for reparations should have learned from the meetings of the preparatory committee that they could not secure a consensus for the statements they wanted, yet, despite many warnings, they persisted to the very end.

A better Declaration could have been prepared had all regions been willing to balance an acknowledgement of racial discrimination within their own regions with their concern about its practice elsewhere. The European and American regional conferences took note of racial issues within their own regions. The African and Asian conferences did not (apart from the Asian concern with the

Palestine issue). The African group tried to define all Africans as victims; this brought certain rhetorical benefits to African governments and helped divert attention from atrocities, like those in Rwanda, for which African governments were responsible. Their strategy was to insinuate that slavery and colonialism were responsible for their lack of development, when the main reason for the slow economic growth of newly independent African states has been political mismanagement. Members of the government and their officials have used their offices to serve their private interests. These states cannot attract the investment of private capital because of the perceived risks deriving from their record of policy reversal. Africans know this well, for they hold a larger share of their wealth abroad than the citizens of any other region; by 1990, 40 per cent of African private wealth was held outside the continent (Collier, 1998:11).

The conflicts over compensation for the transatlantic slave trade and the rights of Palestinians were surface manifestations of deeper problems underlying international relations. The first such problem is that of unequal development, which becomes ever more serious as the inequality increases. African states could insinuate that slavery and colonialism were responsible for their lack of development only because the reasons for unequal development are insufficiently understood. Some of the reasons are to be found in the present regulation of world trade. Others lie within states and in the differential accumulation of human capital. History shows that the effects of economic damage can be overcome, sometimes within a generation, as was demonstrated by the economic recovery of Germany and Japan after World War II. Economists have also shown that countries that respect civil and political rights have enjoyed greater improvements in national income per head, in life expectancy at birth and in the infant survival rate (Dasgupta, 1993).

The second problem lies in the power politics that lead to double standards at the UN. Iraq is punished for not observing Security Council resolutions; Israel is not. The rights of Palestinians have been overridden because the foreign policy of the USA in the Middle East has responded to the political influence that the pro-Israel lobby exerts in the US electoral system. UN resolutions will not change this, but Israel reports on its fulfilment of its obligations as a state party to the Convention, and CERD reports the results of its examination of what the state has to say. Even in these difficult circumstances the legal route can produce a significant and practical contribution that may seem small but could be built upon. The states parties could act on the basis of the Committee's reports were they willing to accept that they, too, might be called to account. In present circumstances that is too much to hope for.

Where does the international anti-racist movement go now? Protest movements have internationalized. Since the gap between developed and undeveloped states is increasing and will continue to increase, they will surely focus on issues of unequal development, using the rhetoric of race and anti-racism when it suits their purposes. To be worthy of its name, social science has to stand aside from the political movement, though it can help by clarifying the issues for political action and by accounting for the changes in progress. These are matters addressed in the next two chapters.

9

Public Policy and Human Rights

The belief that human individuals belong naturally in races, and that this has a determining influence on their lives, offered a beguiling philosophy for Europeans and North Americans in an era of rapidly increasing globalization. Its abuse in Nazi Germany evoked an anti-racism that identified its errors, but, being negative, could not supersede it as a philosophy. Something was needed that could define the nature of the associated abuses while forming part of a positive conception of social life. That synthesis was effected in the doctrine of human rights.

The human rights treaties, and their attendant philosophy, offer the best available approach for the formulation of public policies to overcome wrong ideas about the significance of racial differences. First, in contrast to policies of anti-racism, the conception of human rights is universal. It offers protections for majorities as well as minorities; there is something for everyone. Second, it is global in scope, setting norms that are above national constitutions – norms to which national constitutions increasingly conform. Third, it is flexible, being couched in terms that enable it to apply existing principles to the resolution of problems that could not be envisaged at the time the norms were first identified. Unlike some versions of multiculturalism, it is not tied to historical conceptions of identity. Fourth, it protects individuals from the negative consequences of their being assigned to racial and ethnic categories, while recognizing that individuals' identification with such minorities can be important to their personal dignity. Yet, unlike metaphors of racial dialogue, it does not itself assign them to such categories. It starts from the rights of individuals as members of complex and changing societies.

In Europe this approach, now reinforced by regional and national law, is being employed increasingly. Other world regions could well make more use of it.

Human rights standards

Some political philosophers are not persuaded that human rights can furnish a satisfactory philosophy for regulating the problems that arise in relations between ethnic minorities and majorities. Thus Will Kymlicka (1995:4–5) observes correctly that:

> Traditional human rights standards are simply unable to resolve some of the most important and controversial questions relating to cultural minorities: which languages should be recognised in the parliaments, bureaucracies and courts? Should each ethnic or national group have publicly funded education in its mother tongue? . . . What are the responsibilities of minorities to integrate? What degree of cultural integration can be required of immigrants and refugees before they acquire citizenship?

Bhikhu Parekh (2000a:266) regards human rights as providing only a moral minimum, and contends that as they are essentially individual rights they cannot contend with cultural diversity. In looking for guiding principles, he compares international human rights with the principles of conformity with a society's core values, of avoiding harm, and of dialogue with minority spokespeople.

Human rights standards are applied and developed from case to case. The General Assembly formulates the norms. Then some interested party asks a treaty body or a tribunal to apply it to a particular set of circumstances. Standards can be applied bit by bit to the problems listed by Kymlicka but there has never been any suggestion that they could resolve such big problems in isolation from particular circumstances. For example, to consider whether under any recognized standard the speakers of a particular language have a right to use that language in a parliament, a treaty body would have to consider the nature of the obligation accepted by the state party and the relevance (including cost) of many circumstances. It would have to consider whether any restriction upon use of the language was reasonable. It could take into account the three principles mentioned by Parekh. Even when it finds that there is no established right, a treaty body or a tribunal may express an opinion on the arguments it has heard and in so doing help build an international consensus. As a rule, tribunals decide only those issues that are essential to the decision they have to reach. Other issues that may be raised in a case are usually left for some other occasion. Circumstances change in the course of time, so some of them are superseded by events. This is a kind of benign neglect that has the advantage of economy. The rule of law can be weakened if too much is demanded from laws and courts.

In place of human rights norms Kymlicka and Parekh favour philosophies that rely heavily upon the tricky concept of culture. Parekh (2000a:338) describes a 'multicultural perspective' 'composed of the creative interplay of these three complementary insights, namely the cultural embeddedness of human beings, the inescapability and desirability of cultural diversity and intercultural dialogue, and the internal plurality of each culture'. Yet when describing social patterns in industrial societies it is difficult to decide where one culture begins and another ends; much culture is shared by members of different groups. It is also necessary to give due weight to material culture and the influence of technological change. The last fifty years have seen remarkable changes in transport, with the spread of car ownership and the growth of air transport. Changes in the media of communication have been equally dramatic, with the development of television, audio and video tapes. Mass culture has been based upon forms of mass consumption, both in material goods and in entertainment, and has been sustained by improved means of exchange, such as cash machines, credit cards, faxes, email and the Internet. These innovations have weakened the influence of older institutions, like the churches and trade unions; they have reduced the power of states to control the behaviour of individuals.

A concept like culture – or, for that matter, like race or racism – exists to help explain observations. Some concepts can be used to explain a great variety of observations; others are of restricted utility. As a concept in social science, culture is useful for connoting certain variations in human ways of living, but it needs to be used with care. It cannot always carry the burden imposed upon it in discussions of multiculturalism.

In drafting standards it is important to remember that new technology is continually creating new alternatives and that circumstances change. One frequently quoted example of a problem on the national level is the second amendment to the constitution of the United States, adopted in 1791, which reads: 'A well-regulated militia being necessary to the security of a free State, the right of the people to keep and bear arms shall not be infringed.' A well-regulated militia is not necessary to the security of the modern United States and the present keeping and bearing of arms by private citizens in that country is neither well regulated nor part of a proper militia, yet vested interests have prevented any significant change in the interpretation of this law. This points to the dangers of writing into law rights that cannot be adapted to changing circumstances.

The flexibility of human rights law is illustrated by the case of *Thlimmenos* cited at p. 120. As a member of a religious minority (Jehovah's Witnesses), the applicant had refused to wear military uniform and been convicted and imprisoned for this. Later, he was excluded from becoming a chartered accountant because he was a convicted felon. Noting that the original offence did not disclose any dishonesty, the Court found no reasonable relationship of proportionality between the means employed and the aim sought to be realized by excluding him from his chosen profession. Therefore Greece had violated Article 14 of the Convention. Reference to the principle of proportionality gives human rights law a flexibility that distinguishes it from the use of constitutional law to confer specific rights on a minority. Many of the aims sought by writers like Parekh are being achieved in such ways by human rights law.

What criteria should be used in assessing my claim that human rights law and philosophy offers the best available framework for public policy concerning inter-group relations and can therefore be used to supersede the idiom of race? I suggest that there are two principal issues to be addressed, those of equality of rights and of rights to be different.

Equality in civil and political rights

The enjoyment of rights by individuals is inevitably constrained by differences between societies, particularly in their development. This sets limits to the kinds of rights that can be recognized. It would be wrong to argue for the equality of societies, given that some societies abuse human rights, but in international affairs there is no good alternative to the principle of the sovereign equality of states. That is duly acknowledged at the beginning of the second article of the UN Charter. Formally, therefore, a small state like Nauru, with a population of 8,000, is equal to a very large one like China, with a population of over 1,100 million. In 1948 there were self-governing states and 'territories whose inhabitants have not yet attained a full measure of self-government'. The Charter, in chapters XI to XIII, therefore established institutions to ensure that in their government 'the interests of the inhabitants of these territories are paramount'.

In line with this concern and with the earlier actions of the League of Nations, both Covenants open in Article 1 with the proclamation that all peoples have the right to self-determination, an article that is now to be read together with the 1970 Declaration on Principles of International Law Concerning Friendly Relations and Cooperation Among States in Accordance with the Charter of the United Nations. That Declaration refers to the protection of the territorial integrity or political unity of states 'conducting themselves in compliance with the principle of equal rights and self-determination of peoples . . . *and thus possessed of a government representing the whole people belonging to the territory without distinction as to race, creed or colour'*. One authority (Cassese, 1995:111) refers to the passage I have italicized as a saving clause. He shows that its full meaning can be discovered only by drawing upon the records of the drafting process, the *travaux préparatoires*, to ascertain why a particular formulation was preferred to other proposals considered. The right to self-determination has both an external dimension, as in the right to independence from colonial rule, and an internal dimension, the collective right to authentic self-government, to which peoples can appeal in dispute with the government of the state of which they form part. Since states were suspicious that reference might be made to self-determination in order to claim a right to secession, the clause, by reinforcing the reference to territorial integrity, saved the principle from any such interpretation. It provided that if a government represented the whole people of the territory without discrimination, then it respected the principle. More recent developments suggest that states are increasingly accepting the view that the right of self-determination should be of internal effect, providing for forms of autonomy that fall short of territorial separation (Cassese, 1995:338). They are steps towards recognition of a right to good government.

Before considering other articles, it is well to note that Article 4 permits a state to derogate from certain of its obligations in time of a public emergency that threatens the life of the nation, and that strict limits are set to this permission. Some treaties allow a state to withdraw by denouncing the treaty in question, but there is no such provision in the two Covenants; when a state ratifies one of them it binds its successors for ever.

Article 2 of the ICCPR embodies the principle of non-discrimination and obliges contracting states to ensure that any victim shall have an effective remedy. Articles 6 to 8 define the rights to life and to be free from torture and slavery. Subsequent articles set out rights to liberty, security of person and freedom of movement. Article 14 defines the right to equality before the law. Articles 18 to 22 define the freedoms of thought, expression, peaceful assembly and association. Articles 26 and 27 were described in chapter 3.

The protection of individuals from discrimination requires the legal recognition and prohibition of racial motivation. Article 26 of the ICCPR is supplemented by Article 4(a) of the ICERD, according to which a state party must make punishable certain kinds of action based on ideas of race, and therefore must provide for the application of criminal sanctions. Human rights law recognizes, better than any political philosophy, that one right can conflict with another, so that the resolution of conflicts has usually to be on a case-by-case basis. A case that came before the European Court of Human Rights (*Jersild v. Denmark* 36/1993/431/510), for example, turned on the conflict between the right to freedom of expression and the right to protection from discrimination.

In 1985 a Danish newspaper published an article about the racist attitudes of a group of young men who called themselves 'the Greenjackets'. This stimulated the Danish radio service to produce a television news item for which Mr Jersild was responsible. Rather more than two hours' interviewing of the young men provided material for a transmission lasting a few minutes. Those interviewed described some of their criminal activities, saying that they supported the Ku Klux Klan because:

> niggers . . . are not human beings, they are animals . . . that goes for all the other foreign workers as well, Turks, Yugoslavs and whatever they are called . . . they come up here and sponge on our society . . . that can't be right, Denmark is for the Danes, right? . . . what we don't like is when they walk around in those Zimbabwe-clothes and then speak this hula-hula language in the street . . . it's drugs they are selling . . . We have painted their doors and hoped that they would get fed up with it, so that they would soon leave, and jumped on their cars and thrown paint in their faces.

The youths and the journalist, Mr Jersild, together with Mr Jensen, the head of the news section of Danmarks Radio, were convicted of disseminating statements that insulted or degraded persons on account of their race, colour, national or ethnic origin. The law in question had been designed to meet the state's obligations under Article 4 of the ICERD. Jersild and Jensen were sentenced either to pay fines or to serve five days' imprisonment. Their convictions were upheld on appeal in the High Court and in the Supreme Court. On behalf of the Supreme Court's four-to-one majority judgement, one justice stated that the court had attached importance to the evidence that Jersild had himself contacted the youths and edited the recording to highlight the crude comments, which were defamatory, insulting, and broadcast to a wide circle of people. Their news or information value was not such as to justify dissemination. Reports of extremist views should be presented in a more balanced and comprehensive manner.

Mr Jersild applied to the European Court of Human Rights for a declaration that his conviction violated his right to freedom of expression within the meaning of Article 10 of the ECHR. The Court found that the only point at issue was whether the measures taken in Denmark were 'necessary to a democratic society' as stipulated in that article. It held by twelve votes to seven that in such circumstances it was not necessary to convict the disseminator of the statements of a criminal offence. According to the judgement of the majority, the Court considered the object and purpose pursued by the UN Convention to be of great weight in determining whether the conviction was necessary within the meaning of Article 10 of the ECHR. It reiterated that freedom of expression is one of the essential foundations of a democratic society; nor was it for the Court to substitute its own views for those of the press as to the technique of reporting to be adopted. The Court considered it important to ask whether the item appeared from an objective point of view to have had as its purpose the propagation of racist views and ideas. It found to the contrary that the programme sought to expose, analyse and explain the conduct of these youths by considering a matter that was already of great public concern. Four judges dissented, stating:

> The Danish courts fully recognised that protection of persons whose human dignity is attacked has to be balanced against the right to freedom of expression. They carefully considered the responsibility of the applicant, and the reasons for their conclusions were relevant. The protection of racial minorities cannot have less weight than the right to impart information, and in the concrete circumstances of the present case it is in our opinion not for this Court to substitute its own balancing of the conflicting interests for that of the Danish Supreme Court.

Three other judges dissented in stronger terms, stating:

> We cannot accept that [the freedom of expression] should extend to encouraging racial hatred, contempt for races other than the one to which we belong, and defending violence against those who belong to the races in question. It has been sought to defend the broadcast on the ground that it would provoke a healthy reaction of rejection among the viewers. That is to display an optimism, which to say the least, is belied by experience.

Arguments about freedom of expression raise sensitive issues in the international politics of race. Radio and television reporting appears to have incited racial hatred in Rwanda, Yugoslavia and some other countries. The courts, as in Denmark, are often called upon to decide whether a broadcast or an item in a newspaper has breached a norm and is to be declared illegal. Governments and official agencies may be empowered to license newspapers, radio and television stations, and to withdraw operators' licences, but there is a danger that they may use such powers for their own political ends. Any international norms must be drafted as narrowly as possible to bear in mind the possibilities of abuse by authoritarian governments as well as by private persons.

Protecting the right to equality before the law must go beyond the enactment of laws and ensure that they are equitably applied in practice. Any doubts on this score need to be settled by checks upon equality of treatment at every stage of the criminal process: arrest; prosecution; trial; availability of interpreters; counsel; jury selection; possible prejudice within juries; sentence; imprisonment; police, probation and prison services; and press reporting of proceedings. These may entail the introduction of ethnic monitoring as described in chapter 7. The rights to freedom of thought, expression and association can also be very important to members of minorities, but it is unnecessary to elaborate upon them at this point.

Equality in economic, social and cultural rights

The conflict of rights in the *Jersild* case was considered under the ECHR, a treaty that then covered civil and political rights but not economic, social and cultural rights. These have to be protected by states that are parties to the ICESCR. States parties to the ICERD are obliged in accordance with its Article 5 to protect individuals against discrimination in their exercise of both sets of rights. They can do this by the application of either criminal or civil sanctions. On p. 129, reasons were given for concluding that individuals can be protected more effectively against discrimination in employment by the use of civil procedures. The ICERD requires that whether criminal or civil procedures are used both accuser and accused must be treated fairly, and the case must be proved by reference to the appropriate legal standard of proof. If one person treats another less favourably because he or she believes the other to be of a particular race, that action is unlawful whether or not the other person is of that race. Article 2(2) defines the special measures (sometimes called affirmative action) permitted to assist members of disadvantaged groups to compete on more equal terms with the majority populations.

As already noted, when listing unlawful grounds of action the Convention refers to racial discrimination as including action on grounds of colour, descent, national origin and ethnic origin. Therefore it does not in any way diminish the range and power of the Convention as a weapon against racial discrimination if, in seeking to avoid the idiom of race, victim groups are called ethnic groups rather than racial groups. The Convention does not refer explicitly to racial disadvantage, but it can be helpful to distinguish the two since disadvantage is not necessarily caused by discrimination, and racial disadvantage is not always a product of racism. For example, children brought up speaking the language of an immigrant group, and not the national language, may be at a disadvantage in some circumstances; they may be handicapped from the start of their schooling, but no one has discriminated against them in respect of language.

On p. 37, it was noted that in 1978 the representatives of the world's states, meeting under UNESCO's auspices, agreed that: 'All individuals and groups have the right to be different, to consider themselves as different and to be regarded as such.' This right (which, since it is not clearly defined, cannot be regarded as very compelling) can be exercised in the civil or political fields only if it does not infringe the rights of others to equality of treatment. As a trivial example, an individual might claim it as a justification for attending an official function in folk costume instead of the customary formal attire. More importantly, it could be the basis of a claim made against a state on behalf of an indigenous people or a minority that they must be permitted or assisted to maintain their distinctive culture or features of such a culture. A more secure basis for any such claim is Article 26 of the ICCPR (already quoted in chapter 3), according to which: 'In those States in which ethnic, religious or linguistic minorities exist, persons belonging to such minorities shall not be denied the right, in community with the other members of their group, to enjoy their own culture, to profess and practice their own religion, or to use their own language.' An example of the way this has been used to secure a remedy can be found in the *Lovelace* case, in which Canada was found to be in breach of Article 27 because its law did not allow an Indian woman to return to her natal Indian reserve after her marriage with a non-Indian had broken down.

While, as has also been explained earlier, the UN has been unable to agree a general definition of a minority, for the implementation of Article 27 some definition is essential. The Human Rights Committee, an independent elected body of legal experts that monitors implementation of the Covenant, has addressed the issue. In its

General Comment 23, paragraph 5.2, the Committee has defined the persons on whom Article 27 confers rights:

> Just as they need not be nationals or citizens, they need not be permanent residents. Thus migrant workers or even visitors in a State party constituting such minorities are entitled not to be denied the exercise of those rights. As any other individual in the territory of the State party, they would, also for this purpose, have the general rights, for example, to freedom of association, of assembly, and of expression. The existence of an ethnic, religious or linguistic minority in a State party does not depend upon a decision by that State party but requires to be established by objective criteria.

The implications of such an approach may be considered with respect, first, to indigenous peoples, who, in general, do not wish to be regarded as minorities; second, to national minorities, who are often distinguished by their ethnic origin and their language; and third, to immigrant minorities, who may be distinguished by ethnic origin, religion and language.

Before doing so, it is advisable to note that different uses of the word 'group' can be a source of confusion. Article 27 recognizes that when there is a minority, its members may share culture, religion and language with others in such a way that they constitute a group. Sometimes it is important to distinguish a group from a social category. A social group is defined by the nature of the relations between its members (though the word 'group' is often used more loosely, as when analysts speak of 'grouping data'). A social category is a class the nature of which is determined by the person who defines it; for example, persons earning an income within a certain range may be counted as a category for tax purposes. The members of a minority may constitute either a group or a category, and Article 27 presumably uses the former word because in ordinary language it is not usually necessary to distinguish the two. The concept of a group is of a general nature and at times has to be distinguished from both an association and a community. An association is formed when individuals act together for a defined and limited purpose, sometimes of a commercial character. A community is a collection of individuals who feel bound up with one another for many purposes and are usually identified as such by others. This is grasped by the expression 'a community of fate'. These distinctions matter when considering the nature of the 'right to be different' and the nature of social units that may exercise such a right.

The political philosopher Iris Marion Young (1990:42–8) recognizes many of these distinctions, but is primarily concerned to elaborate upon the implications of a concept of oppression; it is categories of persons who are oppressed, though their experience can lead them to build groups. The same individual may be assigned to many categories and be a member of many groups, different memberships being relevant in different settings. Just as an individual may be treated as a category member contrary to his or her wishes, so may he or she decline to identify himself or herself as a member of a given group. Thus if 'social justice . . . requires . . . institutions that promote reproduction of and respect for group differences without oppression', it may not treat an individual as a member of a social category if he or she does not wish to be identified with that category. That would also be oppression, and it is oppressive to force a person to comply with obligations deriving from someone else's conception of the nature of such a category.

The nature of the group right to be different is less problematic in the case of indigenous peoples, though it is not without difficulties. The *Lovelace* case illustrated one of them. If an indigenous group exercises a right to declare that an individual has surrendered membership rights, or deprives someone of these rights, this can conflict with the state's international obligation to ensure equality of treatment. The group rights of indigenous peoples derive from their position as the original owners of the land. Some entered into treaties as equal parties with the invading groups; others could have done so. They can therefore be regarded, to follow Brian Barry (2001:188), as having become sub-state polities. The most comprehensive international agreement for the protection of the rights of indigenous peoples is the ILO Convention Concerning Indigenous and Tribal Peoples in Independent Countries, 1989 (ILO Convention 169). It obliges states parties to ensure that members of indigenous peoples benefit on an equal footing from the rights and opportunities that national law allows. Most of its provisions strive for the preservation of the identity of indigenous peoples, either by explicitly referring to customs, traditions and values of indigenous peoples, or by providing that decisions that might have an effect upon them are not taken without their consent. The case of the *Mayagna Community of Awas Tingni v. Nicaragua*, mentioned on p. 87, is a notable example of movement in this direction.

A draft Declaration on the Rights of Indigenous Peoples is under consideration by states, and the final adoption of such a Declaration is one of the goals of the International Decade of the World's Indigenous Peoples, due to end in 2004. The draft Declaration emphasizes that indigenous peoples have the right to preserve their group identity. It describes their rights to practise and revitalize their traditions and customs, to manifest, practise, develop and teach their spiritual and religious traditions, to revitalize and transmit to future generations their traditions, to have the dignity of their cultures reflected in public education, to establish their own media, to develop their social systems, to determine priorities for their development and to determine their own citizenship. It describes a specific form for the exercise of the right to self-determination. An authority on these questions (Wolfrum, 1999:382) doubts:

> whether the formulation of classical individual civil, social and cultural rights as collective rights adds substance or is meant to limit the enjoyment of individual rights. Article 34 of the Draft Declaration seems to point in the direction of the latter interpretation. It provides that indigenous peoples have the collective right to determine the responsibilities of their individual members to their communities.

Relatively few states have ratified ILO Convention 169. Australia, New Zealand, Canada and the United States have expressed serious doubts about parts of the draft UN declaration (the last two named states are also involved with proposals for a regional declaration of such rights within the Organization of American States). At UN meetings states in Asia and Africa have maintained that any Declaration must include a definition of the term 'indigenous peoples', whereas representatives of Latin American states and of the peoples themselves believe this unnecessary.

The nature of any group right to be different on the part of national minorities, and any process for invoking that kind of right, may be defined in international treaties. The Hungarian minorities in East European states that resulted from the dissolution of Austro-Hungary provide examples of such minorities. For them, Hungary counts as a 'kin state'. There are also minority nations, like the Welsh within the United Kingdom, who have no kin state but could be accounted minorities for the purposes of Article 27. It can be argued, as it was by some Welsh people in the 1970s, that in present circumstances the maintenance of a distinctive language requires a state-subsidized television channel broadcasting in that language. Since so much will depend upon the cost of any subsidy, such an issue has to be treated as a political matter, not one that can be settled by reference to a human rights standard. Certain individual rights, like those to use of a language and to visit a sacred site, can be exercised only as members of a group. If collective rights are to be conferred on a section of the population the power to exercise those rights must be controlled so that the other rights of group members are not overridden. For example, a right to education in a minority language (which may reasonably be subject to certain conditions, like the presence of enough persons wishing to exercise the right for the provision of the facilities to be an economic proposition) should not lead to a situation in which parents are obliged to send children to a minority school when they would prefer them to make use of available teaching facilities in the majority language.

Roma, or Gypsies, constitute distinctive minorities in European states, sharing some characteristics with national minorities. A case before the European Court of Human Rights, *Buckley v. UK* (23/1995/529/615), touched on the consideration given to Buckley's rights as a Gypsy. Mrs Buckley contended that she was prevented from living with her family in caravans on her own land and from following the traditional life style of a Gypsy contrary to the right to respect for private and family life in Article 8 of the ECHR. She had been unable to secure planning permission for her caravan. The Court, after investigating the circumstances, rejected the claim that the interference with her right under Article 8 could not be justified as 'necessary in a democratic society'. The interests of the community had been satisfactorily balanced against the rights of the applicant. Proceedings before tribunals allow for the examination of the circumstances in which a party advances a claim. For example, in the case of *Sally Chapman v. the UK* the applicant's claim to rights as a Gypsy, an itinerant, were weakened by her having applied for permanent residence, suggesting that she was not committed to an itinerant lifestyle.

Claims based upon the right to be different on the part of members of immigrant minorities raise further issues, the most problematic of which concern religious practice. People who before migration took their religion for granted often find that in a new country it acquires an enhanced significance. By revitalizing their faith they are able to give expression to their unease when confronting some features of the culture of the society in which they have settled. Moreover, they find it easier to organize socially and politically on the basis of their faith when the majority society accepts this as a reasonable and lawful exercise of rights in the private sphere. The inculcation of religious practice is a way in which the parental generation can encourage their children to observe values more important to their parents than to members of the majority, who are often pictured as behaving immorally. Parekh (2000a:198) is uneasy about what he calls 'the religionization of culture':

> Religion acquires a considerable influence over the development of the culture concerned, religious leaders assume undue authority, critical voices are silenced, and easily negotiable cultural demands take on a strident and uncompromising religious character. Frightened by

the spectre of religious militancy, liberal society throws up its own brand of secular militancy, and the consequent polarization of society takes its toll on the normal political process of deliberation and compromise.

This concern for the development of the immigrant culture leads him (Parekh, 2000a:194) to argue that: 'The state need not consist of a single people and could be a community of communities, each enjoying different degrees of autonomy but all held together by shared legal and political bonds.' This defines the policy programme he favours. Since the idea of a community of communities must qualify the idea of national integration it must weaken the emphasis upon common citizenship as a basis for equality of treatment. If different community memberships were officially recognized there is the possibility that this would be exploited by the more powerful communities in their own interest.

If such a proposal entails no more than recognition that most individuals identify with groups, some of them defined by shared ethnic origin, and that these identifications should be respected, the dangers are not great, but it is not clear that the likely benefits would be sufficient to counterbalance the risks. It has also to be remembered that in a free society some identifications will be more respected than others. If adoption of the proposal would enable some members of an ethnic minority to oblige other members to conform to a norm originating in a foreign culture, surrendering a fundamental freedom recognized in the law of the majority society, it is reprehensible. No state can, for example, allow parents unfettered discretion to decide their children's education, because the state must be concerned to see that that all members of the new generation grow up able to assume the duties of citizens. The state must see that, if necessary, children can exercise their rights even against their parents. In Britain this issue has arisen most acutely in respect of parents of Pakistani origin who want their daughters to conform to homeland norms and thereby deny them rights that they should be able to exercise under British law. Parents cannot be permitted to invoke a customary right in order to override the state's obligation, under Article 23(2) of the ICCPR, to ensure that: 'No marriage shall be entered into without the free and full consent of the intending spouses.' Therefore the British state acts to help those who have been forced into marriage, disregarding the assertions of parents and kin that they wish to maintain their group customs.

The right of minority members 'to practise their own religion' cannot easily be adjudicated without agreement about who is to decide what are the obligations of a believer. Members of a minority may regard a customary practice in their homeland (like the expectation that women will conceal their features, as by wearing a *hijab*, the so-called Islamic scarf) as being a requirement of their religion when their co-believers from other countries do not so regard it. Customary practice and religious obligation are not always easily separable, while religious belief does not create a right to be different in all circumstances. The law in Britain, as in some other countries, allows a Sikh man to wear a turban instead of a crash helmet while riding a motorcycle or working on a building site, but a believing Sikh can travel by other means and work in other places. The law on ritual slaughter allows Muslims and Jews to kill animals using methods that expert groups and the general population consider inhumane; believing Muslims and Jews who object to state-approved methods of slaughter do not have to eat meat. If the state has good reasons for its rules about the safety of motorcyclists and building workers, and about animal welfare, their application in these circumstances does not constitute discrimination on grounds of religion. The exemptions given to Sikhs, Muslims and Jews in these connections are political decisions taken, as Barry (2001:33–48, 295–304) describes, because politicians believe that the benefits they can obtain by meeting the wishes of a minority exceed the costs in departing from principle.

From a quite different standpoint it should be remembered that the religions of immigrant minority groups offer a valuable foundation for the criticism of majority culture. There is much to criticize in the social patterns of industrial society, like the deficiencies in the care of the weak and elderly. Several studies have shown that while the children of first-generation immigrants may share some of their parents' criticisms of the unattractive features of the wider society, and therefore value elements of the parental culture, they also want the new consumption goods and are impatient of attempts to make them conform to the norms of an overseas culture. For example, like their age-mates in the ethnic majority, many of the new generation subscribe to the mass media's cult of celebrity, whether it is that of famous footballers or wealthy stars of the screen, and to the transient values that underlie these cults. The critical impetus is soon lost.

The case for religious pluralism is stronger than that for ethnic pluralism because religious identification rests upon individual profession of faith. Rights can more easily be conferred upon religious bodies and congregations than upon ethnic communities since the former are represented by institutions with legal personalities. Members of ethnic communities who do not practise a religion can decide for themselves the extent to which they are represented by such institutions. Little is left of the argument for cultural maintenance once religion is subtracted from culture. Human rights may be a moral minimum in the sense that the representatives of the world's religions cannot agree on a higher moral standard, but human rights law is making up for the deficiencies of organized religion by cultivating international agreement upon common standards of achievement for all peoples and all nations.

Such considerations weaken Iris Young's already quoted argument for the creation of institutions to go beyond action against discrimination in order to safeguard the reproduction of group differences. For example, African-Americans – numerically more numerous than many European nations and not usefully counted as either a national or an immigrant minority – already exert a lot of muscle in US politics. They can take their own decisions about their collective future. The existing institutions for combating discrimination, and the effect of past discrimination, could well be better resourced, but it is difficult to see what new ones might add other than to serve the interests of those who wish to be accepted as group representatives.

In a critical assessment of doctrines of multiculturalism, Brian Barry has highlighted the problems of treating religious communities as sub-state polities by an analysis of legal decisions in the USA concerning groups such as the Amish. Barry (2001:187–93) shows how treating the Amish as a mini-polity, enabled to opt out from national education standards and from the social security and Medicare systems, diminishes the rights of individual Amish as US citizens. It restricts their freedom of choice to leave their community in order to make their way in the national society. Such groups should either be obliged to reproduce internally the features constitutive of a liberal democratic state or be organized as voluntary associations. The example demonstrates how difficult it would be to implement the multiculturalist philosophy without violating the human rights of the members of minority communities.

The individual rights of members of minorities may be protected under other articles and provisions, such as under Article 17 of the ICCPR, providing that everyone shall be protected by law against arbitrary or unlawful interference with his or her privacy, family, home or correspondence and from unlawful attacks on his or her honour and reputation. As the concept of a person is much more than the concept of an individual, human rights law may yet come to recognize a person's faith and community membership as a vital component of his or her personality.

Ethnic relations

The right to be different implies a choice: to identify or not identify with a particular group. The idea of race was inherently a denial of any such right, for it postulated that individuals belonged in objectively determined races whether they accepted this or not. The vocabulary of race which was inspired by this postulate cannot be superseded quickly because it has to be retained for the combating of a particular inequality of treatment, though the Swedish practice of calling their national anti-discrimination law a law against *ethnic* discrimination is a step in the right direction, for a prohibition of ethnic discrimination can comprehend racial discrimination. The recognition of some people's right to be different may not be formulated in any way that reduces the rights of others to equality of treatment. That is readily acknowledged. The difficulties arise because the right is a right to like treatment for like things or like persons. The rights claimed on behalf of African- and Hispanic-Americans are equality rights guaranteed under both international instruments and the US constitution. They and members of the country's ethnic majority are regarded as like persons for this purpose. The rights claimed on behalf of Native Americans and Aboriginal Australians may go beyond those in the US and Australian constitutions, which may explain the hesitations of their governments over the draft UN declaration on the rights of indigenous peoples. Members of indigenous peoples are not 'like persons' in this context because they have rights deriving from their prior occupation of the territory, and the political institutions established subsequently have difficulty acknowledging these.

The right to be different can be better defended if the groups with which humans voluntarily identify are identified as based upon shared ethnic origin. This is a particular instance of the way in which the language of human rights can supersede that of race. Nearly twenty years ago I observed that human groups came about through processes of both inclusion and exclusion, which I represented as analytical concepts useful for uncovering uniformities in social relations independently of folk ideas about the nature of race and ethnicity. The folk ideas could be used for inclusion or exclusion, though in recent times ideas of race had mostly been used for the purpose of exclusion and ideas of ethnicity for inclusion. The language of race had a vocabulary strongly associated with the prejudices of those who wish to exclude others from group membership. The Nazis used it to cultivate a sense of inclusion among those they accounted Aryans and to restrict the range of persons to whom

Aryans should feel moral obligation. That illustrated the dangers of this language.

In the earlier book I noted that the Commission for Racial Equality in Britain was required by statute 'to promote . . . good relations between persons of different racial groups', so that it might be asked: what are good racial relations? My answer was that, if racial grouping was based on exclusive and ethnic grouping on inclusive processes, then good racial relations would be ethnic relations (Banton, 1983:106, 397). When humans identify voluntarily with a group founded upon the sharing of ethnic origin it is better designated an ethnic group.

The language of anti-racism recognizes that victims come together to defend themselves against the prejudices of others, but it has difficulty finding a place for voluntary identification based on shared culture and in coping with the rights of indigenous peoples. The language of human rights has no such handicap and its institutions can balance the claims of one right when it is in conflict with another right. By stressing the common rights of everybody, the language of human rights strikes a positive note. Its emotional and political appeal to the wider public may be strong enough for it to supersede the language of race.

10

Better Explanations

The idea of race was the more influential because it claimed, with some plausibility, to have a scientific basis. The idea's political dimension may be superseded by the philosophy and vocabulary of human rights but these do not touch the scientific claims. In the long run only better explanations can supersede these. That task is the more difficult because racial theories were usually far from specific about just what it was that they claimed to explain.

Attempts to account for the peculiarities of ethnic and racial relations are challenged by a need to overcome the limitations of the language that is used to describe them in everyday life. This is a general problem, for scientific discoveries have often depended upon improving upon prevailing conceptions of the natural world. No one would have discovered that the earth revolves round the sun without breaking with the conventional beliefs of the time, or been able to advance a proper explanation about how it revolved without using the mathematical expressions that represented the movements of heavenly bodies. No one would have been able to explain why there are cycles of economic activity by using only the vocabulary of a shopkeeper. Sociology lacks the sophistication of physics and economics but it has shown (for example, in Durkheim's study of suicide rates) that there are regularities in social life that cannot be uncovered using the practical language of everyday life. The discovery of new knowledge about society often depends upon the development of concepts distinct from ordinary language.

The pioneer sociologists sought to demonstrate that, by borrowing metaphors from other fields and drawing analogies with other things, they could offer a new understanding of social relations.

Herbert Spencer wrote first of social *statics* and in *The Study of Sociology* (1873) drew a famous parallel between the social reformer and the panel beater who, when working a metal sheet back into shape, starts by hammering round the edges of the defect rather than in the middle. He maintained that social reform also had sometimes to start from the edges. Spencer then turned from mechanical to biological analogies and wrote of society as an organism, of social structures and social functions. Robert E. Park, who laid the foundations for a sociology of ethnic and racial relations, drew heavily upon ideas used in the study of plant and animal ecology. Spencer and Park borrowed analytical concepts from the theoretical languages of other subjects in the attempt to create such a language for sociology, but the concepts they borrowed were not very technical and they passed easily into the ordinary language. There they were used more loosely and acquired additional meanings that confused attempts to use them analytically. Race was a failed analytical concept in zoology that was used more confidently as a folk concept by members of the general public than by sociologists.

In the 1940s there were two possible routes by which sociological theory might be developed so as, among other things, to provide a better explanation for the persistence of groups identified by race and ethnic origin. One was the orthodox tradition that led to what was later called structural-functionalism. The other found its inspiration in Marxism.

Talcott Parsons extracted from the work of Max Weber the notion of an ends/means schema and made it into a basic component of the structural-functionalist analysis that was presented to undergraduates in what to my mind was the best textbook of the generation, Kingsley Davis's *Human Society* (1948). Structural-functionalism held that societies were founded upon the sharing of common ultimate ends, while its stress upon the importance of processes of socialization led to a preoccupation with top-down social influences. Davis's textbook had astonishingly little to say about ethnic and racial relations or about the questionable use of concepts of race for social classification. The weakness of the orthodox approach to the sociology of ethnic and racial relations in this period is a reminder that finding the right questions to ask (i.e., those that most help advance knowledge) is much more difficult than finding the answers to unimaginative research questions (though only later can anyone identify which would have been the best questions). Those posed by sociologists at the century's mid-point did not serve to supersede the race-as-species kind of explanation.

The most powerful critique of ordinary language concepts in this field has been that inspired by Marx. It informed the presentation of racial prejudice and discrimination as the products of capitalist expansion and exploitation of peoples set out by Oliver C. Cox in his *Caste, Class and Race* (1948), a book that also neglected possible bottom-up processes. Cox systematically criticized the concepts used by the sociologists of the time, implying that the ways in which they conceptualized social relations were little different from those used by members of the general public, and that therefore their ideas also were ultimately controlled by the ruling class. Popular ideas reflected what some other writers in the same tradition called a false consciousness.

Sociology teaching, especially in the USA, often starts with a discussion of how cultures differ, in order to warn students against assuming that their own society's values are universal and to introduce them to the concept of ethnocentrism. When a lecture course comes to black–white relations, teachers have to explain the processes of status ascription and that the so-called 'one-drop' rule, according to which in the US a person with a small amount of black ancestry is ascribed to the black race, is not natural but cultural. When English-language usage identifies social groups with biological ones, it incorporates and transmits a scientific error. In many other societies differences in physical appearance are recognized as continuous; there is a multitude of names for them without any ascription to either a black or a white category. Sociology students should be taught to look at their society from the outside if they are to understand what is going on inside. This is particularly relevant to ethnic and racial studies.

Race as a social category

Robert E. Park maintained that race relations were not so much the relations that existed between individuals of different races as the relations between individuals conscious of these differences. By treating consciousness as an independent factor, his approach could take account of the differences between the US and Brazil, recognizing that in the former the differences were used to create groups whereas they were not so used in the latter. The nature of racial consciousness varied from one society to another and from one point in time to another. Park's approach did not stimulate sociologists to examine the question of whether, in the US, the groups were properly called races. It accepted the ordinary-language usage of the words 'race' and 'ethnicity', assuming that this usage sufficed for sociological analysis also.

The US assumption that certain large social groups are properly called 'races' is not so strongly established in European countries, partly, perhaps, because in Europe 'race' had often been used as a synonym for nation. So social scientists in Europe have been uneasy about the US assumption. When in 1967 I published a book entitled *Race Relations*, I noted that the apparent independence of race as a social category from its biological meaning had led Charles Wagley (1952:14) to propose a concept of 'social race'. A similar view was expressed a little later by Julian Pitt-Rivers (1970:339), another anthropologist who had undertaken research in Latin America. He asserted: 'To begin with, the biologists' and the sociologists' concepts of race are quite inimical to each other and are connected in fact only by the history of a word. The connection between them must be severed and they must be separated.' Such a course seemed impractical in 1967. The few intellectuals interested in the question did not have the power to effect such a change; they were not agreed on a better alternative, or upon the nature of the connection between the two meanings of the word.

In my book I maintained that the two meanings were connected by more than the history of a word, the social concept of race being based on what was believed to be a biological difference. I drew a parallel with the way the physical differences of sex were used to create what would now be called gender roles. Racial differences were used as a way of dividing up a population, assigning different sets of rights and obligations (or roles) to members of the divisions. Outward differences served as signs telling others to what sorts of privileges and facilities the person in question was conventionally entitled. Race was used as a role sign. My argument was misstated. The main proposition should have been that *physical* differences, rather than racial differences, were used as a way of dividing up a population. The misstatement led Pitt-Rivers to infer that the argument endorsed 'race' as a name for a physical category. This obliged me (Banton, 1967: 130) to clarify my view of race as a folk concept, and to write:

> Where I went wrong was in compressing too much of my argument into the proposition that people utilise racial differences to fashion and allocate roles. People do not perceive racial differences. They perceive phenotypical differences of colour, hair form, underlying bone structure, and so on. Phenotypical differences are a first order abstraction, race is a second order abstraction. It is phenotypical differences which are used as role signs.

This correction still did not go far enough. People use phenotypical differences in classifying those they meet and in answering questions like: 'is this person one of us or one of them?', but in assigning people to groups they also use proper names that reflect belief about national origin. In Britain in the 1950s the groups were named not only as white or coloured (sometimes black), but frequently as West Indian, African, Nigerian, Pakistani, etc. It is the intellectual who decides that certain proper names are racial, ethnic or national classifications. Folk assignments to groups are part of everyday practical language, and in the 1950s ordinary people in Britain did not need to classify others by race.

By the latter part of the 1960s popular usage was changing, until by the end of the century references to race were commonest in situations in which others were being criticized for racial discrimination. Paradoxically, it was the anti-racist movement that heightened racial consciousness in order to overcome it – just as Sartre predicted.

At the time of publication the title *Race Relations* evoked no criticism. This was a generally accepted designation and an author could go on to explain that it referred to social and not biological relations. However, such a title could not avoid implying a dubious demarcation of the field of study. Many features of the relations thought of as 'racial' were common to other kinds of inter-group relations (for example, anti-Semitism was one kind of inter-group prejudice while discrimination against Jews could resemble white discrimination against blacks). Among sociologists there could be little disagreement about this. So there was no real dispute when John Rex objected that my book 'confines the study of race relations somewhat arbitrarily to those situations where there is a clear colour difference' and maintained that the field of study should include that of relations 'between groups recognizable by signs regarded as unalterable, or . . . that there should be ascriptive role allocation' (Rex, 1973:185, 203). The difficulty lay in agreeing a better formulation. To write, as Rex did on another occasion (1973:191), that 'the term "racial" . . . should be used to describe those situations of inter-group differentiation in which men explain the differences between them in terms of determinate biological theories' illustrates the problem. How is the research worker to be sure about the ways in which people explain group differences? Modes of thought can rarely be assessed with enough precision to decide whether or not people are relying upon biological theories. Rex, like others, was struggling with the problems created by ordinary-language usage.

In retrospect, it looks as if many of those who wrote about racial relations in the 1970s were attempting intellectual responses to the political changes embodied in the US civil rights movement of the previous decade. Afro-Caribbeans in Britain followed the changes in the USA very closely. Like African-Americans, they adopted the self-description 'black' and were vehement in disparaging any naming of persons as 'coloured', in part because this recalled a form of graduated discrimination many of them had known in their homelands and in part because it undermined the idea of black unity. This was a moment in time when the concept of race had been intellectually discredited and exposed as politically dangerous. Educated people would have been willing to discard it had they been offered some word, or words, to replace the idiom of race. It was therefore ironical that at this moment many of those who were believed to be the victims of racism discovered the utility of that idiom for new purposes. By appealing to the notion of racial identity and to the racist convention that a person with any ascertainable African ancestry was to be accounted black, they could recruit others to collective action. For them the concept of racism – and associated expressions like that of institutional racism – was empowering because it was a way of reproaching others.

Those, of whatever colour, who had been inspired by the spirit of 1968 expressed a new concern for the victims of racism and were ready to treat them as privileged witnesses in the discussion of its causes and remedies. There was a pressure to make social science serve the ends of liberation. The idea of detached or objective analysis was dismissed as impossible, denying the argument that social science progresses best when its practitioners seek to develop arguments that, because of their cogency, demand acceptance irrespective of a person's political commitments. The insistent call for 'relevance' strengthened impatience with purely conceptual analysis.

Those who used the racial idiom objected to reference to ethnic differences for much the same reasons as they objected to references to colour differences. Describing the anti-racist struggles of the 1970s Stuart Hall claimed that 'all [New Commonwealth settlers] identified themselves politically as Black . . . In that moment, the enemy was ethnicity. The enemy had to be what we called "multi-culturalism" . . . Nobody would talk about racism' (quoted Back and Solomos, 2000:115). The idea of racism was most effective in political contexts when it was defined in an elastic manner, but social scientists were tasked with trying to explain new developments for which sharper concepts, or definitions, were needed. The political activists did not wish to address the arguments of the scholars who found the idiom of ethnicity better than that of race for social science analysis (e.g., Wallman, 1978).

The racism problematic

Robert Miles used my 1979 argument as a springboard when, in the early 1980s, he commenced a sustained critique of the way research workers in Britain had taken over the ordinary-language conception of race. Marxists have long maintained that the ruling class uses ideas like that of race to mystify the real nature of social relations, and thereby to divide the proletariat in order to delay the revolution. Miles's concern was first political, then academic. He directed his fire at what he called 'the race relations problematic', meaning by problematic a set of questions of interest to scholars who share views about the best ways to answer the questions. He named Banton and Rex as the main proponents of this problematic. Through the 1970s sociologists in Britain were still much concerned to criticize the popular use of the idiom of race but had no good alternative to put in its place. Miles completed Cox's criticism of sociologists' use of the ordinary-language concept, complaining that what he called their obsession with this word distorted understanding of the real relations that determined the restricted opportunities open to immigrants to Britain. He insisted that: 'the concepts which we use to analyse the social world cannot be inductively derived in some direct and unmediated way from empirical observations of the world as it presents itself.' By using the language of race sociologists legitimated the world of appearances; they reflected back on it the categories of that world, when they could instead have taken their categories from an understanding of the underlying determinants. He warned: 'we must not unquestioningly incorporate in a scientific analysis the categories of description and analysis used in everyday discourse because, in so far as that discourse is uncritical and confines itself to the direct experience and appearance of the social world, then there is the possibility of creating a false and misleading explanation' (1982:31–2).

Though it appeared as an attack on the race relations problematic, an academic enterprise, the real target was popular misunderstanding. Academic writing may later influence popular speech, and therefore its weakness required correction.

Miles (1989:49–66) attacked the conceptual inflation that resulted when a succession of writers tried to expand the definition of racism. Originally it was defined by its doctrinal content. Rex and others maintained that it should be defined by its function, which meant for some that the exclusion of women was as much a part of it as exclusion on grounds of race. Others argued that racism was present when the exclusion of groups was justified by reference to their biological character. Some counted as racism anything that had the effect of exclusion, without specifying any criteria to be applied when race was just one among many possible causes of exclusion or inequality. Some considered racist any defence of inherited or structural advantage, often maintaining that in the contemporary world racism was a white phenomenon and that, by this definition, blacks could never be racist.

Some of Miles's criticisms could be met were the position he attacked reformulated as a racial discrimination problematic, but this would not address the main charge: that of reinforcing misleading folk ideas about the nature of racial differentiation in society. Miles's proposal was, first, to shift the focus of attention away from race as a marker of social groups towards racism as a concept identifying the forces that led certain groups to be set aside, and, second, to maintain that the underlying reality could be grasped only by deploying a different family of concepts centring upon the ideas of exploitation and class struggle. His criticism of the concepts currently employed was more persuasive than his proposals for developing the alternative set of concepts, though his demonstration in later works of the value of the concept of racialization has been followed with enthusiasm. This concept had been introduced in English (Banton, 1977:18) as a name for a mode of categorization whereby nations and peoples were called races, with the implication that so identifying them opened up a superior way of understanding what went on. If the language of race was used to identify a group, it was racialized; if it was not used, then, on this definition, there was no racialization. This was clear, but Miles (1989:74–5) expanded its use 'to refer to those instances where social relations between people have been structured by the signification of human biological characteristics in such a way as to define and construct differentiated social collectivities'. He considered that racialization had occurred whenever certain effects could be discerned.

Miles was at one with those whose work he attacked in believing that the social scientist's task was to find better explanations of the problems, but he subscribed to a different philosophy of social science. One of the key differences between the two philosophies centres upon the extent to which judgements of fact can be separated from judgements of value. This affects opinion as to the kind of knowledge that is possible in the social sciences. Such disputes should be examined closely because they are the growth points crucial to the advancement of knowledge, but the examination should recognize that those engaged in the controversies have been in agreement about many related matters.

A tutor of my generation of sociologists, Morris Ginsberg (1963:419–20), held that:

> in social investigation judgements of fact and judgements of value are so closely interwoven that in practice it is difficult to keep them apart . . . [but] it is important to remember that detachment is a matter of degree, and that in free societies bias does not remain undetected and that, though a certain relativity of outlook is unavoidable, it admits, in varying measure, of self-correction.

Ginsberg might have agreed that when writing on sensitive subjects there were political as well as academic advantages in being as detached as possible. Many authors hope to persuade readers who at the outset do not share the author's values, and they are more likely to succeed if they present their case in a manner that the reader finds objective. Some questions of fact can be distinguished and from their analysis a body of objective knowledge can be built up.

Both philosophies believe that social science knowledge is cumulative. According to the neo-classical orthodoxy, sociology can follow in the paths of economics and psychology in developing theories that will furnish ever more powerful explanations of social phenomena. According to Marxists, social science has to be a historical science. The material forces of production available in a particular place and time stimulate the creation of the human relations of production and then on this foundation arise legal and political superstructures and corresponding forms of social consciousness. The ruling class exploits the structure in its own interest and cannot avoid provoking revolution. So the analysis of, say, racial conflicts has to be based on an understanding of the epoch and the stage reached in its transformation. This makes it inherently political.

Miles applied this perspective in the study of the migration of workers defined as racially different, boosting the 1970s wave of studies that started from a concept of racism instead of that of race relations. Adoption of the racism problematic brought a change of focus, highlighting the ulterior causes of discrimination and broadening the scope of research, but the new problematic had weaknesses as great as that which it sought to displace.

Within the other intellectual movements starting in the 1970s two particular strains may be discerned, those of critical theory and cultural studies. Both have concentrated on the criticism of contemporary thought and policy about black–white relations in the English-speaking world. Neither has added much to the explanation of the causes, incidence or reactions to racial discrimination.

Both owed much to Marxism, implicitly rejecting the aspiration of orthodox sociologists to cumulate a body of knowledge by keeping judgements of fact and value separate whenever possible. Thus the editors of a recent volume state flatly: 'While . . . some authors have tried to separate the research process from political action, such a separation is in some ways impossible and even undesirable' (Back and Solomos, 2000:23). Given that a *complete* separation is impossible, the editors might have explained why they deny the desirability of such separation as is possible. Nor is the relationship between research and political action so simple an issue that it can be settled by a brief declaration about desirability.

While most authors writing about the racism problematic have abandoned classical Marxism's aspiration to build a historical science, they have retained the study of the history of particular social formations as providing a framework for their work. Critical theory has been developed most in some circles in Germany and the USA. The cultural studies group has taken a special interest in the social conditioning of cultural production and of symbolic forms; in the lived experience of culture, its shaping by class, age, gender and ethnic relations, and in the relationships between economic and political institutions. Its authors range into literary criticism, sharing the postmodernist movement's scepticism about scientific rationality in favour of a focus upon free-floating images and a plurality of viewpoints.

The founding text of the cultural studies version of the racism problematic started from a debate within Marxism about whether ideas of race were determined by economic relations or whether race and ethnicity could be autonomous social features, not reducible to economic determinants. In it Stuart Hall (1980:336) stated that: 'there is as yet no adequate theory of racism which is capable of dealing with both the economic and the superstructural features of such societies, while at the same time giving a historically-concrete and sociologically-specific account of distinctive racial aspects.' Most sociologists outside the Marxist tradition would deny that such a theory is possible. For them social science can answer a limited range of questions but it cannot substitute for a philosophy of history, even though its practitioners will have their private philosophies of history.

Racism was described as a 'rational abstraction which brings out and fixes the common element' and may 'help to distinguish those social features which fix the different positions of social groups and classes on the basis of racial ascription'. Hall warned against 'extrapolating a common and universal structure to racism . . . It is only as the different racisms are historically specified – in their difference

– that they can be properly understood.' A US pioneer of cultural studies, David Theo Goldberg (1993:90–116), argued similarly that 'there is no single characteristic form of racism . . . there may be different racisms in the same place at different times; or different racisms in various different places at the same time'. The main criterion is whether something has the effect of excluding persons deemed to be racially different, so the presence or absence of a folk concept of race is important. In the case of apartheid South Africa, there was such a concept, but the identification of racism in more fluidly structured societies that employ no concept of race is not straightforward. Outside the English-speaking world it can be difficult to identify historically specific racisms without criteria for distinguishing racisms from ethnocentrisms, fascisms, ethnicisms, or other folk ideas of belonging. The basis for deeming other persons to be racially different can also vary. Popular concepts of race as type and race as species generate ideas of permanent difference, whereas ideas of race as lineage and race as sub-species do not.

One exposition of the racism problematic (Solomos and Back, 1996) sets out to show how the idea of race has been used in particular social and historical contexts, but is hampered by the lack of good evidence about the use that ordinary members of the public make of the idea. It would not be easy to collect the necessary information because, while many ordinary English speakers have things to say about the characteristics of minority members living in their localities, they are rarely explicit about what they believe to be the nature of race. While the problem can be approached through the analysis of discourse, many studies within this tradition have been more concerned to expose racism than to analyse the conceptual alternatives available to ordinary members of the public. The problem is the more complex because many analysts maintain that speakers can transmit messages about race without using the word. For example, in 1978 the British prime minister, Margaret Thatcher, said in a radio interview that: 'people are really rather afraid that this country might be swamped by people with a different culture.' One writer (Goldberg, 1993:73) says of this statement: 'Here race is coded as culture, what has been called "the new racism".' Some contend that statements like that include coded references to race by means of what have been called metonymic elaborations:

> This means that racisms may be expressed through a variety of coded signifiers. We have already discussed one such elaboration, that is the coding of race as culture. Contemporary racisms have evolved and adapted to new circumstances. The crucial property of these elaborations is that they can produce a racist effect while denying that this effect is the result of racism. (Solomos and Back, 1996:27–8)

Their example, of references in Birmingham to an 'Asian mafia', is scarcely persuasive.

Where Miles sought to uncover the sources of the biases built into the ordinary-language idiom of race, the approach from cultural studies simply supplies further examples of possible bias. Its arguments about racial coding need to be examined step by step. Mrs Thatcher made reference to a situation in which there was a majority group usually identified as English (or Welsh or Scottish), as white, and as the descendants of others who inhabited the country in previous generations. There were also persons considered as non-members on account of their countries of origin, appearance (both skin colour and dress), religion, or recent settlement in the locality. For some purposes the various groups were best distinguished by their ethnic or national origin. In everyday speech these group differences were sometimes called 'racial', either as a kind of shorthand used by persons with old-fashioned ideas about group difference or by persons concerned to combat discrimination. Members of all groups had their preferences as to the extent to which they wished to reside, work and socialize with co-ethnics. To call Mrs Thatcher's reference to people with a different culture a coded reference to race is to imply that she was soliciting support from members of the majority group by signalling that she understood that they were discomforted when the proportion of minority people in their locality exceeded a threshold. It is to assume that the words 'people of a different culture' were to be interpreted as 'people of a different race', as if the reference to race needed to be hidden. Why should it have been?

A similar formulation appears in the report on *The Future of Multi-Ethnic Britain*. Discussing 'the future of Britishness', this maintained that 'Britishness, as much as Englishness, has systematic, largely unspoken, racial connotations. Whiteness nowhere features as an explicit condition of being British, but it is widely understood that Englishness, and therefore by extension Britishness, is racially coded' (Parekh, 2000b:38). It may be the case that many white English people believe that no one can be really English unless he or she has a complexion like theirs, but this does not, of itself, require any particular belief about the nature of race. A premiss is missing from the syllogism. Those who detect racial coding are assuming that there is a phenotypical dimension to interpersonal relations evoked by reference to race, and that coding is an attempt to strengthen it surreptitiously. They cannot prove that there is a popular idea about race that trumps other conceptions of difference. If – as opinion polls suggest – the significance that white members of the public attach to differences of skin colour is declining, then those who detect racial coding are reinforcing that to which they are opposed. This is part of the anti-racist racism of which Sartre wrote.

One version of the racism problematic is to be found in a text-book by Omi and Winant (1994). Discussing its theses, an expositor of critical theory (Outlaw, 1990:80) wrote: 'For if Omi and Winant are correct: in the United States, the state is *inherently* racial, every state institution is a *racial* institution, and the entire social order is equilibrated (unstably) by the state to preserve the prevailing racial order (i.e. the dominance of "whites" over blacks and other "racial" groups).' The authors describe 'race formation' as a feature of, and a reaction to, this order. From the standpoint of Cox and Miles, by describing the process as one of race formation, rather than of class formation, or of the formation of a new kind of political and economic unit, the authors have accepted the definitions of a ruling class that wants ordinary people to think in terms of race formation instead of looking for the underlying determinants.

If the expression 'race relations' tended to concentrate attention on situations where there was a clear colour difference, so a focus upon racism tended to concentrate attention on abuses for which the state could be held responsible and to neglect human rights abuses within minorities. In Britain numerous such cases have come before the courts. For example, to assess the criminal responsibility of a Muslim Asian woman who has killed her husband after he has abused her, a court may need information about domestic roles in the culture of origin and the ways in which interpersonal relations are changed as a result of migration. Relations between groups are often affected by the relations within these groups, and vice versa.

The moral basis of the stance taken up by those who use racism as a key concept is often uncertain, for they give little attention to the social science techniques that can be used in programmes for the reduction of racial discrimination. It is often unclear whether they believe that racism can be eliminated. By its top-down concentration on the influence of the overall political structure the racism problematic has transmitted a very limited image of the members of ethnic and racial minorities, which represents them only as resisting pressure from elsewhere and neglects what they do for themselves.

As was illustrated in chapter 3, the concept of racism has been made into a powerful political weapon, especially when used in an expression like 'institutional racism'. Those who write of racisms in the plural may likewise find the expression useful for stigmatizing whatever they attach the label to. These are short-term political gains secured at a long-term cost, because any use of the racial idiom divides humans into categories and breathes new life into the obsolete idea of race. When it is proposed to use 'racism' as a concept in social science, it is necessary to consider whether it is used as an explanans, a concept used in producing an explanation, or in order to define an explanandum, something to be explained. Miles used it as an explanans; he sought a better explanation. Other exponents of the racism problematic have seen it as an explanandum, making themselves captives of the ordinary-language folk concept. They have engaged in a Promethean search for total understanding, trying to elaborate a particular kind of theory that seeks the sort of explanation characteristic of the philosophy of history (Banton, 1998a:189–92).

After racism

My response to the objections Miles made explicit has been to maintain that the languages of everyday discourse and scientific analysis must be more sharply differentiated. Some elements of the racial idiom are still needed in law (the introduction of the concept of a *racial group* was in Britain seen as the price to be paid for the prohibition of indirect discrimination). They are needed in social policy for combating discrimination and prejudice, while others of them are useful to the victim groups, so any attempt to eradicate ordinary-language usages would be misguided. When discussing policy issues social scientists cannot avoid using many of the same concepts as those to whom they address their arguments, but they should seek ways of eliminating the racial idiom from their theoretical language by developing better answers to the questions it has purported to answer.

The idiom of race must be retained for the identification and study of an unlawful motivation, but its use in other contexts can lead into the language trap. People are caught in this trap when they assume that membership in some racial group is more important than a person's other attributes. Since there is no way out from this trap, it is better to avoid it by using other words for defining the category in question. A policy of national integration must seek to reduce the significance of classification in racial categories relative to other social categories.

Social science often opens a critical perspective onto social life, but if it is to be social science rather than a form of social criticism, it has to be a process by which knowledge is accumulated. Its scope has to be transnational, not limited to a particular society or a particular moment in historical time. Economics and psychology have shown that this is a feasible enterprise. Sociology, too, can develop a deeper understanding of how societies work, how groups are formed, maintained and dissolved, and how individuals identify themselves socially. To persuade my readers of this I should conclude this chapter by recapitulating briefly the view that I have developed about the best way forward, based on the theory of collective action.

This theory begins from the proposition that humans can attain some of their ends by individual action, but to attain many others they must join in collective action. As societies have changed, from a pastoral economy or agriculture to new times, the balance between individual and collective action has changed. In the industrial era the formation of trade unions and the creation of socialist parties emphasized the importance of collective action to defend the interests of the exploited. In the post-industrial era, an economy based on the cultivation of consumer demand encourages personal desires. The image of the mass society is one of separate individuals manipulated by the media of mass communication, in which the public interest is not always well served.

Collective action is often made the more difficult by the tendency of individuals to take a 'free ride' by benefiting from others' actions while not contributing themselves. Social institutions facilitate the organization of both individual and collective action and they limit the scope for free-riding. No farmer will plant a crop unless there is a reasonable prospect of being able to harvest it. No one will make a deal with another unless there are means of ensuring that the parties keep to their bargain. Legal institutions, like those that regulate contracts, facilitate the pursuit of both individual and collective goals. Ideas about what a husband and wife may expect from one another vary from society to society, but the social institution of marriage always embodies norms about mutual obligations that make it possible for individuals to plan for their futures. Over the course of time, social institutions change, dropping old functions and acquiring new ones. For example, organizations like the freemasons were not formed to undertake charitable activities, but they now refer to these when justifying their existence. Immigrant groups bring homeland social institutions with them and use them for new purposes in the country of settlement. The theory of collective action is therefore much concerned with the action that can result as a by-product of an existing institution (Hechter, 1987:104–24).

When the conduct of others can be predicted, an individual can more easily decide whether it would be worthwhile to sacrifice present gain for the prospect of greater gain later. This can be important to the cultivation of what is often called team spirit. It is well understood that the success of a sporting team depends both upon the talents of individual members and upon the degree to which they combine in subordinating their individual ends to shared ends. The same principle applies widely, for team spirit and high morale can be crucial to the organization of collective action within armies and industrial organizations also. So the theory of collective action brings together in one conceptual framework the behaviour underlying movements that ordinary language separates, like nationalism, feminism, trade unionism, employer organization, political parties, and other forms of mobilization.

Persons ascribed to a social category can, by collective action, make themselves into a social group. The African-American ethnogenesis described at pp. 102–4 was an example of such a transformation. As chapter 9 explained, a social category is a class the nature of which is determined by the person who defines it. A social group is defined by the nature of the relations between its members. The significance of group membership varies. The members may want to be considered as members of a particular group in some circumstances (e.g., in political struggles or when being counted in a census – since many people see the census as an occasion for self-identification). In other circumstances, like standing in a queue to be served, they may insist that their group membership be disregarded as irrelevant. Sometimes a group is contrasted with an aggregate, a concept that should identify a collection of persons assigned to a category. It is said that an aggregate or association model conceives of the individual as ontologically prior to the group, and that both of these are methodologically individualist concepts (Young, 1990:43–5). Yet there is no good reason for regarding either the individual as prior to the group or the group as prior to the individual. The human individual cannot live in isolation. In many circumstances an individual's group affinities help constitute his or her sense of self.

This sort of reference to methodological individualism is also misleading. F. A. von Hayek (1943:41) drew attention to the way that many sociologists generalized about groups as if they had an independent existence. He called this methodological collectivism as opposed to methodological individualism. They were paired concepts, so that it makes no sense to discuss one without the other. The collectivist starts from propositions about groups as constraining individual behaviour. The individualist starts from propositions about how individual behaviour creates and sustains groups. The contrast has sometimes been represented as one between macro-sociology and micro-sociology. It has also been expressed as one between catascopic (or top-down) and anascopic (or bottom-up) approaches. Both are needed. Whichever approach a writer adopts, he or she should take due account of the counter-balancing one.

Social groups are maintained by their shared institutions and by the unconscious daily affirmation of membership, without which they may change into social categories. Solidarity amongst members of a subordinated group is evoked by the shared experience of discrimination. In the case of a group like African-Americans this heightens the members' consciousness of 'race' because it is the word they are accustomed to use to denote their distinctiveness. The institutions that the whites built up to attain their ends incorporated some of the assumptions of their communities and thus gave substance to the charge of 'institutional racism'. Where two groups are opposed a process of polarization can be set in motion that, if it intensifies, must lead towards either resolution or separation. Opposition is rarely clear cut, because while individuals share certain ends with those on their 'side' they share others with people on the opposite 'side'. There are divisions within each of the 'sides', so that an appearance of unanimity is usually a transitory achievement. Any approach in social science that takes the continuity of the 'sides' for granted has to oversimplify, most notably by ignoring the people who do not fit the pattern. Persons of mixed ethnic origin are often in an intermediate position and their experience can throw a different light upon the overall structure.

Political processes determine popular conceptions of race, most obviously in the US 'one-drop' definition of the Negro race. Though the source of the definition was the whites' determination to subordinate blacks, the definition itself gave blacks the opportunity to build the largest possible group by incorporating persons of mixed descent. Elements within the British anti-racist movement in the 1970s tried to follow a similar strategy and create a maximal constituency by counting as black not only persons of Black African, Black Caribbean and Black British origin, but also those of South and South-East Asian and even Chinese origin on the argument that they should combine to resist white oppression. The strategy failed because so many of the groups within the proposed coalition preferred to pursue their distinctive goals, but for a while it influenced conceptions of race.

Partly in reaction to use of the idiom of race, many recent commentators have chosen to describe ethnic groups by their possession of a shared culture. A leading political philosopher begins a discussion of the politics of multiculturalism with the statement that modern societies 'are increasingly confronted with minority groups demanding recognition of their identity, and accommodation of their cultural differences' (Kymlicka, 1995:10). The conceptual short cut implicit in such references to groups may be acceptable for that kind of discussion but it neglects important variables. Any confrontation arises because there are political entrepreneurs who claim to speak for constituencies and may, in varying degree, succeed in mobilizing support for campaigns. Yet they rarely have the support of all those they claim to represent. Only under special conditions are minorities completely united. It may be justified to assume group unity for the purposes of some arguments, but they can be only exceptional.

Others who have written about multiculturalism have adopted an exclusively top-down perspective, overlooking the extent to which groups are the product of continuing collective action. Some groups are temporary coalitions, others have long histories, but all have to be continually renewed if they are to persist. Groups that are distinctive on many dimensions (like appearance, ethnic origin, religion, language, territory, etc.) are more easily renewed. In Britain there have been instances in which children of Asian parents explain to outsiders: 'My religion is Punjabi'; from the child's point of view this is not a confusion of categories but testimony to the multidimensionality of the membership group. The concepts used for the study of groups must allow for the continuing interrelations of individuals assigned to different groups. A mode of reasoning that starts from the assumption that certain groups are oppressed (like that elaborated by Iris Marion Young) cannot come to terms with the many situations of double grievance (like those of relations between Roma and *Gaje*, or non-Roma, in Central Europe).

Ethnic and racial groups are forms of collective action in which individuals combine to seek shared ends, though they are not necessarily conscious of this. Nor is the way individuals think of their group, and the name they give to it, necessarily a good indicator of the pressures that have led to its formation. The most enduring groups – like nations – are those distinctive on many dimensions: territory, political interest, language, ethnic origin, religion, culture and so on. Each dimension serves to include members in the group and to exclude others as outsiders. Attempts to classify groups depend upon the selection of one dimension as the most relevant, and this can be misleading.

The relations between the dimensions vary from case to case. In the nineteenth-century racial theories, race was brought to the forefront as the master concept. At the UN General Assembly in 1965, less favourable treatment on grounds of ethnic origin was treated as a sub-division of racial discrimination, which was seen as the greater evil. The national law of the USA and of Britain has similarly represented race as the more general category. Yet the atrocities of ethnic cleansing and genocidal massacre that followed the break-up of Yugoslavia and the genocide in Rwanda showed that abuses based on ethnic discrimination could be as bad as those based on racial discrimination; they suggested that ethnic discrimination was the more general category, racial discrimination being a sub-division. Had the international law been drafted after the experiences of the early 1990s it might have been formulated differently.

Whereas Huxley and Haddon in 1935 proposed 'ethnic group' as an improvement upon 'race' to identify groups at the national level, social scientists in the USA for a long time neglected this level to concentrate on minority ethnicity. They failed to consider whether a given group can be *both* racial and ethnic. In some other regions ethnic origin and religion are confounded, as in Bosnia, where some people are accounted ethnic Muslims. In Greece, the home of the concept of ethnicity, many criteria are evoked as evidence for the reality of Greek ethnicity. Reviewing the Greek use of ethnicity as a folk concept, one expert (Just, 1989:76) concluded that it was 'a somewhat retrograde step that ethnicity should ever have entered into the *analytical* vocabulary of the social sciences'. Marcus Banks similarly concluded that the concept 'may not be out there in the world of social relations' and that any theory based on a folk concept of ethnicity is unlikely to be useful (Banks, 1996:esp. 100, 186–90). It should also be remembered that, as previous chapters have explained, international law relies on the concept of ethnic *origin*, not of ethnicity. Though ethnic origin is a folk concept, belonging in the ordinary language, it has an objective reference that the abstract conception of ethnicity lacks.

The best way forward is to place the five prohibited grounds of conduct within the larger range of criteria on which humans differentiate one another in interpersonal relations, including those of class, age, religion and even physical attractiveness. One person, A, can see the skin colour of another person, B, but in deciding how to behave towards B, A may be more influenced by B's speech, dress or deportment. Class often trumps colour as a criterion of expected behaviour. A cannot see B's race, descent or national or ethnic origin, and, as criteria, these are all subject to a degree of negotiation. Studies of black–white relations in the Deep South of the USA in the 1930s, where the colour line was drawn especially sharply, emphasized that class could be more important than colour. Different norms came into play when a relationship was defined as one of 'business' rather than as one of black–white inequality. That descent can be negotiated is seen in countries such as India where preferential policies confer privileges on members of backward groups to help them overcome their handicaps. Persons of questionable entitlement can claim membership of such groups to benefit from their quotas. The prohibition of discrimination based upon national origin is wider than one based upon nationality. The latter is decided by the state; it can be changed and a person can acquire a new nationality authenticated in a new passport. National origin is supposed to have been fixed at birth but it can derive from country of birth or from the nationality of either parent. The prohibition of discrimination based upon ethnic origin depends on even less objective criteria than the other grounds, especially because many people's ethnic origins are in some degree mixed.

Consciousness of race and ethnic origin changes over time and differs both from one society to another and within societies. It is no secure foundation on which to build a social science. For example, a study in an Ontario town found that there were residents referred to as Ukrainians. This category included Poles, Romanians, Russians and Yugoslavs. It was called Ukrainian because, apparently, Ukrainians were the most numerous among what appeared to others a category of relatively similar people. The anthropologist who carried out this study (Stymeist, 1975:50) heard someone in a bar referred to as 'Uke'. Instead of treating this name as simply a basis for interpersonal relations, as everyone else did, he asked the man if he was actually a Ukrainian and received the answer 'yes'. The anthropologist then asked, in apparent innocence, 'What part of the Ukraine did your family come from?' and got the reply: 'They didn't. They came from Poland. I'm a Polack.' The man was willing to be taken for a Ukrainian because he thought that in these circumstances it was not relevant or worth the trouble to go into detail. Eriksen (1993:30–2) discusses similar examples to maintain that in interpersonal relations ethnicity may be subject to negotiation between the parties. It is clear that something may be negotiated, but is it ethnicity or assignment to groups recognized by proper names?

Ethnicity is sometimes said to be an extension of kinship, but this does not advance the argument. 'Kinship' is a useful term in the practical language of everyday life, but little more. When it suits them, people create kinship by adoption, by counting as uncles and aunts persons who are not relatives; they may not worry if kin connections are ignored or lost. To understand the actual relations between kinsfolk, it is necessary to consider how close they live to one another, how old they are, their occupations, interests and personalities. In some societies the ownership of land and other valuables is vested in particular descent groups, but the sentiment of obligation associated with closeness of kinship is only one element, which taken by itself, explains very little of the actual relations. Difficulties arise when an author distinguishes groups by a general adjective (like 'ethnic') instead of listing them by proper names. Most readers will know that kinship groups are not very distinctive but they may be misled by references to 'ethnic groups', because grouping them under such an adjective implies that they possess some distinctive quality shared by all groups so designated; it is never clear what this quality might be. The top-down perspective ignores these difficulties.

A theoretical language for the analysis of ethnic and racial relations can rely only on concepts that can explain human conduct independently of the presence or absence of ethnic and racial consciousness. Some of the most important elements for explaining how conduct reflects the relation between shared ends and available means come together in the concept of preference. This can be brought to bear on the problems discussed in this chapter by the analysis of ethnic preferences. Many persons have a preference, in certain circumstances, for associating with co-ethnics, persons regarded as members of the subject's own ethnic group. Others, in the same circumstances, attach no significance to the ethnic origin of their associates; their preference is zero. Some have a preference for associating with members of an ethnic group with higher social status than their own (because they like to be identified in other people's minds with higher-status social circles). Some preferences shared within a group do not involve other persons (a Vietnamese preference for rice over potatoes would be an example); these are not ethnic preferences in the sense used here.

The exercise of an ethnic preference carries a price, for it is always a relative preference. For example, someone who wishes to sell a house may prefer to sell it to someone of the same ethnic group, but may be willing to sell it to a non-member who offers a higher price. How great is the seller's ethnic preference relative to his or her preference for more money? It has happened in some parts of the USA that a white person proposing to sell a house to a black person has been subjected to serious threats, so the seller may sometimes have to take into consideration his or her vulnerability if he or she offends others in the neighbourhood. In some circumstances a person who acts on the basis of an ethnic preference engages in unlawful discrimination and can be subjected to a financial penalty; so in such circumstances a seller could in theory have to calculate whether the possibility of action by others changes the balance of advantage.

One of the merits of the concept of ethnic preference is that it treats the values of members of the majority and of minorities on equal terms, making due allowance for minority members as acting subjects instead of seeing them as driven to behave in a particular way by pressures generated by the majority society. It could be a point of departure for a new approach to the bias that sociologists, for over a century, have called ethnocentrism. All societies and ethnic groups exhibit some degree of ethnocentrism; it may be little more than a manifestation of team spirit and of the solidarity that facilitates collective action, but when a racial idiom is used it can shade into racial prejudice. In some relationships the expression of an ethnic preference is unlawful.

Changes in ethnic preferences can be evident in situations of immigration. Three main processes leading towards national integration can be distinguished. First, immigrants change as they enter the receiving society's system of social stratification, either climbing up through it or being incorporated into a particular part of it. Second, the majority changes, either to make room for them in part of the system or to resist their entry. Third, much of the change is the result of interaction between members of the majority and of the minorities within particular institutions, like those of the workplace, the social services and the political structure, and is channelled by these institutions. The goals of individuals may change, or they may adopt other means to seek their goals.

Changes in relative preferences have been exemplified in studies of Sikh settlement in Britain. The first immigrants, in the 1950s, lived in all-male households. Many were willing to cut their hair (instead of tying it in a turban), and be addressed by English names in order more easily to obtain employment. Their priority was to remit money to their homeland; they enjoyed their freedom from community constraints, not worrying about their status in the eyes of either the British or other Sikhs, though matters could change if stories of disreputable conduct circulated in their homeland villages. After they had arranged for their wives and children to join them their reference groups changed dramatically, and so did their relative preferences. It became more important for a man to protect and advance his reputation in a Sikh community, part of which was now in Britain and part in the Punjab (for an excellent summary of the changes, see Ballard, 1994:13–18 and other essays in that volume).

Change in the majority's ethnic preferences is demonstrated by the results of social distance tests that show that in Britain, as in the US, the proportion of white people who say they would object to having a non-white neighbour has dropped very considerably.

Majority and minority preferences can interact, as illustrated by US studies of tipping points in housing. Studies have found that some Jewish people would prefer to live in neighbourhoods that were half Jewish and half Gentile, whereas non-Jewish persons when questioned said they would want to leave any neighbourhood that became more than one-third Jewish. Both parties could not be satisfied, because as soon as the Jews started to approach their ideal mix, the non-Jews would leave. The situation has since changed, but the example illustrates one difficulty, as does that in US cities in which the population is so largely black, or white, that particular levels of mixture are not attainable.

The ethnic preferences of the first-generation settlers in Britain, particularly those in Asian groups, were challenged by their children, who could share them only in part. The conflicts were sharpest when their daughters insisted that they should enjoy the same liberties as those enjoyed by their English age-mates. Some of the conflicts were over arranged marriages, either arranged within Britain or with a spouse selected in the homeland. The government appointed a working group to develop a strategy on the prevention of forced marriage. Since there had been cases in which the father arranged for his daughter to travel to Pakistan, ostensibly to visit kinsfolk, but in reality to be forced into marriage with a cousin who would thereby acquire a right to domicile in Britain, UK diplomats in Pakistan had to take special measures to protect them. Among Hindus, also, the choice of a marriage partner was at times restricted by considerations of the caste status of a possible spouse.

A desire on the part of immigrants to maintain the customs of their homeland culture has sometimes meant that abuses within an immigrant community are concealed from the authorities and are difficult for the police to investigate. The first generation of settlers experience pressure to conform to the customs of the majority but at the same time they are very conscious of the failure of members of the majority themselves to conform to their professed standards, as exemplified in crime and sexual immorality. A collective reaction to this situation is shown in the intensification of religious practice. The majority recognizes the legitimacy of minority religious institutions that become vehicles for collective action of an ethnic rather than a strictly religious character. This leads to what in the previous chapter was called the ethnicization of religion.

Most of the sociological writing about ethnic and racial relations has taken the form of interpretations after the event. Theoretical development requires an ability to predict events and to test hypotheses. From this standpoint the analysis of collective action does not yet qualify as a proper theory, but it has many merits by comparison with other kinds of analysis that sociologists are accustomed to call theories. It has the potential to become a theory of aggregate behaviour comparable, in this respect, to the theory of suicide (Durkheim, 1897) that has inspired much subsequent research. There is a parallel with studies of consumer behaviour. Manufacturers with products to sell want to be able to predict what change there will be in demand for them if they change their price or if the government changes the level of taxation. They wish to predict aggregate changes, not whether a particular person will buy more or less. In like manner it should be possible to predict whether people will continue to act in accordance with an ethnic preference if the costs are increased. Those who seek to influence the course of international politics would be helped if analysts could predict when groups will mobilize along the lines of ethnic origin or colour and how far group members will go in solidarity with their peers. These are questions of relative preference.

The atrocities in the Balkans and the Great Lakes region of central Africa were the result of one kind of collective action, raising questions about why it seems easier to mobilize groups for the negative end of defence (or presumed defence) than for positive ends. Remarkably, many atrocities were committed by persons who had lived in the same neighbourhoods as their victims and who knew them personally. This suggests that while living together in the same neighbourhood encourages feelings of mutual obligation, in certain circumstances these effects can be quickly undone. A critical element appears to be the psychology satirized in the expression 'we must get our retaliation in first'. The top-down influence of the state, the mass media and other institutions can easily instil fear and override less emotional considerations.

As a small step towards the development of a theory of ethnic collective action it has been found possible in research in Malaysia to measure the strength of ethnic preferences relative to preferences for money, status, and the observance of personal obligation (Banton, 2000). It is difficult to generalize from the findings, but the technique has potential. Comparable studies could be conducted in the many countries in which parents can choose a school for a child. Interviewees can be asked whether they would prefer a school attended by children of their ethnic group only, or one with a given proportion of co-ethnics and the balance of children from other groups. Having ascertained a preference for a certain mixture, they can then be asked about how important they believe this to be, either for themselves or other members of their group, relative to a preference for a neighbourhood school or one that will entail a journey of a particular length; they can be asked about the strength of the ethnic preference relative to any preference for a school with an outstanding or an average record of examination success. The results of such studies could be of value to any authorities that have to decide the boundaries within which schools are to recruit pupils.

This brief summary has claimed that by utilizing the theory of collective action it becomes possible to offer better explanations of many forms of inter-group relations. At the head of the list are analyses of processes of discrimination in housing, employment and other markets, and of responses to discrimination, either on the part of victims or by policy-makers who wish to prevent it. Similar analyses can elucidate the processes by which majority and minority candidates try to win the votes of electors in ethnically mixed constituencies. At the other extreme, the theory can cast a little light on the suspension or destruction of norms of mutual obligation. Instead of assuming that all persons are motivated by sentiments common to members of their group, the theory of collective action takes account of the multiplicity of motives, the significance vested in particular social attributes, and the interaction between different patterns of goal-seeking behaviour.

Postface

The preceding chapters have tried to show that behind the idea that some races were superior to others lay an apparently innocent yet equally dangerous idea. This was the assumption that humans belonged naturally in races. As the preface stated, to ascribe individuals to 'races' was to:

- assign them to discontinuous categories, distracting attention from differences within categories and from characteristics shared across categories;
- identify biological differences with social and political differences, suggesting that the former caused the latter.

In 1926 the British Institute of Philosophical Studies used the expression 'the problem of colour' in choosing a title for the symposium mentioned in chapter 1. This was more accurate than the expression 'the race problem' (which was current then and for the next three decades), because 'colour' designates a form of continuous variation that does not by itself assign individuals to categories or identify physical with social differences (though it can be made to do so, as when 'coloured' is used as a category opposed to 'white' or 'black'). Whereas it is fairly evident that the significance attributed to colour is social in origin, the description of phenotypical differences as 'racial' sustains the idea that humans belong in races. Members of groups that consider themselves oppressed often dislike reference to differences of colour; they see them as divisive. It is easier to mobilize for collective action on the basis of presumed racial difference because this can be made to imply clear lines of difference. Where 'races' exist in social life they are the products of collective action, not of nature.

The idea that humans belong in races was boosted by the belief that this could explain why some sections of the human species had attained a higher degree of economic development than others. These inequalities stemmed from the efforts of the various groups to make the best use of their physical, social and political environments and their differential resources. The use of *race* as a name by which to identify and classify such groups built false associations into the ordinary-language use of the word. Anti-racist movements have found it extremely difficult to get ordinary people to revise assumptions built into what seem innocent words.

In any ideological struggle the parties cannot avoid publicizing the ideas they oppose as well as those that they support, which is one reason why struggle often follows a dialectic of thesis and antithesis. Therefore it is not very remarkable to contend that the international anti-racist movement has tended to recycle some of the very ideas it set out to eliminate. It has often acted in line with Thesis Two and constructed a bogey figure of racism as an evil that acts like an opponent in a contest, when what matters most is to transcend the opposition by reformulating it in more satisfactory terms. This is the task of synthesis.

The international anti-racist movement has been partly scientific and partly political. The scientific component has been part of another movement, the attempt to account for human variation. In the popular mind the really scientific contribution has been that from genetics, which has uncovered the common inheritance of all humans and identified genes that are responsible for particular variations. The social scientific contribution does not qualify as equally scientific, partly because its subject matter is more difficult to analyse objectively and partly because some authors make their academic work a vehicle for their political commitments. Yet compared with the explicitly political work of drafting and implementing legislation, the study of the nature and operation of the causes of cultural variation is a scientific enterprise. Much of this study has entailed analysis of what people think they know about racial differences and their social implications, trying to sort out the confusions that, with the benefit of hindsight, can be seen to have confounded the 1926 symposium. Social science has been engaged in the elaboration of a conceptual scheme that leads to better explanations. That scheme has to be genuinely international. It cannot be built upon British, Chinese, French or US assumptions about racial differences, and has to be one that can be used by research workers of different political persuasion.

The political component of the international anti-racist movement has also been part of another movement, reacting to the horrors of World War II. It has succeeded beyond any of the hopes entertained in the late 1940s, most notably by the creation of institutions that facilitate collective action. Beginning with an antithesis, the attack on doctrines of racial superiority, it has gradually incorporated anti-racism into the wider movement for the protection of human rights. The World Conference Against Racism in 2001 showed that those who energize the international and national anti-racist movements are likely to continue employing words deriving from the idea of 'race' whenever these serve their purposes. For perhaps another generation they will believe that the advantages of the racial idiom outweigh its disadvantages. Though they will be impatient with academic objections, their rhetoric will be aligned increasingly with the human rights movement and concentrate upon the international fault lines.

If the twentieth century was the century of the colour line, reactions to the events of 11 September 2001 in the USA make it look as if the twenty-first century may be marked by what appears to be an opposition between Muslim and Christian nations. The assumption that people belong in religious categories can be as misleading as that of racial categories. If at one point in time there appears to be a Muslim bloc and a Christian bloc, this should not prevent recognition of their internal divisions. Each bloc will be a coalition of groups and persons differing on social dimensions other than a Muslim/Christian opposition.

The human rights movement must lead ultimately to the creation of an international court able to take over the adjudication of complaints of the kind provided for in Article 14 of the ICERD and empowered to invoke action by the Security Council to ensure that its adjudications are heeded. The Security Council will have to intervene when states fail persistently and grossly to honour the obligations they have accepted, and act speedily when disasters threaten. Progress towards these objectives can be only slow because the world's states are very unequal in size and power and frequently cannot trust each other. They cannot be sure that the Security Council will act impartially. Indeed, it can be difficult to apply the concept of impartiality when the framework for decision-taking is so much weaker than that in a court of law. Though state representatives will increasingly use the rhetoric of human rights, the reality of international politics is that only a few states have the military and economic power to serve as international police. These states operate with short-term perspectives because democratic governments are restrained by the desire to remain in office after their country's next election. This is particularly noticeable where there is a two-party political system and the winner of an election can govern independently of the other party, rather than a system based upon proportional representation. With 'winner takes all', the time perspective is dictated by the date of the next election. The bottom-up influence is then strong. Though the electorate can vote a party out of office it may have little understanding of the long-term considerations that are so important in foreign affairs. To cite a recent and prominent example, after its ill-judged intervention in Somalia the US government was for eight years unwilling to commit troops to any situation that carried the possibility that the TV cameras would in due course be filming the unloading of 'body bags' containing the remains of slain soldiers. It feared the effect this could have on the electorate. The attack on the World Trade Center in 2001 changed those attitudes but did little to lengthen the electoral time perspective.

In addressing these issues the academic analysis of collective action links up with the practical problems of international politics. The UN Charter in Article 1 declares that: 'the purposes of the UN are: 1. To maintain international peace and security, and to that end: to take effective *collective* measures for the prevention and removal of threats to the peace', and that it is to harmonize actions for the attainment of 'common ends'. Globalization proceeds rapidly wherever individuals have opportunities to make money, but the cultivation of common ends advances only slowly. The most important of these ends find expression in the law of human rights. In an epoch of rapid change humans across the world are coming to appreciate how important these rights are to them and to others also. They are the same for everyone, irrespective of race, colour, or national or ethnic origin. The realization of that principle could some day displace any assumption that humans belong naturally in races.

Bibliography

Printed sources

Australia 2000 *Sixteenth Report of the Parliamentary Joint Committee on Native Title and the Aboriginal and Torres Strait Islander Land Fund. CERD and the Native Title Amendment Act 1998*. Canberra: Parliament of the Commonwealth of Australia.

Back, Les, and John Solomos, eds 2000 *Theories of Race and Racism. A Reader*. London: Routledge.

Ballard, Roger, ed. 1994 *Desh Pardesh. The South Asian Presence in Britain*. London: Hurst.

Banks, Marcus 1996 *Ethnicity: Anthropological Constructions*. London: Routledge.

Banton, Michael 1967 *Race Relations*. London: Tavistock.

——1970 'The Concept of Racism', pp. 17–34 in Sami Zubaida, ed., *Race and Racialism*. London: Tavistock.

——1977 *The Idea of Race*. London: Tavistock.

——1979 'Analytical and Folk Concepts of Race and Ethnicity', *Ethnic and Racial Studies*, 2:127–38.

——1983 *Racial and Ethnic Competition*. Cambridge: Cambridge University Press. Reprinted. Aldershot: Gregg Revivals, 1992.

——1985 *Promoting Racial Harmony*. Cambridge: Cambridge University Press.

——1986 'The Historical Context of Racial Classification', pp. 79–127 in *UNESCO Yearbook on Peace and Conflict Studies 1984*. Paris: UNESCO; Westport, Conn.: Greenwood.

——1994 *Discrimination*. Buckingham: Open University Press.

——1996 *International Action against Racial Discrimination*. Oxford: Clarendon Press.

——1998a *Racial Theories*. Second edition. Cambridge: Cambridge University Press.

——1998b 'Judicial Training in Ethnic Minority Issues in England and Wales', *Journal of Ethnic and Migration Studies*, 24:561–72.

——2000 *Combating Racial Discrimination. The UN and its Member States.* London: Minority Rights International.

Barkan, Elazar 1992 *The Retreat of Scientific Racism.* Cambridge: Cambridge University Press.

Barker, Anthony J. 1978 *The African Link. British Attitudes to the Negro in the Era of the Atlantic Slave Trade, 1550–1807.* London: Frank Cass.

Barot, Rohit, ed. 1996 *The Racism Problematic: Contemporary Sociological Debates on Race and Ethnicity.* Lewiston, N.Y.: Edwin Mellen.

Barry, Brian 2001 *Culture and Equality.* Cambridge: Polity.

Bendick, M. 1996 *Discrimination against Racial/Ethnic Minorities in Access to Employment in the United States: Empirical Findings from Situation Testing.* International Migration Papers 12. Geneva: ILO.

Bendick, M., M. L. Egan, and S. Lofhjelm 1998 *The Documentation and Evaluation of Anti-Discrimination Training in the United States.* International Migration Papers 29. Geneva: ILO.

Benedict, Ruth 1942 *Race and Racism.* London: Labour Book Service. First published as *Race: Science and Politics.* New York: Modern Age Books, 1940.

Bibby, Cyril 1959 *Race, Prejudice and Education.* London: Heinemann.

Biddiss, Michael D. 1979 *Images of Race: A Selection from Mid-Victorian Periodicals.* Leicester: Leicester University Press.

Bossuyt, Marc 2000 'The Concept and Practice of Affirmative Action', UN document E/CN.4/Sub.2/2000/11.

Boven, Theo van 1998 'Prevention, Early-Warning and Urgent Procedures: A New Approach by the Committee on the Elimination of Racial Discrimination', pp. 165–82 in Eric Denters and Nico Schrijver, eds, *Reflections on International Law from the Low Countries in Honour of Paul de Waart.* The Hague: Kluwer Law International. Reprinted at pp. 199–217 in Fons Coomans, Cees Flinterman, Fred Grünfeld, Ingrid Westendorp and Jan Willems, eds, *Human Rights from Exclusion to Inclusion: Principles and Practice. An Anthology from the Work of Theo van Boven.* The Hague: Kluwer Law International, 2000.

Boxill, Bernard, ed. 2001 *Race and Racism.* Oxford: Oxford University Press.

Bulmer, Martin, and John Solomos, eds 1999a *Racism.* Oxford: Oxford University Press.

——1999b *Ethnic and Racial Studies Today.* London: Routledge.

Cannon, David T. 1999 *Race, Redistricting, and Representation. The Unintended Consequences of Black Majority Districts.* Chicago: University of Chicago Press.

Carmichael, Stokely, and Charles W. Hamilton 1967 *Black Power: The Politics of Black Liberation in America.* New York: Vintage; London: Penguin, 1968.

Cassese, Antonio 1995 *Self-Determination of Peoples. A Legal Reappraisal.* Cambridge: Cambridge University Press.

Cathcart, Brian 1999 *The Case of Stephen Lawrence.* London: Viking.

Clark, Jennifer 1997 ' "Something to Hide": Aborigines and the Department of External Affairs, January 1961–January 1962', *Journal of the Royal Australian Historical Society*, 87:71–84.

Collier, Paul 1998 *Living Down the Past: How Europe can Help Africa Grow*. London: Institute of Economic Affairs.

Commissariat Royal à la Politique des Immigrés 1993 *Rapport final. Desseins d'Égalité*. Brussels: INBEL.

Cox, Oliver C. 1948 *Caste, Class and Race: A Study in Social Dynamics*. New York: Monthly Review Press.

Crawford, James 2000 'The UN Human Rights Treaty System: A System in Crisis?', pp. 1–12 in Philip Alston and James Crawford, eds, *The Future of UN Human Rights Treaty Reporting*. Cambridge: Cambridge University Press.

Dasgupta, Partha 1993 *An Inquiry into Well-Being and Destitution*. Oxford: Clarendon Press.

Davis, Kingsley 1948 *Human Society*. New York: Macmillan.

Dennis, Norman, George Erdos, and Ahmed Al-Shahi 2000 *Racist Murder and Pressure Group Politics: The Macpherson Report and the Police*. London: Institute for the Study of Civil Society.

Dir. 1999: 49 *Översyn av lagstiftningen om olaga diskriminering m.m. Beslut vid regeringssammanträde den 17 juni 1999*. Stockholm.

Dowden, Richard 2001 'Don't Compensate Africa for Slavery', *Independent*, 28 March.

Durkheim, Émile 1897 *Le Suicide: étude sociologique*. Paris: Alcan.

Edmonston, Barry, Joshua Goldstein, and Juanita Tamayo Lott, eds 1996 *Spotlight on Heterogeneity. The Federal Standards for Racial and Ethnic Classification*. Washington, D.C.: National Academy Press.

Eriksen, Thomas Hylland 1993 *Ethnicity and Nationalism: Anthropological Perspectives*. London: Pluto Press.

Finger, Seymour M. 1972 'A New Approach to Colonial Problems at the United Nations', *International Organization*, 26:143–54.

Franklin, John Hope (chairman) 1998 *One America in the 21st Century. Forging a New Future. The Advisory Board's Report to the President*. Washington, D.C.: US Government Printing Office.

Freeman, E. A. 1877 'Race and Language', reprinted at pp. 205–35 in Biddiss (1979).

Füredi, Frank 1998 *The Silent War. Imperialism and the Changing Perception of Race*. London: Pluto Press.

Ginsberg, Morris 1947 *Reason and Unreason in Society. Essays in Sociology and Social Philosophy*. London: Longmans, Green.

——1963 'Facts and Values', *Advancement of Science*, 19(81):407–20.

Goering, John 1994 'Anti-Discrimination Law on the Grounds of Race in the United States: Enforcement and Research Concerns', *New Community*, 20:393–414.

——2001 'An Assessment of President Clinton's Initiative on Race', *Ethnic and Racial Studies*, 24:472–84.

Goldberg, David Theo 1993 *Racist Culture: Philosophy and the Politics of Meaning*. Oxford: Blackwell.

Grant, Stefanie 2000 'The United States and the International Human Rights Treaty System: For Export Only?', pp. 317–29 in Philip Alston and

James Crawford, eds, *The Future of UN Human Rights Treaty Monitoring*. Cambridge: Cambridge University Press.

Greene, John C. 1961 *The Death of Adam. Evolution and its Impact on Western Thought*. New York: Mentor Book.

Hall, Stuart 1980 'Race, Articulation and Societies Structured in Dominance', pp. 305–45 in *Sociological Theories: Race and Colonialism*. Paris: UNESCO.

——2000 'Old and New Identities, Old and New Ethnicities', pp. 144–53 in Back and Solomos (2000).

Haut Conseil à l'Intégration 1993 *L'intégration à la française*. Paris: La documentation française.

Hayek, F. A. von 1943 'Scientism and the Study of Society Part II', *Economica*, 10:34–63.

Hechter, Michael 1987 *Principles of Group Solidarity*. Berkeley: University of California Press.

Hiernaux, Jean 1969 'Biological Aspects of the Racial Question', pp. 9–16 in *Four Statements on the Race Question*. Paris: UNESCO.

Hutchinson, John, and Anthony D. Smith 1996 *Ethnicity*. Oxford: Oxford University Press.

Huxley, Julian S., and A. C. Haddon 1935 *We Europeans: A Survey of 'Racial' Problems*. London: Cape.

Jacobsen, Michael, and Ole Bruun, eds 2000 *Human Rights and Asian Values: Contesting National Identities and Cultural Representations in Asia*. Richmond: Curzon Press.

James, H. E. O., and Cora Tenen 1953 *The Teacher Was Black*. London: Heinemann.

Jary, David, and Julia Jary, eds 1991 *Collins Dictionary of Sociology*. London: HarperCollins.

Just, Roger 1989 'Triumph of the Ethnos', pp. 71–88 in Elizabeth Tonkin, Maryon McDonald and Malcolm Chapman, eds, *History and Ethnicity*. ASA Monograph 27. London: Routledge.

Kohn, Marek 1995 *The Race Gallery. The Return of Racial Science*. London: Cape.

Kuper, Leo, ed. 1975 *Race, Science and Society*. London: Allen and Unwin.

Kymlicka, Will 1995 *Multicultural Citizenship: A Liberal Theory of Minority Rights*. Oxford: Clarendon Press.

Lauren, Paul Gordon 1996 *Power and Prejudice: The Politics and Diplomacy of Racial Discrimination*. Second edition. Boulder, Col.: Westview Press.

Layton, Azza Salama 2000 *International Politics and Civil Rights Policies in the United States*. Cambridge: Cambridge University Press.

Lester, Anthony, and Geoffrey Bindman 1972 *Race and Law*. Harmondsworth: Penguin.

Lévi-Strauss, Claude 1952 *Race and History*. Paris: UNESCO.

Lugard, Sir Frederick, Morris Ginsberg, and H. A. Wyndham 1926 *The Problem of Colour in Relation to the Idea of Equality*. Supplement to *Journal of Philosophical Studies*, 1(2):208–37.

McKean, Warwick 1983 *Equality and Discrimination under International Law*. Oxford: Clarendon Press.

Macpherson of Cluny, Sir William 1999 *The Stephen Lawrence Inquiry*, vol. 1. London: Home Office, CM 4262-1.

Markus, Andrew 1979 *Fear and Hatred: Purifying Australia and California, 1850–1901*. Sydney: Hole and Iremonger.

Martucelli, Danilo 1994 'L'expérience italienne', pp. 215–33 in Michel Wieviorka, Philippe Bataille, Kristin Couper, Danilo Martucelli and Angelina Peralua, *Racisme et xénophobie en Europe: une comparaison internationale*. Paris: La Découverte.

Mason, Philip 1970 *Patterns of Dominance*. London: Oxford University Press.

Massey, Douglas S., and Nancy A. Denton 1993 *American Apartheid. Segregation and the Making of the Underclass*. Cambridge, Mass.: Harvard University Press.

Mazower, Mark 1998 *Dark Continent: Europe's Twentieth Century*. London: Penguin.

Miles, Robert 1982 *Racism and Migrant Labour*. London: Routledge.

——1989 *Racism*. London: Routledge.

——1993 *Racism after 'Race Relations'*. London: Routledge.

Modood, Tariq 1988 '"Black", Racial Equality and Asian Identity', *New Community*, 14:397–404.

——1996a 'If Races Don't Exist, then What Does? Racial Categorisation and Ethnic Realities', pp. 89–105 in Barot (1996).

——1996b '"Race" in Britain and the Politics of Difference', pp. 177–90 in D. Archard, ed., *Philosophy and Pluralism*. Cambridge: Cambridge University Press.

Myrdal, Gunnar 1944 *An American Dilemma: The Negro Problem and Modern Democracy*. New York: Harper.

Omi, Michael, and Harold Winant 1994 *Racial Formation in the United States, from the 1960s to the 1990s*. Second edition. London: Routledge.

Outlaw, Lucius 1990 'Toward a Critical Theory of Race', in David Theo Goldberg, ed., *The Anatomy of Racism*. Minneapolis: University of Minnesota Press. Reprinted at pp. 58–82 in Boxill (2001) (page references in text to this version).

Parekh, Bhikhu (Lord Parekh) 2000a *Rethinking Multiculturalism. Cultural Diversity and Political Theory*. Basingstoke: Macmillan.

——(chair) 2000b *The Future of Multi-Ethnic Britain*. Report of Commission established by the Runnymede Trust. London: Profile Books.

Patterson, Orlando 1997 *The Ordeal of Integration*. New York: Basic Civitas.

Pitt-Rivers, Julian 1970 'Race Relations as a Science: A Review of Michael Banton's *Race Relations*', *Race*, 11:335–42.

Popper, K. R. 1945 *The Open Society and its Enemies*. London: Routledge. Fifth edition 1966.

Rex, John 1973 *Race, Colonialism and the City*. London: Routledge.

Reynolds, Henry 1998 *This Whispering in Our Hearts*. St Leonards: Allen and Unwin.

Rosenberg, Alfred 1970 *Selected Writings*, ed. Robert Pois. London: Cape.

Sartre, Jean-Paul 1948 'Orphée Noir', pp. ix–xliv in Léopold Sédar-Senghor, ed., *Anthologie de la nouvelle poésie nègre et malgache de langue française*. Paris: Presses Universitaires de France.

Singer, Lester 1962 'Ethnogenesis and Negro-Americans Today', *Social Research*, 29:419–32.

Solomos, John, and Les Back 1996 *Racism and Society*. Basingstoke: Macmillan.

Sowell, Thomas 1984 *Civil Rights: Rhetoric or Reality?* New York: Morrow.

Stymeist, David H. 1975 *Ethnics and Indians: Social Relationships in a Northwestern Ontario Town*. Toronto: Peter Martin Associates.

Thernstrom, Stephen, and Abigail Thernstrom 1997 *America in Black and White. One Nation, Indivisible*. New York: Simon and Schuster.

UN 1949 *The Main Types and Causes of Discrimination*. Memorandum submitted by the Secretary-General. E/CN.4/Sub.2/40/Rev.1.

——1972 *Review of Studies of Problems of Race Relations and of the Creation and Maintenance of Racial Attitudes*. Report by the Secretary-General. E/CN.4/1105.

——2002 *Declaration Adopted on 8 September 2001 in Durban, South Africa*. A/CONF.189/12.

UNESCO 1953 *The Race Concept. Results of an Inquiry*. Paris: UNESCO.

——1969 *Four Statements on the Race Question*. Paris: UNESCO.

USA 2000 *Initial/Third Report of the United States of America*. UN document CERD/C/351/Add.1. Also available on www.state.gov/www/global/human_rights/cerd_report/cerd_index.html

Vermeulen, Hans 1999 'Essentializing Difference? The Census, Multiculturalism and the Multiracials in the USA', pp. 81–98 in Marie-Claire Foblets and Pang Chin Lin, eds, *Cultuur, etniciteit en migratie. Liber amicorum E. Roosens*. Leuven: Acco.

Wagley, Charles, ed. 1952 *Race and Class in Rural Brazil*. Paris: UNESCO.

Wallman, Sandra 1978 'The Boundaries of Race: Processes of Ethnicity in England', *Man*, 13:200–17.

Weiler, J. H. H. 1999 *The Constitution of Europe*. Cambridge: Cambridge University Press.

Wolfrum, Rüdiger 1999 'The Protection of Indigenous Peoples in International Law', *Zeitschrift für ausländisches Recht und Völkerrecht*, 59:369–81.

Wolton, Suke 2000 *Lord Hailey, the Colonial Office and the Politics of Race and Empire in the Second World War. The Loss of White Prestige*. Basingstoke: Macmillan.

Wrench, John 2000 'Combating Employment Discrimination in Europe: National Variation and the Dawn of "Good Practice"', pp. 259–78 in Erna Appelt and Monika Jarosch, *Combating Racial Discrimination. Affirmative Action as a Model for Europe*. Oxford: Berg.

Yinger, John 1995 *Closed Doors, Opportunities Lost. The Continuing Costs of Housing Discrimination*. New York: Russell Sage Foundation.

Young, Iris Marion 1990 *Justice and the Politics of Difference*. Princeton, N.J.: Princeton University Press.

Zegers de Beijl, Roger, Irene McClure, and Patrick Taran, 2001 'Inequality in Access to Employment: A Statement of the Challenge', pp. 153–67 in UNESCO, *United to Combat Racism*. Paris: UNESCO.

Zubrzycki, Jerzy 1995 'The Evolution of the Policy of Multiculturalism in Australia, 1968–1995', presentation to Global Cultural Diversity Conference, Sydney, April.

Websites

European Commission on Racism and Intolerance: www.coe.fr
European Monitoring Centre on Racism and Xenophobia:
    http://eumc.eu.int
United Nations High Commissioner for Human Rights: www.unhchr.ch

Index

trap, language, 5, 7, 8, 24, 116, 126, 201
treaties, 40–1, 107–8
  reservations to, 68, 100–2, 106
Tsarmerian, I. P., and S. L. Ronin, 32
Tumin, Melvin, 32
Turkey, 119
typology, racial, 13–16

Union of Soviet Socialist Republics (USSR), 35, 53
United Kingdom, 6, 14, 15, 17, 57, 58, 60, 126–30
United Nations
  Charter, 23, 39, 73, 173, 216
  Commission on Human Rights (CHR), 40, 53, 60–5, 142
  Conference on Human Settlements, 162–3
  Economic and Social Council, 6, 55
  General Assembly, 6, 39–44, 51–8, 142, 145, 167
  High Commissioner for Human Rights, 144, 153
  Human Rights Committee, 101, 178–9
  Research Institute for Social Development, 162
  Security Council, 40, 215
  Special Rapporteur on Racism and Xenophobia, 62–5, 161, 162
  Sub-Commission on Prevention of Discrimination and Protection of Minorities (afterwards Sub-Commission on Promotion and Protection of Human Rights), 43, 62–5
  Universal Declaration of Human Rights, 39–41, 75, 81
  World Conferences Against Racism, 7, 37, 38, 55, 56, 86, 142–69

World Conferences on Human Rights, 53, 59
United Nations Educational, Scientific and Cultural Organization (UNESCO), 1, 2, 6, 7, 28–38, 57, 152, 161, 163, 178
United States of America (USA), 2, 4, 6, 12, 16, 24, 56, 57, 60, 70, 98–117, 147, 216
  Advisory Board on Race, 4, 5
  Civil Rights Act, 2, 17–18, 108
  Constitution, 3, 5, 102, 172–3

Vermeulen, Hans, 104
Verstegan, Richard, 10

Wagley, Charles, 32, 191
Wales, 181
Wallman, Sandra, 193
Weber, Max, 189
Weiler, J. H. H., 119
West European and Other group of states, 68, 147
Wik case, 91
Wolfrum, Rüdiger, 181
Wolton, Suke, 24
World Health Organization (WHO), 152, 162
Wrench, John, 124–5
Wyndham, H. A., 21

xenophobia, 134

Yinger, John, 112
Young, Iris Marion, 179–80, 185, 204, 205

Zavala, Sylvio, 32
Zegers de Beijl, Roger, 58
Zimbabwe, 84
Zimbardo, Philip, 46
Zionism, 56, 153
Zubrzycki, Jerzy, 95